Capitalism & Slavery

Eric Williams

with a New Introduction by

COLIN A. PALMER

Ian Randle Publishers
Kingston · Miami

Published in Jamaica 2005 by
Ian Randle Publishers
11 Cunningham Avenue
Box 686, Kingston 6
www.ianrandlepublishers.com

Capitalism & Slavery by Eric Williams
with a new introduction by Colin A. Palmer
Published under licence from University of North Carolina Press

© 1944, 1994 the University of North Carolina Press

A catalogue record for this book is available from the National Library of Jamaica

ISBN 976-637-210-1

Printed and bound in the United States of America

To Professor Lowell Joseph Ragatz
Whose monumental labors in this field
may be amplified and developed
but can never be superseded

CONTENTS

Preface   ix
Introduction *by Colin A. Palmer*   xi
1. The Origin of Negro Slavery   3
2. The Development of the Negro Slave Trade   30
3. British Commerce and the Triangular Trade   51
4. The West India Interest   85
5. British Industry and the Triangular Trade   98
6. The American Revolution   108
7. The Development of British Capitalism, 1783–1833   126
8. The New Industrial Order   135
9. British Capitalism and the West Indies   154
10. "The Commercial Part of the Nation" and Slavery   169
11. The "Saints" and Slavery   178
12. The Slaves and Slavery   197
13. Conclusion   209
    Notes   213
    Bibliography   262
    Index   271

PREFACE

THE PRESENT STUDY is an attempt to place in historical perspective the relationship between early capitalism as exemplified by Great Britain, and the Negro slave trade, Negro slavery and the general colonial trade of the seventeenth and eighteenth centuries. Every age rewrites history, but particularly ours, which has been forced by events to re-evaluate our conceptions of history and economic and political development. The progress of the Industrial Revolution has been treated more or less adequately in many books both learned and popular, and its lessons are fairly well established in the consciousness of the educated class in general and of those people in particular who are responsible for the creation and guidance of informed opinion. On the other hand, while material has been accumulated and books have been written about the period which preceded the Industrial Revolution, the world-wide and interrelated nature of the commerce of that period, its direct effect upon the development of the Industrial Revolution, and the heritage which it has left even upon the civilization of today have not anywhere been placed in compact and yet comprehensive perspective. This study is an attempt to do so, without, however, failing to give indications of the economic origin of well-known social, political, and even intellectual currents.

The book, however, is not an essay in ideas or interpretation. It is strictly an economic study of the role of Negro slavery and the slave trade in providing the capital which financed the Industrial Revolution in England and of mature industrial capitalism in destroying the slave system. It is therefore first a study in English economic history and second in West Indian and Negro history. It is not a study of the institution of slavery but of the contribution of slavery to the development of British capitalism.

ix

Many debts must be acknowledged. The staffs of the following institutions were very kind and helpful to me: British Museum; Public Record Office; India Office Library; West India Committee; Rhodes House Library, Oxford; Bank of England Record Office; the British Anti-Slavery and Aborigines Protection Society; Friends' House, London; John Rylands Library, Manchester; Central Library, Manchester; Public Library, Liverpool; Wilberforce Museum, Hull; Library of Congress; Biblioteca Nacional, Havana; Sociedad Económica de Amigos del País, Havana. I wish to thank the Newberry Library, Chicago, for its kindness in making it possible for me, through an inter-library loan with Founders' Library, Howard University, to see Sir Charles Whitworth's valuable statistics on "State of the Trade of Great Britain in its imports and exports, progressively from the year 1697–1773."

My research has been facilitated by grants from different sources: the Trinidad Government, which extended an original scholarship; Oxford University, which awarded me two Senior Studentships; the Beit Fund for the study of British Colonial History, which made two grants; and the Julius Rosenwald Foundation, which awarded me fellowships in 1940 and 1942. Professor Lowell J. Ragatz of George Washington University in this city, Professor Frank W. Pitman of Pomona College, Claremont, California, and Professor Melville J. Herskovits of Northwestern University, very kindly read the manuscript and made many suggestions. So did my senior colleague at Howard University, Professor Charles Burch. Dr. Vincent Harlow, now Rhodes Professor of Imperial History in the University of London, supervised my doctoral dissertation at Oxford and was always very helpful. Finally, my wife was of great assistance to me in taking my notes and typing the manuscript.

Eric Williams
Howard University
Washington, D.C.
September 12, 1943

INTRODUCTION

Colin A. Palmer

FEW MODERN HISTORICAL works have enjoyed the enduring intellectual impact and appeal of Eric Williams's *Capitalism and Slavery*. Its publication in 1944 was greeted by acclaim in some quarters and severe criticism in others. The scholarly debate over its conclusions continues fifty years later with no sign of abating. This classic work by a West Indian scholar remains the most provocative contribution to the study of the complex relationship between the African slave trade, slavery, the rise of British capitalism, and the emancipation of the slave population in the West Indies.

Eric Eustace Williams was born in Trinidad in 1911. An intellectually gifted young man, he attended Queen's Royal College, one of the best secondary schools on the island. In 1931 he was awarded the lone Island Scholarship and in 1932 enrolled at Oxford University, where he read for a degree in modern history. At Oxford, as in Trinidad, Williams was exposed to intellectual currents that celebrated the imperial connection and gave little agency to the peoples of African descent in the colonies. Recalling his formative years in Trinidad, Williams noted, "The intellectual equipment with which I was endowed by the Trinidad school system had two principal characteristics—quantitatively it was rich; qualitatively it was British. 'Be British' was the slogan not only of the Legislature but also of the school."[1]

As he grew intellectually at Oxford, the young colonial came to question, and ultimately reject, an imperial-centered analysis of his people's history. In his meetings with his tutor, R. Trevor Davies, for example, Williams reported that he consistently "took an independent line."[2] The intellectually curious student spent nearly seven years at Oxford, receiving the Ph.D. in December 1938. His dissertation,

"The Economic Aspects of the Abolition of the West Indian Slave Trade and Slavery," would be revised, expanded, and published five years later.

Williams accepted a teaching appointment at Howard University in 1939. There, he continued his research, elaborating on his dissertation and placing special emphasis on the relationship between slavery and the rise of British capitalism. Williams also established contact with Professors Lowell Ragatz of George Washington University and Frank Pitman of Pomona College. The two scholars were leading authorities on the pre-emancipation history of the British West Indies.

Acting upon the advice of Ragatz, Williams submitted his completed manuscript to the University of North Carolina Press on February 17, 1943. In his letter to William T. Couch, the director, the author wrote that he hoped the book "lives up to the high standards of your Press as much as it would seem to fit in with the general run of works on Negro Slavery which the intellectual world has learned to associate with the University of North Carolina."[3] He noted that the manuscript had been read by Pitman and Ragatz and that his research had been supported by two Rosenwald Fellowships that he received in 1940–41 and in 1942.

Williams's letter was accompanied by a one-page prospectus describing the book and its principal thesis. The book, he said, "attempts to place in historical perspective the relation between early capitalism in Europe, as exemplified by Great Britain, and the Negro slave trade and Negro slavery in the West Indies. It shows how the commercial capitalism of the eighteenth century was built up on slavery and monopoly, while the Industrial capitalism of the nineteenth century destroyed slavery and monopoly." He stressed that the West Indian colonies "are put in a general colonial framework" and that "British West Indian development is seen always in relation to the development of other Caribbean areas, e.g., Cuba and St. Domingue, as well as other sugar producing areas, Brazil and India." Williams emphasized that he saw the humanitarian movement "not, as is customary, as something abstract, but as essentially a part of the age and the general economic struggle against slavery and monopoly."[4]

Upon receipt of the manuscript, the Press solicited the opinions of four scholars regarding its scholarly merit. Ragatz and Pitman were obvious choices; the others were Professors Hugh Lefler and Charles B. Robson of the University of North Carolina. Lefler was a distinguished historian of colonial America and Robson was a political scientist.

Ragatz, to whom the manuscript was dedicated, responded with a brief but strong endorsement of the work. He had, he reported, "carefully read Dr. Eric Williams' manuscript Capitalism and Slavery, both in first draft and in final form as submitted to you, and consider it a highly meritorious piece of work."[5] Pitman's report was longer and somewhat less enthusiastic. He indicated that he had met with Williams twice and found him "a very well trained (Oxford University) young man." The Pomona scholar thought the manuscript "was a sound piece of work. I suggested that in a few places he soften a somewhat caustic racial bias against capitalism which I detected. I told him to let the facts alone constitute, in the main, the judgment against capitalist malpractices."

Pitman did not consider Williams's ideas original. "His work adds little to what scholars in the field know," he wrote. On the other hand, "for the layman it is a fresh, rather well written and sound synthesis." Pitman also had other reasons for recommending the book's publication. "Literary work *from the minority group* to which Eric Williams belongs should be encouraged— *especially at this time*," he advised. Williams was, he continued, "very energetic and shows promise of making a name for himself. I want to help him and hope you feel the same way."[6]

The two University of North Carolina readers also endorsed the publication of the book, but they completely misunderstood Williams's arguments and, like Pitman, failed to appreciate the book's refreshing originality. Lefler found the study "to be interesting, readable, and quite scholarly." He concluded, however, that the manuscript had "the wrong title." In his opinion, the work was "really a study of slavery in the West Indies rather than of capitalism and slavery." Lefler thought, nonetheless, that Williams had made "a good analysis of the influence of the West Indian planter class in British pol-

itics." He suggested the revision of "a few sentimental para-
graphs in the manuscript."[7]

Robson also found the manuscript to be "a straight history
of slavery in the West Indies and as such quite interesting."
He found the manuscript "OK," although he had only "read a
couple of chapters." He confessed, "I'd like to read the rest but
see no need to do so." Robson "found no trace, in the chapters
I read, of the kind of treatment that I thought the title might
indicate. . . . I found nothing objectionable to the 'tone.'"[8]

Robson's comment was sent to the Press on May 10, 1943.
Evidently influenced by the earlier recommendations of Ragatz,
Pitman, and Lefler, William Couch wrote to Williams on April
22 predicting that the "work will be approved, so far as editorial
considerations are concerned, for publication." Since the Press
expected that the book would have a limited market, the author
was required to pay a $700 subsidy to finance its publication.
Couch estimated that 400 to 500 copies of the book would be
sold during the first year and a few copies annually thereafter.[9]

Williams responded to Couch on June 9, expressing his
delight that the Press planned to publish the book. He noted,
optimistically, that he would be able to raise the subsidy.[10]
But the assistant professor found the task substantially more
difficult than he had anticipated. When Couch prodded him in
the late summer, he admitted that his "tardiness" in "replying
to the terms of publication" was due partly to "an addition to
our family which introduced me to slavery of another sort [and]
partly illness." But there were other difficulties. Although he
had been "negotiating" in an attempt to raise the subsidy, he
had been unsuccessful. Williams was "confident," however, that
he would be able to secure the funds "in the very near future."
He indicated that some of "my West Indian friends are making
efforts to raise the money through the West Indian community
in the United States. But at the same time I am trying to obtain
the subsidy through the usual academic sources."[11]

Williams was eventually successful in raising the funds. On December 18, 1943, he informed Couch that some of his West Indian
friends had loaned him the money to cover the subsidy, which was to

be paid in three installments, and he advised the director to "go ahead" inaccordance with the terms of the April 22 letter.[12] Williams would later struggle to repay his benefactors from the modest royalties he received. Furthermore, the efforts by the author and the Press to obtain a publication subsidy from the American Council of Learned Societies (ACLS) were to no avail. After delaying a decision on the matter for six months, Donald Goodchild, the secretary for grants-in-aid of the ACLS, informed Williams that his request for funding had been rejected. Goodchild reported "confidentially" that "the Advisory Board in this matter did not concur in the recommendation of our Committee on Negro Studies. . . . Some of our consultants felt that your manuscript, though of high quality, was directed rather to the nonspecialist in the field of history."[13]

Although Williams acceded to the request to subsidize the publication of the book, he was not immediately very responsive to the suggestion that the title should be changed. After promising to address the matter more fully at a later date, the author informed Couch on September 4, 1943, that "with respect to the change of title suggested by your readers, I am wholly in disagreement with your suggestion."[14]

Williams had sought the advice of Professor Melville Herskovits, the distinguished anthropologist and sensitive student of Africans in the diaspora. He hoped that Herskovits would be sympathetic to the title that he had proposed. Although Herskovits found the manuscript "an interesting piece of work with a thesis that I regard as important to present," he did not endorse its title. According to Williams, Herskovits "was inclined to agree with your reader, when I told him of it, that the title ought to be changed. I disagree." Displaying the pugnacity that characterized him as a scholar and a politician, Williams outlined his objections vigorously. To those who suggested that the book was about slavery in the West Indies, he responded: "That is not the book I set out to write, and the book has nothing of the treatment or conditions of the slaves. It deals with what the slaves produced, how they were purchased, and the consequences of these points for capitalism."

Williams was not, however, averse to a compromise, provided that the new title reflected the principal arguments and content of the work. Herskovits had proposed two titles, which Williams noted in his December 18 letter to Couch:

> The first is "Slavery in the Industrial Revolution." To my mind this is inadequate, as it excludes the role of slavery in the period of commercial capitalism, to which I devote many pages. The second is "Slavery in the Development of Capitalism." That satisfies me. But it seems too long. I have not yet been convinced by anyone that I am not justified in speaking in general terms of Capitalism when the book deals with British Capitalism which was the model and parent of Capitalism elsewhere. . . . It is important to note too that two scholars like Professor Ragatz and Professor Pitman entirely approved of my choice. I do not wish to labour the point. But my choice expresses the book I intended to write and have written. If you insist on changing it, then Professor Herskovits' "Slavery in the Development of Capitalism" I am prepared to accept as a compromise. But "Slavery in the West Indies" is out of the question.[15]

The Press probably saw little point in contesting the author's forceful arguments and decided to retain the original title. As editorial work began on the manuscript in 1944, Williams took an active interest in its progress, suggesting changes from time to time. In fact, chapter 12 was added in June when the manuscript was already in page proofs. Williams informed his editor, May Littlejohn, on June 3 that he was adding a new chapter entitled "The Slaves and Emancipation." He noted that he had found some "wonderful" information on the role of the slaves in furthering the cause of emancipation, explaining,

> I have discussed the attitude of the government, the absentee planter, the capitalists, the humanitarians. Now I discuss the slaves. I have discussed the battle in England, now I discuss the battle in the West Indies. And as the book begins with the origin of Negro slavery, it would be effective to end it with the slaves' attempt to end slavery. . . . The general theme is that the pressure from the capitalists and humanitarians at home on the planters was aggravated in the colonies by pressures from the slaves, and that by 1833 if slav-

ery was not abolished from above it would have been abolished from below.[16]

When Williams submitted the completed chapter on June 19, he elaborated on his reasons for writing it. "As I read over the manuscript," he confessed, "it struck me that I had dealt with all aspects of the problem for over two centuries, but the people who are the objects and basis of the movement [for emancipation] I had left untouched. I therefore laid myself open to the devastating criticism that my history was old style, because my eyes were glued entirely upon those above. Chapter 12 makes this criticism impossible."[17]

The book was finally published on November 11, 1944. The Press had originally intended to print 1,000 copies, but because of the author's insistence that there would be a substantial market for the work, and probably as a result of its own market surveys, the number was increased to 1,500. The West Indian author was particularly sensitive on the question of how he would be described in the Press's marketing materials. When he submitted the biographical sketch that the Press requested, he wrote that he hoped he would be characterized as a "West Indian" rather than as a "Trinidadian" in the advertisements. He explained to Couch, "I have put down that I was born in Trinidad, but I should appreciate it if somewhere you can arrange to describe me as a West Indian born in Trinidad rather than as a Trinidadian. It might seem a trifle, but we West Indians set much store by it."[18] This assertion of a West Indian identity, in contradistinction to a more narrowly constructed Trinidadian one, remained an important feature of Williams's life and work.

Williams also sought to ensure that the book would derive its intellectual respectability from the strength of its arguments and not from the personality of its author or his academic qualifications. After he saw the first proofs of the book, he hastened to assure his editor that he was "so happy to see the galleys with the simple statement 'By Eric Williams.' I have such a horror of all these high sounding titles and lengthy degrees."[19] Still, Williams was extraordinarily active in promoting the sale of the book in the United States, the West Indies, and Canada. On April 25, 1944, nearly seven months before the book appeared, Williams wrote to Couch that he had just returned from a tour of the West Indies, where

> I found, as I had expected, a tremendous interest in the history of the West Indies. I was asked to speak to the subscribers of the Public Library of Trinidad and chose for my topic "The British West Indies in World History," giving the audience, so to speak, a preview of the book. The Governor was in the chair, so it was a gala occasion. A hall meant for 300 had to accommodate 700, and on all sides I have been told that there never has been anything comparable in Trinidad history. I am not so modest as to deny that some part of the interest was due to the speaker, but at the same time the subject exercised a great attention. I was told afterwards that my book would sell 1,000 copies in Trinidad, and whilst the figure appears to be a little high, the exaggeration is not as great as it might appear to the outsider. I had been given some publicity in Barbados and British Guiana, and I found there, too, a great interest in the book.[20]

Williams was able to persuade the Press to sell the book in the West Indies for $1.00 instead of the $3.00 that it cost in the United States. He also purchased several copies at a discount rate for authors and sold them in the United States and Canada, particularly to West Indian students. Four months after the book's publication, he stressed to Couch that he was "very keen on West Indians in particular reading the book," believing that they would profit intellectually and in other ways from it. "I have taken a political line in the book," Williams reminded Couch, "which West Indians more than anyone else need to understand."[21] Williams was so successful in selling the book that Porter Cowles, the executive assistant to the director of the Press, complimented him for his role. "Most authors who buy a number of copies of their own works seem to do it for themselves," wrote Cowles. "You are the exception in that you persuade other people to buy them," she added.[22]

The remarkable success of the book led the Press to order a second printing of 1,500 copies in the summer of 1945. Williams was very pleased. Writing to Couch on August 18, 1945, he exulted, "I am of course very happy that the book is going so well. Without wishing to appear conceited, however, I am not surprised. Not only slavery but also the West Indies are subjects of great interest in the United States and England; and of course the West Indies today."[23] By December 31, 1949, the Press had sold 2,412 copies of the book and had distributed 95 complimentary copies. The royalties amounted to $271.80, a sum that fell far short of the author's obligations to his benefactors.

Capitalism and Slavery was widely reviewed. Scholarly journals, literary magazines, and the popular press took note of its appearance. The reviews were, understandably, mixed. Reviewers of African descent uniformly praised the work, while those who claimed a European heritage were much less enthusiastic and more divided in their reception. Writing in the *Negro College Quarterly*, noted black scholar Lorenzo Greene called the book "a scholarly study." He commented that "a work of this kind has been long overdue and Dr. Williams has filled the need in brilliant fashion." The reviewer for the *Crisis*, historian J. A. Rogers, complimented the author for showing "better than I can recall ever having seen what the New World owes to the Negro, the victim of slavery and the slave trade, for its development; particularly in its pioneer stages; as well as England for its rise from a small power to the world's greatest empire." Carter J. Woodson in the *Journal of Negro History* praised the book for marking "the beginning of the scientific study of slavery from the international point of view."[24]

Among the white reviewers, Elizabeth Donnan was "sometimes troubled by the feeling that the thesis, plausible as it is, may be too simple. The rigidity of the economic interpretation makes small allowance for the complexity of man's motives and for the play of circumstances which often create utterly unplanned and unexpected situations," she asserted. In a very hostile review, Frank Tannenbaum found that the book was tainted "with a strongly flavored faith in the economic interpretation of history, given strident enthusiasm by a visible notion of Negro nationalism." The reviewer for the *Times Literary Supplement*, D. W. Brogan, charged that "some of the sections of this book are more brilliant guesses than complete demonstrations of incontestable claims of cause and effect." Nevertheless, Brogan continued, "this is an admirably written, argued and original piece of work." Henry Steele Commager found the work "one of the most learned, most penetrating and most significant that has appeared in this field of history."[25]

It is hardly surprising that a few English historians sought to dismiss Williams's arguments with venomous assaults rather than with reasoned arguments, careful research, and analysis. D. A. Farnie, an economic historian, suggested that the book had presented the author's "own community with the sustaining myth that 'capitalism' was responsible for their condition, a view that has not found favor in Western Europe, where history has been separated from its tap-root in myth, but has been found highly acceptable to the educated *élites* of Africa and Asia."[26] Much less critical, but blatantly patronizing, was J. D. Fage, the Africanist, who felt that Williams's assault on the "humanitarian argument" for the abolition of slavery was "inevitable in the late 1930s and early 1940s, when a young Negro radical from the colonies, still more one from the bitterly depressed West Indies, found himself working in the shadow of the school of imperial history that [Sir Reginald] Coupland had established within the calm walls of Oxford University."[27]

The first extended scholarly critique of *Capitalism and Slavery* did not appear until 1968. Writing in the *Economic History Review*, English historian Roger Anstey challenged the argument that a mature capitalism destroyed slavery.[28] Other scholars, benefiting from decades of research since the publication of the book in 1944, soon attempted to undermine its principal conclusions. As one measure of the debates that the book continues to generate, some of the world's leading students of the economics of slavery gathered at Bellagio, Italy, in 1984 to discuss the ideas that Williams advanced in his classic work.[29]

Capitalism and Slavery appeared when the author was only thirty-three years old—a fact that is sometimes overlooked. Despite his youth, it is a work of conceptual brilliance, intellectually mature, bold, incisive, and immensely provocative. Some contemporary scholars have chipped away at the edges of the book's arguments, and others have attacked its core, but the central contentions have not been vanquished intellectually. In fact, Williams's conceptualization of the problematic remains even if some later scholars have refined his questions and offered other answers.

The publication of *Capitalism and Slavery* marked an important watershed in the historiography of the Caribbean. It inaugurated a new phase in the study of the relationship between the colonial power and the colonies, permanently altering the terms of the analysis and the subsequent discourse. But its ramifications extended beyond the Caribbean. Williams established the centrality of African slavery and the slave trade to the English economy, challenging the traditional view that the colonies were more the recipients of metropolitan benevolence and less the principal agents in the construction of the imperial power's prosperity. His conclusions may be rejected, but no serious scholar can avoid confronting the important questions the book poses. *Capitalism and Slavery* will remain a historical treasure.

NOTES

1. Eric Williams, *Inward Hunger: The Education of a Prime Minister* (Chicago: University of Chicago Press, 1971), p. 33.
2. Ibid., p. 41.
3. Eric Williams to W. T. Couch, February 17, 1943, University of North Carolina Press Records, subgroup 4, Southern Historical Collection, University of North Carolina at Chapel Hill. All records concerning the publication of *Capitalism and Slavery* are located in this collection.
4. Ibid.
5. Lowell Ragatz to May T. Littlejohn, March 14, 1943.
6. Frank Pitman to May T. Littlejohn, n.d. (original emphasis).
7. Hugh Lefler to W. T. Couch, April 17, 1943.
8. Charles Robson to W. T. Couch, May 10, 1943.
9. W. T. Couch to Eric Williams, April 22, 1943.
10. Eric Williams to W. T. Couch, June 9, 1943.
11. Eric Williams to W. T. Couch, September 14, 1943.
12. Eric Williams to W. T. Couch, December 18, 1943.
13. Donald Goodchild to Eric Williams, March 27, 1944.
14. Eric Williams to W. T. Couch, September 4, 1943.
15. Eric Williams to W. T. Couch, December 18, 1943.
16. Eric Williams to May T. Littlejohn, June 3, 1944.
17. Eric Williams to May T. Littlejohn, June 19, 1944.
18. Eric Williams to W. T. Couch, March 13, 1944.

19. Eric Williams to May T. Littlejohn, March 29, 1944.
20. Eric Williams to W. T. Couch, April 25, 1944.
21. Eric Williams to W. T. Couch, March 14, 1945.
22. Porter Cowles to Eric Williams, April 19, 1947.
23. Eric Williams to W. T. Couch, August 18, 1945.
24. *Negro College Quarterly* 3, no. 1 (March 1945): 46–48; *Crisis*, July 10, 1945, 203–4; *Journal of Negro History* 30 (1945): 93–95.
25. *Journal of Economic History* 6, no. 2 (November 1946): 228; *Political Science Quarterly* 61 (1946): 247–53; *Times Literary Supplement*, May 26, 1945, 250; *Weekly Book Review*, February 4, 1945, 5.
26. D. A. Farnie, "The Commercial Empire of the Atlantic, 1607–1783," *Economic History Review*, 2d ser., 15 (1962): 212.
27. J. D. Fage, introduction to *The British Anti-Slavery Movement*, 2d ed., by Sir Reginald Coupland (New York: Barnes and Noble, 1964), xvii–xxi. Coupland emphasized the humanitarian impulse in British emancipation in his works.
28. Roger T. Anstey, "'Capitalism and Slavery': A Critique," *Economic History Review*, 2d ser., 21 (1968): 307–20.
29. Some of the papers presented at this conference appeared in Barbara L. Solow and Stanley L. Engerman, eds., *British Capitalism and Caribbean Slavery: The Legacy of Eric Williams* (New York: Cambridge University Press, 1987). See, in particular, Richard B. Sheridan, "Eric Williams and *Capitalism and Slavery*: A Biographical and Historiographical Essay," in ibid., pp. 317–45.

Capitalism & Slavery

THE ORIGIN

OF

NEGRO SLAVERY

WHEN IN 1492 COLUMBUS, representing the Spanish monarchy, discovered the New World, he set in train the long and
bitter international rivalry over colonial possessions for which,
after four and a half centuries, no solution has yet been found.
Portugal, which had initiated the movement of international
expansion, claimed the new territories on the ground that they
fell within the scope of a papal bull of 1455 authorizing her to
reduce to servitude all infidel peoples. The two powers, to avoid
controversy, sought arbitration and, as Catholics, turned to the
Pope—a natural and logical step in an age when the universal
claims of the Papacy were still unchallenged by individuals and
governments. After carefully sifting the rival claims, the Pope
issued in 1493 a series of papal bulls which established a line of
demarcation between the colonial possessions of the two states:
the East went to Portugal and the West to Spain. The partition,
however, failed to satisfy Portuguese aspirations and in the subsequent year the contending parties reached a more satisfactory
compromise in the Treaty of Tordesillas, which rectified the
papal judgment to permit Portuguese ownership of Brazil.

Neither the papal arbitration nor the formal treaty was intended to be binding on other powers, and both were in fact
repudiated. Cabot's voyage to North America in 1497 was Eng-

land's immediate reply to the partition. Francis I of France voiced his celebrated protest: "The sun shines for me as for others. I should very much like to see the clause in Adam's will that excludes me from a share of the world." The king of Denmark refused to accept the Pope's ruling as far as the East Indies were concerned. Sir William Cecil, the famous Elizabethan statesman, denied the Pope's right "to give and take kingdoms to whomsoever he pleased." In 1580 the English government countered with the principle of effective occupation as the determinant of sovereignty.[1] Thereafter, in the parlance of the day, there was "no peace below the line." It was a dispute, in the words of a later governor of Barbados, as to "whether the King of England or of France shall be monarch of the West Indies, for the King of Spain cannot hold it long. . . ."[2] England, France, and even Holland, began to challenge the Iberian Axis and claim their place in the sun. The Negro, too, was to have his place, though he did not ask for it: it was the broiling sun of the sugar, tobacco and cotton plantations of the New World.

According to Adam Smith, the prosperity of a new colony depends upon one simple economic factor—"plenty of good land."[3] The British colonial possessions up to 1776, however, can broadly be divided into two types. The first is the self-sufficient and diversified economy of small farmers, "mere earth-scratchers" as Gibbon Wakefield derisively called them,[4] living on a soil which, as Canada was described in 1840, was "no lottery, with a few exorbitant prizes and a large number of blanks, but a secure and certain investment."[5] The second type is the colony which has facilities for the production of staple articles on a large scale for an export market. In the first category fell the Northern colonies of the American mainland; in the second, the mainland tobacco colonies and the sugar islands of the Caribbean. In colonies of the latter type, as Merivale pointed out, land and capital were both useless unless labor could be commanded.[6] Labor, that is, must be constant and must work, or be made to work, in co-operation. In such colonies the rugged individualism of the Massachusetts farmer, practising his intensive agriculture and wringing by the sweat of his brow niggardly returns from a grudging soil, must yield to the disciplined gang of the big capitalist practising extensive agriculture and producing on a large scale. Without this compulsion, the laborer would otherwise exercise his natural inclination to work his own land and toil on his own account. The story is frequently told of the great English capitalist, Mr. Peel, who took £50,000 and three hundred laborers with him to the Swan River colony in Australia. His plan was that his laborers would work for him, as in the old country. Arrived in Australia, however, where land was plentiful—too plentiful —the laborers preferred to work for themselves as small proprietors, rather than under the capitalist for wages. Australia was not England, and the capitalist was left without a servant to make his bed or fetch him water.[7]

For the Caribbean colonies the solution for this dispersion and "earth-scratching" was slavery. The lesson of the early history of Georgia is instructive. Prohibited from employing slave labor by trustees who, in some instances, themselves owned slaves in other colonies, the Georgian planters found themselves in the position, as Whitefield phrased it, of people whose legs were tied and were told to walk. So the Georgia magistrates drank toasts "to the one thing needful"—slavery—until the ban was lifted.[8] "Odious resource" though it might be, as Merivale called it,[9] slavery was an economic institution of the first importance. It had been the basis of Greek economy and had built up the Roman Empire. In modern times it provided the sugar for the tea and the coffee cups of the Western world. It produced the cotton to serve as a base for modern capitalism. It made the American South and the Caribbean islands. Seen in historical perspective, it forms a part of that general picture of the harsh treatment of the underprivileged classes, the unsympathetic poor laws and severe feudal laws, and the indifference with which the rising capitalist class was "beginning to reckon prosperity in terms of pounds sterling, and . . . becoming used to the idea of sacrificing human life to the deity of increased production."[10]

Adam Smith, the intellectual champion of the industrial middle class with its new-found doctrine of freedom, later propagated the argument that it was, in general, pride and love of power in the master that led to slavery and that, in those countries where slaves were employed, free labor would be more profitable. Universal experience demonstrated conclusively that "the work done by slaves, though it appears to cost only their maintenance, is in the end the dearest of any. A person who can acquire no property can have no other interest than to eat as much, and to labour as little as possible."[11]

Adam Smith thereby treated as an abstract proposition what is a specific question of time, place, labor and soil. The economic superiority of free hired labor over slave is obvious even to the slave owner. Slave labor is given reluctantly, it is unskilful, it lacks versatility.[12] Other things being equal, free men would be preferred. But in the early stages of colonial development, other things are not equal. When slavery is adopted, it is not adopted as the choice over free labor; there is no choice at all. The reasons for slavery, wrote Gibbon Wakefield, "are not moral, but economical circumstances; they relate not to vice and virtue, but to production."[13] With the limited population of Europe in the sixteenth century, the free laborers necessary to cultivate the staple crops of sugar, tobacco and cotton in the New World could not have been supplied in quantities adequate to permit large-scale production. Slavery was necessary for this, and to get slaves the Europeans turned first to the aborigines and then to Africa.

Under certain circumstances slavery has some obvious advantages. In the cultivation of crops like sugar, cotton and tobacco, where the cost of production is appreciably reduced on larger units, the slaveowner, with his large-scale production and his organized slave gang, can make more profitable use of the land than the small farmer or peasant proprietor. For such staple crops, the vast profits can well stand the greater expense of inefficient slave labor.[14] Where all the knowledge required is simple and a matter of routine, constancy and cooperation in labor—slavery—is essential, until, by importation of new recruits and breeding, the population has reached the point of density and the land available for appropriation has been already apportioned. When that stage is reached, and only then, the expenses of slavery, in the form of the cost and maintenance of slaves, productive and unproductive, exceed the cost of hired laborers. As Merivale wrote: "Slave labour is dearer than free *wherever abundance of free labour can be procured.*"[15]

From the standpoint of the grower, the greatest defect of slavery lies in the fact that it quickly exhausts the soil. The labor supply of low social status, docile and cheap, can be maintained in subjection only by systematic degradation and by deliberate efforts to suppress its intelligence. Rotation of crops and scientific farming are therefore alien to slave societies. As Jefferson wrote of Virginia, "we can buy an acre of new land cheaper than we can manure an old one."[16] The slave planter, in the picturesque nomenclature of the South, is a "land-killer." This serious defect of slavery can be counter-balanced and postponed for a time if fertile soil is practically unlimited. Expansion is a necessity of slave societies; the slave power requires ever fresh conquests.[17] "It is more profitable," wrote Merivale, "to cultivate a fresh soil by the dear labour of slaves, than an exhausted one by the cheap labour of freemen."[18] From Virginia and Maryland to Carolina, Georgia, Texas and the Middle West; from Barbados to Jamaica to Saint Domingue and then to Cuba; the logic was inexorable and the same. It was a relay race; the first to start passed the baton, unwillingly we may be sure, to another and then limped sadly behind.

Slavery in the Caribbean has been too narrowly identified with the Negro. A racial twist has thereby been given to what is basically an economic phenomenon. Slavery was not born of racism: rather, racism was the consequence of slavery. Unfree labor in the New World was brown, white, black, and yellow; Catholic, Protestant and pagan.

The first instance of slave trading and slave labor developed in the New World involved, racially, not the Negro but the Indian. The Indians rapidly succumbed to the excessive labor demanded of them, the insufficient diet, the white man's diseases, and their inability to adjust themselves to the new way of life. Accustomed to a life of liberty, their constitution and temperament were ill-adapted to the rigors of plantation slavery. As Fernando Ortíz writes: "To subject the Indian to the mines, to their monotonous, insane and severe labor, without tribal sense, without religious ritual, . . . was like taking away from him the meaning of his life. . . . It was to enslave not only his muscles but also his collective spirit."[19]

The visitor to Ciudad Trujillo, capital of the Dominican Republic (the present-day name of half of the island formerly called Hispaniola), will see a statue of Columbus, with the figure of an Indian woman gratefully writing (so reads the caption) the name of the Discoverer. The story is told, on the other hand, of the Indian chieftain, Hatuey, who, doomed to die for resisting the invaders, staunchly refused to accept the Christian faith as the gateway to salvation when he learned that his executioners, too, hoped to get to Heaven. It is far more probable that Hatuey, rather than the anonymous woman, represented contemporary Indian opinion of their new overlords.

England and France, in their colonies, followed the Spanish practice of enslavement of the Indians. There was one conspicuous difference—the attempts of the Spanish Crown, however ineffective, to restrict Indian slavery to those who refused to accept Christianity and to the warlike Caribs on the specious plea that they were cannibals. From the standpoint of the British government Indian slavery, unlike later Negro slavery which involved vital imperial interests, was a purely colonial matter. As Lauber writes: "The home government was interested in colonial slave conditions and legislation only when the African slave trade was involved. . . . Since it (Indian slavery) was never sufficiently extensive to interfere with Negro slavery and the slave trade, it never received any attention from the home government, and so existed as legal because never declared illegal."[20]

But Indian slavery never was extensive in the British dominions. Ballagh, writing of Virginia, says that popular sentiment had never "demanded the subjection of the Indian race *per se*, as was practically the case with the Negro in the first slave act of 1661, but only of a portion of it, and that admittedly a very small portion.... In the case of the Indian ... slavery was viewed as of an occasional nature, a preventive penalty and not as a normal and permanent condition."[21] In the New England colonies Indian slavery was unprofitable, for slavery of any kind was unprofitable because it was unsuited to the diversified agriculture of these colonies. In addition the Indian slave was inefficient. The Spaniards discovered that one Negro was worth four Indians.[22] A prominent official in Hispaniola insisted in 1518 that "permission be given to bring Negroes, a race robust for labor, instead of natives, so weak that they can only be employed in tasks requiring little endurance, such as taking care of maize fields or farms."[23] The future staples of the New World, sugar and cotton, required strength which the Indian lacked, and demanded the robust "cotton nigger" as sugar's need of strong mules produced in Louisiana the epithet "sugar mules." According to Lauber, "When compared with sums paid for Negroes at the same time and place the prices of Indian slaves are found to have been considerably lower."[24]

The Indian reservoir, too, was limited, the African inexhaustible. Negroes therefore were stolen in Africa to work the lands stolen from the Indians in America. The voyages of Prince Henry the Navigator complemented those of Columbus, West African history became the complement of West Indian.

The immediate successor of the Indian, however, was not the Negro but the poor white. These white servants included a variety of types. Some were indentured servants, so called because, before departure from the homeland, they had signed a contract, indented by law, binding them to service for a stipulated time in return for their passage. Still others, known as "redemptioners," arranged with the captain of the ship to pay for their passage on arrival or within a specified time thereafter; if they did not, they were sold by the captain to the highest bidder. Others were convicts, sent out by the deliberate policy of the home government, to serve for a specified period.

This emigration was in tune with mercantilist theories of the day which strongly advocated putting the poor to industrious and useful labor and favored emigration, voluntary or involuntary, as relieving the poor rates and finding more profitable occupations abroad for idlers and vagrants at home. "Indentured servitude," writes C. M. Haar, "was called into existence by two different though complementary forces: there was both a positive attraction from the New World and a negative repulsion from the Old."[25] In a state paper delivered to James I in 1606 Bacon emphasized that by emigration England would gain "a double commodity, in the avoidance of people here, and in making use of them there."[26]

This temporary service at the outset denoted no inferiority or degradation. Many of the servants were manorial tenants fleeing from the irksome restrictions of feudalism, Irishmen seeking freedom from the oppression of landlords and bishops, Germans running away from the devastation of the Thirty Years' War. They transplanted in their hearts a burning desire for land, an ardent passion for independence. They came to the land of opportunity to be free men, their imaginations powerfully wrought upon by glowing and extravagant descriptions in the home country.[27] It was only later when, in the words of Dr. Williamson, "all ideals of a decent colonial society, of a better and greater England overseas, were swamped in the pursuit of an immediate gain,"[28] that the introduction of disreputable elements became a general feature of indentured service.

A regular traffic developed in these indentured servants. Between 1654 and 1685 ten thousand sailed from Bristol alone, chiefly for the West Indies and Virginia.[29] In 1683 white servants represented one-sixth of Virginia's population. Two-thirds of the immigrants to Pennsylvania during the eighteenth century were white servants; in four years 25,000 came to Philadelphia alone. It has been estimated that more than a quarter of a million persons were of this class during the colonial period,[30] and that they probably constituted one-half of all English immigrants, the majority going to the middle colonies.[31]

As commercial speculation entered the picture, abuses crept in. Kidnaping was encouraged to a great degree and became a regular business in such towns as London and Bristol. Adults would be plied with liquor, children enticed with sweetmeats. The kidnapers were called "spirits," defined as "one that taketh upp men and women and children and sells them on a shipp to be conveyed beyond the sea." The captain of a ship trading to Jamaica would visit the Clerkenwell House of Correction, ply with drink the girls who had been imprisoned there as disorderly, and "invite" them to go to the West Indies.[32] The temptations held out to the unwary and the credulous were so attractive that, as the mayor of Bristol complained, husbands were induced to forsake their wives, wives their husbands, and apprentices their masters, while wanted criminals found on the transport ships a refuge from the arms of the law.[33] The wave of German immigration developed the "newlander," the labor agent of those days, who traveled up and down the Rhine Valley persuading the feudal peasants to sell their belongings and emigrate to America, receiving a commission for each emigrant.[34]

Much has been written about the trickery these "newlanders" were not averse to employing.[35] But whatever the deceptions practised, it remains true, as Friedrich Kapp has written, that "the real ground for the emigration fever lay in the unhealthy political and economic conditions. . . . The misery and oppression of the conditions of the little (German) states promoted emigration much more dangerously and continuously than the worst 'newlander.' "[36]

Convicts provided another steady source of white labor. The harsh feudal laws of England recognized three hundred capital crimes. Typical hanging offences included: picking a pocket for more than a shilling; shoplifting to the value of five shillings; stealing a horse or a sheep; poaching rabbits on a gentleman's estate.[37] Offences for which the punishment prescribed by law was transportation comprised the stealing of cloth, burning stacks of corn, the maiming and killing of cattle, hindering customs officers in the execution of their duty, and corrupt legal practices.[38] Proposals made in 1664 would have banished to the colonies all vagrants, rogues and idlers, petty thieves, gipsies, and loose persons frequenting unlicensed brothels.[39] A piteous petition in 1667 prayed for transportation instead of the death sentence for a wife convicted of stealing goods valued at three shillings and four pence.[40] In 1745 transportation was the penalty for the theft of a silver spoon and a gold watch.[41] One year after the emancipation of the Negro slaves, transportation was the penalty for trade union activity. It is difficult to resist the conclusion that there was some connection between the law and the labor needs of the plantations, and the marvel is that so few people ended up in the colonies overseas.

Benjamin Franklin opposed this "dumping upon the New World of the outcasts of the Old" as the most cruel insult ever offered by one nation to another, and asked, if England was justified in sending her convicts to the colonies, whether the latter were justified in sending to England their rattlesnakes in exchange?[42] It is not clear why Franklin should have been so sensitive. Even if the convicts were hardened criminals, the great increase of indentured servants and free emigrants would have tended to render the convict influence innocuous, as increasing quantities of water poured in a glass containing poison. Without convicts the early development of the Australian colonies in the nineteenth century would have been impossible. Only a few of the colonists, however, were so particular. The general attitude was summed up by a contemporary: "Their labor would be more beneficial in an infant settlement, than their vices could be pernicious."[43] There was nothing strange about this attitude. The great problem in a new country is the problem of labor, and convict labor, as Merivale has pointed out, was equivalent to a free present by the government to the settlers without burdening the latter with the expense of importation.[44] The governor of Virginia in 1611 was willing to welcome convicts reprieved from death as "a readie way to furnish us with men and not allways with the worst kind of men."[45] The West Indies were prepared to accept all and sundry, even the spawn of Newgate and Bridewell, for "no goale-bird [sic] can be so incorrigible, but there is hope of his conformity here, as well as of his preferment, which some have happily experimented."[46]

The political and civil disturbances in England between 1640 and 1740 augmented the supply of white servants. Political and religious nonconformists paid for their unorthodoxy by transportation, mostly to the sugar islands. Such was the fate of many of Cromwell's Irish prisoners, who were sent to the West Indies.[47] So thoroughly was this policy pursued that an active verb was added to the English language—to "barbadoes" a person.[48] Montserrat became largely an Irish colony,[49] and the Irish brogue is still frequently heard today in many parts of the British West Indies. The Irish, however, were poor servants. They hated the English, were always ready to aid England's enemies, and in a revolt in the Leeward Islands in 1689[50] we can already see signs of that burning indignation which, according to Lecky, gave Washington some of his best soldiers.[51] The vanquished in Cromwell's Scottish campaigns were treated like the Irish before them, and Scotsmen came to be regarded as "the general travaillers and soldiers in most foreign parts."[52] Religious intolerance sent more workers to the plantations. In 1661 Quakers refusing to take the oath for the third time were to be transported; in 1664 transportation, to any plantation except Virginia or New England, or a fine of one hundred pounds was decreed for the third offence for persons over sixteen assembling in groups of five or more under pretence of religion.[53] Many of Monmouth's adherents were sent to Barbados, with orders to be detained as servants for ten years. The prisoners were granted in batches to favorite courtiers, who made handsome profits from the traffic in which, it is alleged, even the Queen shared.[54] A similar policy was resorted to after the Jacobite risings of the eighteenth century.

The transportation of these white servants shows in its true light the horrors of the Middle Passage—not as something unusual or inhuman but as a part of the age. The emigrants were packed like herrings. According to Mittelberger, each servant was allowed about two feet in width and six feet in length in bed.[55] The boats were small, the voyage long, the food, in the absence of refrigeration, bad, disease inevitable. A petition to Parliament in 1659 describes how seventy-two servants had been locked up below deck during the whole voyage of five and a half weeks, "amongst horses, that their souls, through heat and steam under the tropic, fainted in them."[56] Inevitably abuses crept into the system and Fearon was shocked by "the horrible picture of human suffering which this living sepulchre" of an emigrant vessel in Philadelphia afforded.[57] But conditions even for the free passengers were not much better in those days, and the comment of a Lady of Quality describing a voyage from Scotland to the West Indies on a ship full of indentured servants should banish any ideas that the horrors of the slave ship are to be accounted for by the fact that the victims were Negroes. "It is hardly possible," she writes, "to believe that human nature could be so depraved, as to treat fellow creatures in such a manner for so little gain."[58]

The transportation of servants and convicts produced a powerful vested interest in England. When the Colonial Board was created in 1661, not the least important of its duties was the control of the trade in indentured servants. In 1664 a commission was appointed, headed by the King's brother, to examine and report upon the exportation of servants. In 1670 an act prohibiting the transportation of English prisoners overseas was rejected; another bill against the stealing of children came to nothing. In the transportation of felons, a whole hierarchy, from courtly secretaries and grave judges down to the jailors and turnkeys, insisted on having a share in the spoils.[59] It has been suggested that it was humanity for his fellow countrymen and men of his own color which dictated the planter's preference for the Negro slave.[60] Of this humanity there is not a trace in the records of the time, at least as far as the plantation colonies and commercial production were concerned. Attempts to register emigrant servants and regularize the procedure of transportation—thereby giving full legal recognition to the system—were evaded. The leading merchants and public officials were all involved in the practice. The penalty for man-stealing was exposure in the pillory, but no missiles from the spectators were tolerated. Such opposition as there was came from the masses. It was enough to point a finger at a woman in the streets of London and call her a "spirit" to start a riot.

This was the situation in England when Jeffreys came to Bristol on his tour of the West to clean up the remnants of

Monmouth's rebellion. Jeffreys has been handed down to posterity as a "butcher," the tyrannical deputy of an arbitrary king, and his legal visitation is recorded in the textbooks as the "Bloody Assizes." They had one redeeming feature. Jeffreys vowed that he had come to Bristol with a broom to sweep the city clean, and his wrath fell on the kidnapers who infested the highest municipal offices. The merchants and justices were in the habit of straining the law to increase the number of felons who could be transported to the sugar plantations they owned in the West Indies. They would terrify petty offenders with the prospect of hanging and then induce them to plead for transportation. Jeffreys turned upon the mayor, complete in scarlet and furs, who was about to sentence a pickpocket to transportation to Jamaica, forced him, to the great astonishment of Bristol's worthy citizens, to enter the prisoners' dock, like a common felon, to plead guilty or not guilty, and hectored him in characteristic language: "Sir, Mr. Mayor, you I meane, Kidnapper, and an old Justice of the Peace on the bench. ... I doe not knowe him, an old knave: he goes to the taverne, and for a pint of sack he will bind people servants to the Indies at the taverne. A kidnapping knave! I will have his ears off, before I goe forth of towne. ... Kidnapper, you, I mean, Sir. ... If it were not in respect of the sword, which is over your head, I would send you to Newgate, you kidnapping knave. You are worse than the pick-pockett who stands there. ... I hear the trade of kidnapping is of great request. They can discharge a felon or a traitor, provided they will go to Mr. Alderman's plantation at the West Indies." The mayor was fined one thousand pounds, but apart from the loss of dignity and the fear aroused in their hearts, the merchants lost nothing—their gains were left inviolate.[61]

According to one explanation, Jeffreys' insults were the result of intoxication or insanity.[62] It is not improbable that they were connected with a complete reversal of mercantilist thought on the question of emigration, as a result of the internal development of Britain herself. By the end of the seventeenth century the stress had shifted from the accumulation of the precious metals as the aim of national economic policy to the develop-

ment of industry within the country, the promotion of employment and the encouragement of exports. The mercantilists
argued that the best way to reduce costs, and thereby compete with other countries, was to pay low wages, which a large
population tended to ensure. The fear of overpopulation at
the beginning of the seventeenth century gave way to a fear
of under-population in the middle of the same century. The
essential condition of colonization—emigration from the home
country—now ran counter to the principle that national interest
demanded a large population at home. Sir Josiah Child denied
that emigration to America had weakened England, but he
was forced to admit that in this view he was in a minority
of possibly one in a thousand, while he endorsed the general
opinion that "whatever tends to the depopulating of a kingdom
tends to the impoverishment of it."[63] Jeffreys' unusual humanitarianism appears less strange and may be attributed rather to
economic than to spirituous considerations. His patrons, the
Royal Family, had already given their patronage to the Royal
African Company and the Negro slave trade. For the surplus
population needed to people the colonies in the New World
the British had turned to Africa, and by 1680 they already had
positive evidence, in Barbados, that the African was satisfying
the necessities of production better than the European.

The status of these servants became progressively worse in
the plantation colonies. Servitude, originally a free personal
relation based on voluntary contract for a definite period of
service, in lieu of transportation and maintenance, tended to
pass into a property relation which asserted a control of varying
extent over the bodies and liberties of the person during service as if he were a thing.[64] Eddis, writing on the eve of the
Revolution, found the servants groaning "beneath a worse than
Egyptian bondage."[65] In Maryland servitude developed into an
institution approaching in some respects chattel slavery.[66] Of
Pennsylvania it has been said that "no matter how kindly they
may have been treated in particular cases, or how voluntarily
they may have entered into the relation, as a class and when
once bound, indentured servants were temporarily chattels."[67]
On the sugar plantations of Barbados the servants spent their

time "grinding at the mills and attending the furnaces, or digging in this scorching island; having nothing to feed on (notwithstanding their hard labour) but potatoe roots, nor to drink, but water with such roots washed in it, besides the bread and tears of their own afflictions; being bought and sold still from one planter to another, or attached as horses and beasts for the debts of their masters, being whipt at the whipping posts (as rogues,) for their masters' pleasure, and sleeping in sties worse than hogs in England...."[68] As Professor Harlow concludes, the weight of evidence proves incontestably that the conditions under which white labor was procured and utilized in Barbados were "persistently severe, occasionally dishonourable, and generally a disgrace to the English name."[69]

English officialdom, however, took the view that servitude was not too bad, and the servant in Jamaica was better off than the husbandman in England. "It is a place as grateful to you for trade as any part of the world. It is not so odious as it is represented."[70] But there was some sensitiveness on the question. The Lords of Trade and Plantations, in 1676, opposed the use of the word "servitude" as a mark of bondage and slavery, and suggested "service" instead.[71] The institution was not affected by the change. The hope has been expressed that the white servants were spared the lash so liberally bestowed upon their Negro comrades.[72] They had no such good fortune. Since they were bound for a limited period, the planter had less interest in their welfare than in that of the Negroes who were perpetual servants and therefore "the most useful appurtenances" of a plantation.[73] Eddis found the Negroes "almost in every instance, under more comfortable circumstances than the miserable European, over whom the rigid planter exercises an inflexible severity."[74] The servants were regarded by the planters as "white trash," and were bracketed with the Negroes as laborers. "Not one of these colonies ever was or ever can be brought to any considerable improvement without a supply of white servants and Negroes," declared the Council of Montserrat in 1680.[75] In a European society in which subordination was considered essential, in which Burke could speak of the working classes as "miserable sheep" and Voltaire as "canaille," and Linguet condemn the worker to the use of his physical strength alone, for "everything would be lost once he knew that he had a mind"[76]—in such a society it is unnecessary to seek for apologies for the condition of the white servant in the colonies. Defoe bluntly stated that the white servant was a slave.[77] He was not. The servant's loss of liberty was of limited duration, the Negro was slave for life. The servant's status could not descend to his offspring, Negro children took the status of the mother. The master at no time had absolute control over the person and liberty of his servant as he had over his slave. The servant had rights, limited but recognized by law and inserted in a contract. He enjoyed, for instance, a limited right to property. In actual law the conception of the servant as a piece of property never went beyond that of personal estate and never reached the stage of a chattel or real estate. The laws in the colonies maintained this rigid distinction and visited cohabitation between the races with severe penalties. The servant could aspire, at the end of his term, to a plot of land, though, as Wertenbaker points out for Virginia, it was not a legal right,[78] and conditions varied from colony to colony. The serf in Europe could therefore hope for an early freedom in America which villeinage could not afford. The freed servants became small yeomen farmers, settled in the back country, a democratic force in a society of large aristocratic plantation owners, and were the pioneers in westward expansion. That was why Jefferson in America, as Saco in Cuba, favored the introduction of European servants instead of African slaves—as tending to democracy rather than aristocracy.[79]

The institution of white servitude, however, had grave disadvantages. Postlethwayt, a rigid mercantilist, argued that white laborers in the colonies would tend to create rivalry with the mother country in manufacturing. Better black slaves on plantations than white servants in industry, which would encourage aspirations to independence.[80] The supply moreover was becoming increasingly difficult, and the need of the plantations outstripped the English convictions. In addition, merchants were involved in many vexatious and costly proceedings arising from people signifying their willingness to emigrate, accepting food and clothes in advance, and then sueing for unlawful detention.[81] Indentured servants were not forthcoming in sufficient quantities to replace those who had served their term. On the plantations, escape was easy for the white servant; less easy for the Negro who, if freed, tended, in self-defence, to stay in his locality where he was well known and less likely to be apprehended as a vagrant or runaway slave. The servant expected land at the end of his contract; the Negro, in a strange environment, conspicuous by his color and features, and ignorant of the white man's language and ways, could be kept permanently divorced from the land. Racial differences made it easier to justify and rationalize Negro slavery, to exact the mechanical obedience of a plough-ox or a cart-horse, to demand that resignation and that complete moral and intellectual subjection which alone make slave labor possible. Finally, and this was the decisive factor, the Negro slave was cheaper. The money which procured a white man's services for ten years could buy a Negro for life.[82] As the governor of Barbados stated, the Barbadian planters found by experience that "three blacks work better and cheaper than one white man."[83]

But the experience with white servitude had been invaluable. Kidnaping in Africa encountered no such difficulties as were encountered in England. Captains and ships had the experience of the one trade to guide them in the other. Bristol, the center of the servant trade, became one of the centers of the slave trade. Capital accumulated from the one financed the other. White servitude was the historic base upon which Negro slavery was constructed. The felon-drivers in the plantations became without effort slave-drivers. "In significant numbers," writes Professor Phillips, "the Africans were latecomers fitted into a system already developed."[84]

Here, then, is the origin of Negro slavery. The reason was economic, not racial; it had to do not with the color of the laborer, but the cheapness of the labor. As compared with Indian and white labor, Negro slavery was eminently superior. "In each case," writes Bassett, discussing North Carolina, "it was a survival of the fittest. Both Indian slavery and white servitude were to go down before the black man's superior endurance, docility, and labor capacity."[85] The features of the man, his hair, color and dentifrice, his "subhuman" characteristics so widely pleaded, were only the later rationalizations to justify a simple economic fact: that the colonies needed labor and resorted to Negro labor because it was cheapest and best. This was not a theory, it was a practical conclusion deduced from the personal experience of the planter. He would have gone to the moon, if necessary, for labor. Africa was nearer than the moon, nearer too than the more populous countries of India and China. But their turn was to come.

This white servitude is of cardinal importance for an understanding of the development of the New World and the Negro's place in that development. It completely explodes the old myth that the whites could not stand the strain of manual labor in the climate of the New World and that, for this reason and this reason alone, the European powers had recourse to Africans. The argument is quite untenable. A Mississippi dictum will have it that "only black men and mules can face the sun in July." But the whites faced the sun for well over a hundred years in Barbados, and the Salzburgers of Georgia indignantly denied that rice cultivation was harmful to them.[86] The Caribbean islands are well within the tropical zone, but their climate is more equable than tropical, the temperature rarely exceeds 80 degrees though it remains uniform the whole year round, and they are exposed to the gentle winds from the sea. The unbearable humidity of an August day in some parts of the United States has no equal in the islands. Moreover only the southern tip of Florida in the United States is actually tropical, yet Negro labor flourished in Virginia and Carolina. The southern parts of the United States are not hotter than South Italy or Spain, and de Tocqueville asked why the European could not work there as well as in those two countries?[87] When Whitney invented his cotton gin, it was confidently expected that cotton would be produced by free labor on small farms, and it was, in fact, so produced.[88] Where the white farmer was ousted, the enemy was not the climate but the slave plantation, and the white farmer moved westward, until the expanding plantation sent him on his wanderings again. Writing in 1857, Weston pointed out that labor in the fields of the extreme South and all the heavy outdoor work in New Orleans were performed by whites, without any ill consequences. "No part of the continental borders of the Gulf of Mexico," he wrote, "and none of the islands which separate it from the ocean, need be abandoned to the barbarism of negro slavery."[89] In our own time we who have witnessed the dispossession of Negroes by white sharecroppers in the South and the mass migration of Negroes from the South to the colder climates of Detroit, New York, Pittsburgh and other industrial centers of the North, can no longer accept the convenient rationalization that Negro labor was employed on the slave plantations because the climate was too rigorous for the constitution of the white man.

A constant and steady emigration of poor whites from Spain to Cuba, to the very end of Spanish dominion, characterized Spanish colonial policy. Fernando Ortíz has drawn a striking contrast between the role of tobacco and sugar in Cuban history. Tobacco was a free white industry intensively cultivated on small farms; sugar was a black slave industry extensively cultivated on large plantations. He further compared the free Cuban tobacco industry with its slave Virginian counterpart.[90] What determined the difference was not climate but the economic structure of the two areas. The whites could hardly have endured the tropical heat of Cuba and succumbed to the tropical heat of Barbados. In Puerto Rico, the jíbaro, the poor white peasant, is still the basic type, demonstrating, in the words of Grenfell Price, how erroneous is the belief that after three generations the white man cannot breed in the tropics.[91] Similar white communities have survived in the Caribbean, from the earliest settlements right down to our own times, in the Dutch West Indian islands of Saba and St. Martin. For some sixty years French settlers have lived in St. Thomas not only as fishermen but as agriculturalists, forming today the "largest single farming class" in the island.[92] As Dr. Price concludes: "It appears that northern whites can retain a fair standard for generations in the trade-wind tropics if the location is free from the worst forms of tropical disease, if the economic return is adequate, and if the community is prepared to undertake hard, physical work."[93] Over one hundred years ago a number of German emigrants settled in Seaford, Jamaica. They survive today, with no visible signs of deterioration, flatly contradicting the popular belief as to the possibility of survival of the northern white in the tropics.[94] Wherever, in short, tropical agriculture remained on a small farming basis, whites not only survived but prospered. Where the whites disappeared, the cause was not the climate but the supersession of the small farm by the large plantation, with its consequent demand for a large and steady supply of labor.

The climatic theory of the plantation is thus nothing but a rationalization. In an excellent essay on the subject Professor Edgar Thompson writes: "The plantation is not to be accounted for by climate. It is a political institution." It is, we might add, more: it is an economic institution. The climatic theory "is part of an ideology which rationalizes and naturalizes an existing social and economic order, and this everywhere seems to be an order in which there is a race problem."[95]

The history of Australia clinches the argument. Nearly half of this island continent lies within the tropical zone. In part of this tropical area, the state of Queensland, the chief crop is sugar. When the industry began to develop, Australia had a choice of two alternatives: black labor or white labor. The commonwealth began its sugar cultivation in the usual way—with imported black labor from the Pacific islands. Increasing demands, however, were made for a white Australia policy, and in the twentieth century non-white immigration was prohibited. It is irrelevant to consider here that as a result the cost of production of Australian sugar is prohibitive, that the industry is artificial and survives only behind the Chinese wall of Australian autarchy. Australia was willing to pay a high price in order to remain a white man's country. Our sole concern here with the question is that this price was paid from the pockets of the Australian consumer and not in the physical degeneration of the Australian worker.

Labor in the Queensland sugar industry today is wholly white. "Queensland," writes H. L. Wilkinson, "affords the only example in the world of European colonization in the tropics on an extensive scale. It does more; it shows a large European population doing the whole of the work of its civilization from the meanest service, and most exacting manual labor, to the highest form of intellectualism."[96] To such an extent has science exploded superstition that Australian scientists today argue that the only condition on which white men and women can remain healthy in the tropics is that they must engage in hard manual work. Where they have done so, as in Queensland, "the most rigorous scientific examination," according to the Australian Medical Congress in 1920, "failed to show any organic changes in white residents which enabled them to be distinguished from residents of temperate climates."[97]

Negro slavery, thus, had nothing to do with climate. Its origin can be expressed in three words: in the Caribbean, Sugar; on the mainland, Tobacco and Cotton. A change in the economic structure produced a corresponding change in the labor supply. The fundamental fact was "the creation of an inferior social and economic organization of exploiters and exploited."[98] Sugar, tobacco, and cotton required the large plantation and hordes of cheap labor, and the small farm of the ex-indentured white servant could not possibly survive. The tobacco of the small farm in Barbados was displaced by the sugar of the large plantation. The rise of the sugar industry in the Caribbean was the signal for a gigantic dispossession of the small farmer. Barbados in 1645 had 11,200 small white farmers and 5,680 Negro slaves; in 1667 there were 745 large plantation owners and 82,023 slaves. In 1645 the island had 18,300 whites fit to bear arms, in 1667 only 8,300.[99] The white farmers were squeezed out. The planters continued to offer inducements to newcomers, but they could no longer offer the main inducement, land. White servants preferred the other islands where they could hope for land, to Barbados, where they were sure there was none.[100] In desperation the planters proposed legislation which would prevent a landowner from purchasing more land, compel Negroes and servants to wear dimity manufactured in Barbados (what would English mercantilists have said?) to provide employment for the poor whites, and prevent Negroes from being taught a trade.[101] The governor of Barbados in 1695 drew a pitiful picture of these ex-servants. Without fresh meat or rum, "they are domineered over and used like dogs, and this in time will undoubtedly drive away all the commonalty of the white people." His only suggestion was to give the right to elect members of the Assembly to every white man owning two acres of land. Candidates for election would "sometimes give the poor miserable creatures a little rum and fresh provisions and such things as would be of nourishment to them," in order to get their votes—and elections were held every year.[102] It is not surprising that the exodus continued.

The poor whites began their travels, disputing their way all over the Caribbean, from Barbados to Nevis, to Antigua, and thence to Guiana and Trinidad, and ultimately Carolina. Everywhere they were pursued and dispossessed by the same inexorable economic force, sugar; and in Carolina they were safe from cotton only for a hundred years. Between 1672 and 1708 the white men in Nevis decreased by more than three-fifths, the black population more than doubled. Between 1672 and 1727 the white males of Montserrat declined by more than two-thirds, in the same period the black population increased more than eleven times.[103] "The more they buie," said the Barbadians, referring to their slaves, "the more they are able to buye, for in a yeare and a halfe they will earne with God's blessing as much as they cost."[104] King Sugar had begun his depredations, changing flourishing commonwealths of small farmers into vast sugar factories owned by a camarilla of absentee capitalist magnates and worked by a mass of alien proletarians. The plantation economy had no room for poor whites; the proprietor or overseer, a physician on the more prosperous plantations, possibly their families, these were sufficient. "If a state," wrote Weston, "could be supposed to be made up of continuous plantations, the white race would be not merely starved out, but literally squeezed out."[105] The resident planters, apprehensive of the growing disproportion between whites and blacks, passed Deficiency Laws to compel absentees, under penalty of fines, to keep white servants. The absentees preferred to pay the fines. In the West Indies today the poor whites survive in the "Redlegs" of Barbados, pallid, weak and depraved from in-breeding, strong rum, insufficient food and abstinence from manual labor. For, as Merivale wrote, "in a country where Negro slavery prevails extensively, no white is industrious."[106]

It was the triumph, not of geographical conditions, as Harlow contends,[107] but of economic. The victims were the Negroes in Africa and the small white farmers. The increase of wealth for the few whites was as phenomenal as the increase of misery for the many blacks. The Barbados crops in 1650, over a twenty-month period, were worth over three million pounds,[108] about fifteen millions in modern money. In 1666 Barbados was computed to be seventeen times as rich as it had been before the planting of sugar. "The buildings in 1643 were mean, with things only for necessity, but in 1666, plate, jewels, and household stuff were estimated at £500,000, their buildings very fair and beautiful, and their houses like castles, their sugar houses and negroes huts show themselves from the sea like so many small towns, each defended by its castle."[109] The price of land skyrocketed. A plantation of five hundred acres which sold for £400 in 1640 fetched £7,000 for a half-share in 1648.[110] The estate of one Captain Waterman, comprising eight hundred acres, had at one time been split up among no less than forty proprietors.[111] For sugar was and is essentially a capitalist undertaking, involving not only agricultural operations but the crude stages of refining as well. A report on the French sugar islands stated that to make ten hogsheads of sugar required as great an expenditure in beasts of burden, mills and utensils as to make a hundred.[112] James Knight of Jamaica estimated that it required four hundred acres to start a sugar plantation.[113] According to Edward Long, another planter and the historian of the island, it needed £5,000 to start a small plantation of three hundred acres, producing from thirty to fifty hogsheads of sugar a year, £14,000 for a plantation of the same size producing one hundred hogsheads.[114] There could be only two classes in such a society, wealthy planters and oppressed slaves.

The moral is reinforced by a consideration of the history of Virginia, where the plantation economy was based not on sugar but on tobacco. The researches of Professor Wertenbaker have exploded the legend that Virginia from the outset was an aristocratic dominion. In the early seventeenth century about two-thirds of the landholders had neither slaves nor indentured servants. The strength of the colony lay in its numerous white yeomanry. Conditions became worse as the market for tobacco was glutted by Spanish competition and the Virginians demanded in wrath that something be done about "those petty English plantations in the savage islands in the West Indies" through which quantities of Spanish tobacco reached England.[115] None the less, though prices continued to fall, the exports of Virginia and Maryland increased more than six times between 1663 and 1699. The explanation lay in two words—Negro slavery, which cheapened the cost of production. Negro slaves, one-twentieth of the population in 1670, were one-fourth in 1730. "Slavery, from being an insignificant factor in the economic life of the colony, had become the very foundation upon which it was established." There was still room in Virginia, as there was not in Barbados, for the small farmer, but land was useless to him if he could not compete with slave labor. So the Virginian peasant, like the Barbadian, was squeezed out. "The Virginia which had formerly been so largely the land of the little farmer, had become the land of Masters and Slaves. For aught else there was no room."[116]

The whole future history of the Caribbean is nothing more than a dotting of the i's and a crossing of the t's. It happened earlier in the British and French than in the Spanish islands, where the process was delayed until the advent of the dollar diplomacy of our own time. Under American capital we have witnessed the transformation of Cuba, Puerto Rico and the Dominican Republic into huge sugar factories (though the large plantation, especially in Cuba, was not unknown under the Spanish regime), owned abroad and operated by alien labor, on the British West Indian pattern. That this process is taking place with free labor and in nominally independent areas (Puerto Rico excepted) helps us to see in its true light the first importation of Negro slave labor in the British Caribbean—a phase in the history of the plantation. In the words of Professor Phillips, the plantation system was "less dependent upon slavery than slavery was upon it. . . . The plantation system formed, so to speak, the industrial and social frame of government. . ., while slavery was a code of written laws enacted for that purpose."[117]

Where the plantation did not develop, as in the Cuban tobacco industry, Negro labor was rare and white labor predominated. The liberal section of the Cuban population consistently advocated the cessation of the Negro slave trade and the introduction of white immigrants. Saco, mouthpiece of the liberals, called for the immigration of workers "white and free, from all parts of the world, of all races, provided they have a white face and can do honest labor."[118] Sugar defeated Saco. It was the sugar plantation, with its servile base, which retarded white immigration in nineteenth century Cuba as it had banned it in seventeenth century Barbados and eighteenth century Saint Domingue. No sugar, no Negroes. In Puerto Rico, which developed relatively late as a genuine plantation, and where, before the American regime, sugar never dominated the lives and thoughts of the population as it did elsewhere, the poor white peasants survived and the Negro slaves never exceeded fourteen per cent of the population.[119] Saco wanted to "whiten" the Cuban social structure.[120] Negro slavery blackened that structure all over the Caribbean while the blood of the Negro slaves reddened the Atlantic and both its shores. Strange that an article like sugar, so sweet and necessary to human existence, should have occasioned such crimes and bloodshed!

After emancipation the British planters thought of white immigration, even convicts. The governor of British Guiana wrote in glowing terms in 1845 about Portuguese immigrants from Madeira.[121] But though the Portuguese came in large numbers, as is attested by their strength even today in Trinidad and British Guiana, they preferred retail trade to plantation labor. The governor of Jamaica was somewhat more cautious in his opinion of British and Irish immigrants. Sickness had broken out, wages were too low, the experiment could only be partially useful in making an immediate addition to the laboring population, and therefore indiscriminate importation was inadvisable.[122] The European immigrants in St. Christopher bewailed their fate piteously, and begged to be permitted to return home. "There is not the slightest reluctance on our part to continue in the island for an honest livelihood by pleasing our employers by our industrious labour if the climate agreed with us, but unfortunately it do not; and we are much afraid if we continue longer in this injurious hot climate (the West Indies) death will be the consequence to the principal part of us...."[123]

It was not the climate which was against the experiment. Slavery had created the pernicious tradition that manual labor was the badge of the slave and the sphere of influence of the Negro. The first thought of the Negro slave after emancipation was to desert the plantation, where he could, and set up for himself where land was available. White plantation workers could hardly have existed in a society side by side with Negro peasants. The whites would have prospered if small farms had been encouraged. But the abolition of slavery did not mean the destruction of the sugar plantation. The emancipation of the Negro and the inadequacy of the white worker put the sugar planter back to where he had been in the seventeenth century. He still needed labor. Then he had moved from Indian to white to Negro. Now, deprived of his Negro, he turned back to white and then to Indian, this time the Indian from the East. India replaced Africa; between 1833 and 1917, Trinidad imported 145,000 East Indians* and British Guiana 238,000. The pattern was the same for the other Caribbean colonies. Between 1854 and 1883 39,000 Indians were introduced into Guadeloupe; between 1853 and 1924, over 22,000 laborers from the Dutch East Indies and 34,000 from British India were carried to Dutch Guiana.[124] Cuba, faced with a shortage of Negro slaves, adopted the interesting experiment of using

---

*This is the correct West Indian description. It is quite incorrect to call them, as is done in this country, "Hindus." Not all East Indians are Hindus. There are many Moslems in the West Indies.

Negro slaves side by side with indentured Chinese coolies,[125] and after emancipation turned to the teeming thousands of Haiti and the British West Indies. Between 1913 and 1924 Cuba imported 217,000 laborers from Haiti, Jamaica and Puerto Rico.[126] What Saco wrote a hundred years ago was still true, sixty years after Cuba's abolition of slavery.

Negro slavery therefore was only a solution, in certain historical circumstances, of the Caribbean labor problem. Sugar meant labor—at times that labor has been slave, at other times nominally free; at times black, at other times white or brown or yellow. Slavery in no way implied, in any scientific sense, the inferiority of the Negro. Without it the great development of the Caribbean sugar plantations, between 1650 and 1850, would have been impossible.

THE DEVELOPMENT

OF THE

NEGRO SLAVE TRADE

THE NEGRO SLAVES were "the strength and sinews of this west-tern world."[1] Negro slavery demanded the Negro slave trade. Therefore the preservation and improvement of the trade to Africa was "a matter of very high importance to this king-dom and the plantations thereunto belonging."[2] And thus it remained, up to 1783, a cardinal object of British foreign policy.

The first English slave-trading expedition was that of Sir John Hawkins in 1562. Like so many Elizabethan ventures, it was a buccaneering expedition, encroaching on the papal arbitra-tion of 1493 which made Africa a Portuguese monopoly. The slaves obtained were sold to the Spaniards in the West Indies. The English slave trade remained desultory and perfunctory in character until the establishment of British colonies in the Caribbean and the introduction of the sugar industry. When by 1660 the political and social upheavals of the Civil War period came to an end, England was ready to embark wholeheartedly on a branch of commerce whose importance to her sugar and her tobacco colonies in the New World was beginning to be fully appreciated.

In accordance with the economic policies of the Stuart mon-archy, the slave trade was entrusted to a monopolistic com-pany, the Company of Royal Adventurers trading to Africa, incorporated in 1663 for a period of one thousand years. The Earl of Clarendon voiced the enthusiasm current at the time, that the company would "be found a model equally to advance the trade of England with that of any other company, even that of the East Indies."[3] The optimistic prediction was not realized, largely as a result of losses and dislocations caused by war with the Dutch, and in 1672 a new company, the Royal African Company, was created.

The policy of monopoly however remained unchanged and provoked determined resistance in two quarters—the merchants in the outports, struggling to break down the monopoly of the capital; and the planters in the colonies, demanding free trade in blacks as vociferously and with as much gusto as one hundred and fifty years later they opposed free trade in sugar. The mercantilist intelligentsia were divided on the question. Postlethwayt, most prolific of the mercantilist writers, wanted the company, the whole company and nothing but the company.[4] Joshua Gee emphasized the frugality and good management of the private trader.[5] Davenant, one of the ablest economists and financial experts of his day, at first opposed the monopoly,[6] and then later changed his mind, arguing that other nations found organized companies necessary, and that the company would "stand in place of an academy, for training an indefinite number of people in the regular knowledge of all matters relating to the several branches of the African trade."[7]

The case against monopoly was succinctly stated by the free traders—or interlopers as they were then called—to the Board of Trade in 1711. The monopoly meant that the purchase of British manufactures for sale on the coast of Africa, control of ships employed in the slave trade, sale of Negroes to the plantations, importation of plantation produce—"this great circle of trade and navigation," on which the livelihood, direct and indirect, of many thousands depended, would be under the control of a single company.[8] The planters in their turn complained of the quality, prices, and irregular deliveries, and refused to pay their debts to the company.[9]

There was nothing unique in this opposition to the monopoly of the slave trade. Monopoly was an ugly word, which conjured up memories of the political tyranny of Charles I, though no "free trader" of the time could have had the slightest idea of the still uglier visions the word would conjure up one hundred and fifty years later when it was associated with the economic tyranny of the West Indian sugar planter. But in the last decade of the seventeenth century the economic current was flowing definitely against monopoly. In 1672 the Baltic trade was thrown open and the monopoly of the Eastland Company overthrown. One of the most important consequences of the Glorious Revolution of 1688 and the expulsion of the Stuarts was the impetus it gave to the principle of free trade. In 1698 the Royal African Company lost its monopoly and the right of a free trade in slaves was recognized as a fundamental and natural right of Englishmen. In the same year the Merchant Adventurers of London were deprived of their monopoly of the export trade in cloth, and a year later the monopoly of the Muscovy Company was abrogated and trade to Russia made free. Only in one particular did the freedom accorded in the slave trade differ from the freedom accorded in other trades—the commodity involved was man.

The Royal African Company was powerless against the competition of the free traders. It soon went bankrupt and had to depend on parliamentary subsidy. In 1731 it abandoned the slave trade and confined itself to the trade in ivory and gold dust. In 1750 a new organization was established, called the Company of Merchants trading to Africa, with a board of nine directors, three each from London, Bristol and Liverpool. Of the slave traders listed in 1755, 237 belonged to Bristol, 147 to London, and 89 to Liverpool.[10]

With free trade and the increasing demands of the sugar plantations, the volume of the British slave trade rose enormously. The Royal African Company, between 1680 and 1686, transported an annual average of 5,000 slaves.[11] In the first nine years of free trade Bristol alone shipped 160,950 Negroes to the sugar plantations.[12] In 1760, 146 ships sailed from British ports for Africa, with a capacity for 36,000 slaves;[13] in 1771, the number of ships had increased to 190 and the number of slaves to 47,000.[14] The importation into Jamaica from 1700 to 1786 was 610,000, and it has been estimated that the total import of slaves into all the British colonies between 1680 and 1786 was over two million.[15]

But the slave trade was more than a means to an end, it was also an end in itself. The British slave traders provided the necessary laborers not only for their own plantations but for those of their rivals. The encouragement thereby given to foreigners was contrary not only to common sense but to strict mercantilism, but, in so far as this foreign slave trade meant the Spanish colonies, there was some defence for it. Spain was always, up to the nineteenth century, dependent on foreigners for her slaves, either because she adhered to the papal arbitration which excluded her from Africa, or because of a lack of capital and the necessary goods for the slave trade. The privilege of supplying these slaves to the Spanish colonies, called the Asiento, became one of the most highly coveted and bitterly contested plums of international diplomacy. British mercantilists defended the trade, legal or illegal, with the Spanish colonies, in Negroes and manufactured goods, as of distinct value in that the Spaniards paid in coin, and thus the supply of bullion in England was increased. The supply of slaves to the French colonies could plead no such justification. Here it was clearly a clash of interest between the British slave trader and the British sugar planter, as the trade in the export of British machinery after 1825 led to a clash of interests between British shippers and British producers.

The sugar planter was right and the slave trader wrong. But in the first half of the eighteenth century this was noticed only by the very discerning. Postlethwayt condemned the Asiento of 1713 as scandalous and ruinous, an exchange of the substance for the shadow: "a treaty could scarce have been contrived of so little benefit to the nation."[16] During the nine months of British occupation of Cuba in the Seven Years' War, 10,700 slaves were introduced, over one-sixth of the importations from 1512 to 1763, over one-third of the importations from 1763 to 1789.[17] Forty thousand Negroes were introduced into Guadeloupe by the British in three years during the same

war.[18] The Privy Council Committee of 1788 paid special attention to the fact that of the annual British export of slaves from
Africa two-thirds were disposed of to foreigners.[19] During the
whole of the eighteenth century, according to Bryan Edwards,
British slave traders furnished the sugar planters of France and
Spain with half a million Negroes, justifying his doubts of "the
wisdom and policy of this branch of the African commerce."[20]
Britain was not only the foremost slave trading country in the
world; she had become, in Ramsay's phrase, the "honourable
slave carriers" of her rivals.[21]

The story of this increase in the slave trade is mainly the
story of the rise of Liverpool. Liverpool's first slave trader, a
modest vessel of thirty tons, sailed for Africa in 1709. This was
the first step on a road which, by the end of the century, gained
Liverpool the distinction of being the greatest slave trading port
in the Old World. Progress at first was slow. The town was more
interested in the smuggling trade to the Spanish colonies and
the tobacco trade. But, according to a historian of the town,
it soon forged ahead by its policy of cutting down expenses
to a minimum, which enabled it to undersell its English and
continental rivals. In 1730 it had fifteen ships in the slave trade;
in 1771 seven times as many. The proportion of slave ships to
the total shipping owned by the port was slightly over one
in a hundred in 1709; in 1730 it was one-eleventh; in 1763,
one-fourth; in 1771, one-third.[22] In 1795 Liverpool had five-
eighths of the British slave trade and three-sevenths of the whole
European slave trade.[23]

The "horrors" of the Middle Passage have been exaggerated.
For this the British abolitionists are in large part responsible.
There is something that smacks of ignorance or hypocrisy or
both in the invectives heaped by these men upon a traffic which
had in their day become less profitable and less vital to England.
A West Indian planter once reminded Parliament that it ill
became the elected representative of a country which had pock-
eted the gains from the slave trade to stigmatize it as a crime.[24]
The age which had seen the mortality among indentured servants saw no reason for squeamishness about the mortality
among slaves, nor did the exploitation of the slaves on the

plantations differ fundamentally from the exploitation of the feudal peasant or the treatment of the poor in European cities.

Mutinies and suicides were obviously far more common on slave ships than on other vessels, and the brutal treatment and greater restrictions on the movements of the slaves would doubtless have tended to increase their mortality. But the fundamental causes of this high mortality on the slave ships, as on ships carrying indentured servants and even free passengers, must be found firstly in epidemics, the inevitable result of the long voyages and the difficulty of preserving food and water, and secondly in the practice of overcrowding the vessels. The sole aim of the slave merchants was to have their decks "well coverd with black ones."[25] It is not uncommon to read of a vessel of 90 tons carrying 390 slaves or one of 100 tons carrying 414.[26] Clarkson's investigations in Bristol revealed a sloop of twenty-five tons destined for seventy human beings, and another of a mere eleven tons for thirty slaves.[27] The space allotted to each slave on the Atlantic crossing measured five and a half feet in length by sixteen inches in breadth. Packed like "rows of books on shelves," as Clarkson said, chained two by two, right leg and left leg, right hand and left hand, each slave had less room than a man in a coffin. It was like the transportation of black cattle, and where sufficient Negroes were not available cattle were taken on.[28] The slave trader's aim was profit and not the comfort of his victims, and a modest measure in 1788 to regulate the transportation of the slaves in accordance with the capacity of the vessel evoked a loud howl from the slave traders. "If the alteration takes place," wrote one to his agent, "it will hurt the trade, so hope you will make hay while the sun shines."[29]

The journal of one slave dealer during his residence in Africa admits that he had "found no place in all these several countrys of England, Ireland, America, Portugall, the Caribes, the Cape de Verd, the Azores or all the places I have been in . . . where I can inlarge my fortune so soon as where I now live." Money made the man. The prodigal who returned home empty-handed would have to be content with the common name of "the Mallato just come from Guinea." If, however, he returned with his pockets well stuffed with gold, "that very perticular hides all other infirmities, then you have hapes of frinds of all kinds thronging and wateing for your commands. Then your known by the name of 'the African gentleman' at every great man's house, and your discource is set down as perticular as Cristopher Culumbus's expedition in America."[30]

About 1730 in Bristol it was estimated that on a fortunate voyage the profit on a cargo of about 270 slaves reached £7,000 or £8,000, exclusive of the returns from ivory. In the same year the net return from an "indifferent" cargo which arrived in poor condition was over £5,700.[31] Profits of 100 per cent were not uncommon in Liverpool, and one voyage netted a clear profit of at least 300 per cent. The *Lively*, fitted out in 1737 with a cargo worth £1,307, returned to Liverpool with colonial produce and bills of exchange totalling £3,080, in addition to cotton and sugar remitted later. The *Ann*, another Liverpool ship, sailed in 1751 with an outfit and a cargo costing £1,604; altogether the voyage produced £3,287 net. A second voyage in 1753 produced £8,000 on a cargo and outfit amounting to £3,153.[32]

An eighteenth century writer has estimated the sterling value of the 303,737 slaves carried in 878 Liverpool ships between 1783 and 1793 at over fifteen million pounds. Deducting commissions and other charges and the cost of the outfit of the ships and maintenance of the slaves, he concluded that the average annual profit was over thirty per cent.[33] Modern scholarship has tended to reproach contemporary observers with undue exaggeration. But even taking the reduced estimates of Professor Dumbell, the net profit of the *Enterprise* in 1803, estimated on cost of outfit and cost of cargo, was 38 per cent, while that of the *Fortune* in 1803, for a cargo of poor slaves, was over 16 per cent. Again with these reduced estimates the profit of the *Lottery* in 1802 was thirty-six pounds per slave, the *Enterprise* sixteen pounds, and the *Fortune* five.[34] The slave trade on the whole was estimated to bring Liverpool alone in the eighties a clear profit of £300,000 a year; and it was a common saying in the town of the far less profitable West Indian trade that if one ship in three came in a man was no loser, while if two came in he was a good gainer. On an average only one ship in five miscarried.[35]

Such profits seem small and insignificant compared with the fabulous five thousand per cent the Dutch East India Company cleared at times in its history. It is even probable that the profits from the slave trade were smaller than those made by the British East India Company. Yet these trades were far less important than the slave trade. The explanation lies in the fact that from the mercantilist standpoint the India trade was a bad trade. It drained Britain of bullion to buy unnecessary wares, which led many at the time to think that "it were a happie thing for Christendome that the navigation to the East Indies, by way of the Cape of Good Hope, had never bene found out."[36] The slave trade, on the contrary, was ideal in that it was carried on by means of British manufactured goods and was, as far as the British colonies were concerned, inseparably connected with the plantation trade which rendered Britain independent of foreigners for her supply of tropical products. The enormous profits of the Dutch spice trade, moreover, were based on a severe restriction of production to ensure high prices, whereas the slave trade created British industry at home and tropical agriculture in the colonies.

The "attractive African meteor,"[37] as a contemporary Liverpool historian called it, therefore became immensely popular. Though a large part of the Liverpool slave traffic was monopolized by about ten large firms, many of the small vessels in the trade were fitted out by attorneys, drapers, grocers, barbers and tailors. The shares in the ventures were subdivided, one having one-eighth, another one-fifteenth, a third one-thirty-second part of a share and so on. "Almost every man in Liverpool is a merchant, and he who cannot send a bale will send a band-box . . . almost every order of people is interested in a Guinea cargo, it is to this influenza that (there are) so many small ships."[38]

The purchase of slaves called for a business sense and shrewd discrimination. An Angolan Negro was a proverb for worthlessness; Coromantines (Ashantis), from the Gold Coast, were good workers but too rebellious; Mandingoes (Senegal) were too prone to theft; the Eboes (Nigeria) were timid and despondent; the Pawpaws or Whydahs (Dahomey) were the most docile and best-disposed.[39] The slaves were required for arduous field work, hence women and children were less valuable than robust males, the former because they were liable to interruptions from work through pregnancies, the latter because they required some attention until able to care for themselves. One Liverpool merchant cautioned his agents against buying ruptured slaves, idiots or any "old spider leged quality."[40] A West Indian poet advised the slave trader to see that the slave's tongue was red, his chest broad and his belly not prominent.[41] Buy them young, counselled one overseer from Nevis; "them full grown fellers think it hard to work never being brought up to it they take it to heart and dye or is never good for any thing. ..."[42]

But the slave trade was always a risky business. "The African Commerce," it was written in 1795, "holds forward one constant train of uncertainty, the time of slaving is precarious, the length of the middle passage uncertain, a vessel may be in part, or wholly cut off, mortalities may be great, and various other incidents may arise impossible to be foreseen."[43] Sugar cultivation, moreover, was a lottery. The debts of the planters, their bankruptcies and demand for long credits gave the merchants many worries. "As you know," wrote one of them, "quick dispatch is the life of trade, I have had many anxious hours this year, I wou'd not wish the same again for double the profits I may get if any."[44] From 1763 to 1778 the London merchants avoided all connection with the Liverpool slave traders, on the conviction that the slave trade was being conducted at a loss; between 1772 and 1778 the Liverpool merchants were alleged to have lost £700,000.[45] Of thirty leading houses which dominated the slave trade from 1773, twelve had by 1788 gone bankrupt, while many others had sustained considerable losses.[46] The American Revolution seriously interrupted the trade. "Our once extensive trade to Africa is at a stand," lamented a Liverpool paper in 1775. Her "gallant ships laid up and useless," Liverpool's slave traders turned to privateering,[47] anxiously awaiting the return of peace, with never a thought that they were witnessing the death rattles of an old epoch and the birth pangs of a new.

Prior to 1783, however, all classes in English society presented a united front with regard to the slave trade. The monarchy, the government, the church, public opinion in general, supported the slave trade. There were few protests, and those were ineffective.

The Spanish monarchy set the fashion which European royalty followed to the very last. The palace-fortresses of Madrid and Toledo were built out of the payment to the Spanish Crown for licences to transport Negroes. One meeting of the two sovereigns of Spain and Portugal was held in 1701 to discuss the arithmetical problem posed by a contract for ten thousand "tons" of Negroes granted the Portuguese.[48] The Spanish queen, Christina, in the middle of the nineteenth century, openly participated in the slave trade to Cuba. The royal court of Portugal, when it moved to Brazil to avoid capture by Napoleon, did not find the slave atmosphere of its colonial territory uncongenial. Louis XIV fully appreciated the importance of the slave trade to metropolitan France and France overseas. The plans of the Great Elector for Prussian aggrandizement included the African slave trade.[49]

Hawkins' slave trading expedition was launched under the patronage of Queen Elizabeth. She expressed the hope that the Negroes would not be carried off without their free consent, which "would be detestable and call down the vengeance of Heaven upon the undertakers." But there was as much possibility that the transportation of the Negroes would be effected in democratic fashion as there was of collective bargaining. The Company of Royal Adventurers and the Royal African Company had, as their names imply, royal patronage and, not infrequently, investments by members of the royal family.[50] According to Wilberforce, George III later opposed abolition,[51] and great was the joy of the Liverpool slave traders and Jamaican sugar planters when the royal Duke of Clarence, the future William IV, "took up the cudgills" against abolition[52] and attacked Wilberforce as either a fanatic or a hyprocrite.[53]

The British government, prior to 1783, was uniformly consistent in its encouragement of the slave trade. The first great rivals were the Dutch, who monopolized the carrying trade of the British colonies. The bitter commercial warfare of the second half of the seventeenth century between England and Holland represented an effort on the part of England to break the commercial net the Dutch had woven about England and her colonies. "What we want," said Monk with military bluntness, "is more of the trade the Dutch now have."[54] Whether it was nominal peace or actual war, a sort of private war was maintained, for thirty years, between the Dutch West India Company and the Royal African Company.

England's victory over Holland left her face to face with France. Anglo-French warfare, colonial and commercial, is the dominant theme in the history of the eighteenth century. It was a conflict of rival mercantilisms. The struggle was fought out in the Caribbean, Africa, India, Canada and on the banks of the Mississippi, for the privilege of looting India and for the control of certain vital and strategic commodities—Negroes; sugar and tobacco; fish; furs and naval stores.[55] Of these areas the most important were the Caribbean and Africa; of these commodities the most important were Negroes and sugar. The outstanding single issue was the control of the Asiento. This privilege was conceded to England by the Treaty of Utrecht in 1713 as one result of her victory in the War of the Spanish Succession, and produced popular rejoicings in the country. It was the proud boast of Chatham that his war with France had given England almost the entire control of the African coast and of the slave trade.

Colonial assemblies frequently impeded the slave traders by imposing high duties on imported slaves, partly to raise revenue, partly out of their fear of the growing slave population. All such laws were frustrated by the home government, on the insistence of British merchants, who opposed taxes on British trade. The Board of Trade ruled in 1708 that it was "absolutely necessary that a trade so beneficial to the kingdom should be carried on to the greatest advantage. The well supplying of the plantations and colonies with a sufficient number of negroes at reasonable prices is in our opinion the chief point to be considered."[56] In 1773 the Jamaica Assembly, for the purpose of raising revenue and to reduce the fear of slave rebellions, imposed a duty on every Negro imported. The merchants of London, Liverpool and Bristol protested, and the Board of Trade condemned the law as unjustifiable, improper and prejudicial to British commerce. The governor was sharply reprimanded for his failure to stop efforts made to "check and discourage a traffic so beneficial to the nation."[57] As counsel for the sugar planters later argued: "in every variation of our administration of public affairs, in every variation of parties, the policy, in respect to that trade, has been the same. ... In every period of our history, in almost every variation of our politics, each side and description of party men have, in terms, approved this very trade, voted its encouragement, and considered it as beneficial to the nation."[58]

Parliament appreciated the importance of slavery and the slave trade to Britain and her plantations. In 1750 Horace Walpole wrote scornfully of "the British Senate, that temple of liberty, and bulwark of Protestant Christianity, ... pondering methods to make more effectual that horrid traffic of selling negroes."[59] Parliament heard many debates in its stately halls over abolition and emancipation, and its records show the doughty defenders the slave traders and slave owners possessed. Among them was Edmund Burke. The champion of conciliation of America was an accessory to the crucifixion of Africa. In 1772 a bill came before the House of Commons to prohibit the control of the African Committee by outsiders who were not engaged in the slave trade. Burke protested, not against the slave trade, however, but against depriving of the right to vote those who had legally purchased that right. Only a few, he argued, were so accused. "Ought we not rather to imitate the pattern set us in sacred writ, and if we find ten just persons among them, to spare the whole? ... Let us not then counteract the wisdom of our ancestors, who considered and reconsidered this subject, nor place upon the footing of a monopoly what was intended for a free trade."[60] Bristol could well afford to share in the general admiration of the great Liberal.

The Church also supported the slave trade. The Spaniards saw in it an opportunity of converting the heathen, and the Jesuits, Dominicans and Franciscans were heavily involved in sugar cultivation which meant slave-holding. The story is told of an old elder of the Church in Newport who would invariably, the Sunday following the arrival of a slaver from the coast, thank God that "another cargo of benighted beings had been brought to a land where they could have the benefit of a gospel dispensation."[61] But in general the British planters opposed Christianity for their slaves. It made them more perverse and intractable and therefore less valuable. It meant also instruction in the English language, which allowed diverse tribes to get together and plot sedition.[62] There were more material reasons for this opposition. The governor of Barbados in 1695 attributed it to the planters' refusal to give the slaves Sundays and feast days off,[63] and as late as 1823 British public opinion was shocked by the planters' rejection of a proposal to give the Negroes one day in the week in order to permit the abolition of the Negro Sunday market.[64] The Church obediently toed the line. The Society for the Propagation of the Gospel prohibited Christian instruction to its slaves in Barbados,[65] and branded "Society" on its new slaves to distinguish them from those of the laity;[66] the original slaves were the legacy of Christopher Codrington.[67] Sherlock, later Bishop of London, assured the planters that "Christianity and the embracing of the Gospel does not make the least difference in civil property."[68] Neither did it impose any barriers to clerical activity; for his labors with regard to the Asiento, which he helped to draw up as a British plenipotentiary at Utrecht, Bishop Robinson of Bristol was promoted to the see of London.[69] The bells of the Bristol churches pealed merrily on the news of the rejection by Parliament of Wilberforce's bill for the abolition of the slave trade.[70] The slave trader, John Newton, gave thanks in the Liverpool churches for the success of his last venture before his conversion and implored God's blessing on his next. He established public worship twice every day on his slaver, officiating himself, and kept a day of fasting and prayer, not for the slaves but for the crew. "I never knew," he confessed, "sweeter or more frequent hours of divine communion than in the last two voyages to Guinea."[71] The famous Cardinal Manning of the nineteenth century was the son of a rich West Indian merchant dealing in slave-grown produce.[77] Many missionaries found it profitable to drive out Beelzebub by Beelzebub. According to the most recent English writer on the slave trade, they "considered that the best way in which to remedy abuse of negro slaves was to set the plantation owners a good example by keeping slaves and estates themselves, accomplishing in this practical manner the salvation of the planters and the advancement of their foundations."[73] The Moravian missionaries in the islands held slaves without hesitation; the Baptists, one historian writes with charming delicacy, would not allow their earlier missionaries to deprecate ownership of slaves.[74] To the very end the Bishop of Exeter retained his 655 slaves, for whom he received over £12,700 compensation in 1833.[75]

Church historians make awkward apologies, that conscience awoke very slowly to the appreciation of the wrongs inflicted by slavery and that the defence of slavery by churchmen "simply arose from want of delicacy of moral perception."[76] There is no need to make such apologies. The attitude of the churchman was the attitude of the layman. The eighteenth century, like any other century, could not rise above its economic limitations. As Whitefield argued in advocating the repeal of that article of the Georgia charter which forbade slavery, "it is plain to demonstration that hot countries cannot be cultivated without negroes."[77]

Quaker nonconformity did not extend to the slave trade. In 1756 there were eighty-four Quakers listed as members of the Company trading to Africa, among them the Barclay and Baring families.[78] Slave dealing was one of the most lucrative investments of English as of American Quakers, and the name of a slaver, *The Willing Quaker*, reported from Boston at Sierra Leone in 1793,[79] symbolizes the approval with which the slave trade was regarded in Quaker circles. The Quaker opposition to the slave trade came first and largely not from England but from America, and there from the small rural communities of the North, independent of slave labor. "It is difficult," writes

Dr. Gary, "to avoid the assumption that opposition to the slave system was at first confined to a group who gained no direct advantage from it, and consequently possessed an objective attitude."[80]

The Navy was impressed with the value of the West Indian colonies and refused to hazard or jeopardize their security. The West Indian station was the "station for honour," and many an admiral had been feted by the slave owners. Rodney opposed abolition.[81] Earl St. Vincent pleaded that life on the plantations was for the Negro a veritable paradise as compared with his existence in Africa.[82] Abolition was a "damned and cursed doctrine, held only by hypocrites."[83] The gallant admiral's sentiments were not entirely divorced from more material considerations. He received over £6,000 compensation in 1837 for the ownership of 418 slaves in Jamaica.[84] Nelson's wife was a West Indian, and his views on the slave trade were unequivocal. "I was bred in the good old school, and taught to appreciate the value of our West Indian possessions, and neither in the field nor the Senate shall their just rights be infringed, while I have an arm to fight in their defence, or a tongue to launch my voice against the damnable doctrine of Wilberforce and his hypocritical allies."[85]

Slavery existed under the very eyes of eighteenth century Englishmen. An English coin, the guinea, rare though it was and is, had its origin in the trade to Africa.[86] A Westminster goldsmith made silver padlocks for blacks and dogs.[87] Busts of blackamoors and elephants, emblematical of the slave trade, adorned the Liverpool Town Hall. The insignia and equipment of the slave traders were boldly exhibited for sale in the shops and advertised in the press. Slaves were sold openly at auction.[88] Slaves being valuable property, with title recognized by law, the postmaster was the agent employed on occasions to recapture runaway slaves and advertisements were published in the official organ of the government.[89] Negro servants were common. Little black boys were the appendages of slave captains, fashionable ladies or women of easy virtue. Hogarth's heroine, in *The Harlot's Progress*, is attended by a Negro boy, and Marguerite Steen's Orabella Burmester typifies eighteenth century English opinion in her desire for a little black boy whom she could love as her long-haired kitten.[90] Freed Negroes were conspicuous among London beggars and were known as St. Giles blackbirds. So numerous were they that a parliamentary committee was set up in 1786 for relieving the black poor.[91]

"Slaves cannot breathe in England," wrote the poet Cowper. This was license of the poet. It was held in 1677 that "Negroes being usually bought and sold among merchants, so merchandise, and also being infidels, there might be a property in them." In 1729 the Attorney General ruled that baptism did not bestow freedom or make any alteration in the temporal condition of the slave; in addition the slave did not become free by being brought to England, and once in England the owner could legally compel his return to the plantations.[92] So eminent an authority as Sir William Blackstone held that "with respect to any right the master may have lawfully acquired to the perpetual service of John or Thomas, this will remain exactly in the same state of subjection for life," in England or elsewhere.[93]

When, therefore, the assiduous zeal of Granville Sharp brought before Chief Justice Mansfield in 1772 the case of the Negro James Somersett who was about to be returned by his owner to Jamaica, there were abundant precedents to prove the impurity of the English air. Mansfield tried hard to evade the issue by suggesting manumission of the slave, and contented himself with the modest statement that the case was not "allowed or approved by the law of England" and the Negro must be discharged. Much has been made of this case, by people constantly seeking for triumphs of humanitarianism. Professor Coupland contends that behind the legal judgment lay the moral judgment and that the Somersett case marked the beginning of the end of slavery throughout the British Empire.[94] This is merely poetic sentimentality translated into modern history. Benjamin Franklin pointed scornfully to "the hypoccrisy of this country, which encourages such a detestable commerce, while it piqued itself on its virtue, love of liberty, and the equity of its courts in setting free a single negro."[95] Two years after the Somersett case the British government disallowed the Jamaican Acts restricting the slave trade. In 1783 a Quaker petition for abolition was solemnly rejected by Parliament.

In 1783, moreover, the same Mansfield handed down a decision in the case of the ship *Zong*. Short of water, the captain had thrown 132 slaves overboard, and now the owners brought an action for insurance alleging that the loss of the slaves fell within the clause of the policy which insured against "perils of the sea." In Mansfield's view "the case of slaves was the same as if horses had been thrown overboard." Damages of thirty pounds were awarded for each slave, and the idea that the captain and crew should be prosecuted for mass homicide never entered into the head of any humanitarian. In 1785 another insurance case, involving a British ship and mutiny among the slaves, came before Mansfield. His Daniel judgment was that all the slaves who were killed in the mutiny or had died of their wounds and bruises were to be paid for by the underwriters; those who had died from jumping overboard or from swallowing water or from "chagrin" were not to be paid for on the ground that they had not died from injuries received in the mutiny; and the underwriters were not responsible for any depreciation in price which resulted to the survivors from the mutiny.[96]

The prosecution of the slave trade was not the work of the dregs of English society. The daughter of a slave trader has assured us that her father, though a slave captain and privateer, was a kind and just man, a good father, husband, and friend.[97] This was probably true. The men most active in this traffic were worthy men, fathers of families and excellent citizens. The abolitionist Ramsay acknowledged this with real sorrow, but pleaded that "they had never examined the nature of this commerce and went into it, and acted as others had done before them in it, as a thing of course, for which no account was to be given in this world or the next."[98] The apology is unnecessary. The slave trade was a branch of trade and a very important branch. An officer in the trade once said that "one real view, one minute absolutely spent in the slave rooms on the middle passage would do more for the cause of humanity than the pen of a Robertson, or the whole collective eloquence of the British

senate."[99] This is dubious. As it was argued later about the
Cuban and Brazilian slave trade, it was no use saying it was
an unholy or unchristian occupation. It was a lucrative trade,
and that was enough.[100] The slave trade has even been justified
as a great education. "Think of the effect, the result of a slave
voyage on a youngster starting in his teens. ... What an education was such a voyage for the farmer lad. What an enlargement
of experience for a country boy. If he returned to the farm his
whole outlook on life would be changed. He went out a boy; he
returned a man."[101]

The slave traders were among the leading humanitarians of
their age. John Cary, advocate of the slave trade, was conspicuous
for his integrity and humanity and was the founder of a society known as the "Incorporation of the Poor."[102] The Bristol
slaver "Southwell" was named after a Bristol parliamentarian,
whose monument depicts him as true to king and country and
steady to what he thought right.[103] Bryan Blundell of Liverpool, one of Liverpool's most prosperous merchants, engaged
in both the slave and West Indian trades, was for many years
trustee, treasurer, chief patron and most active supporter of a
charity school, the Blue Coat Hospital, founded in 1709.[104]
To this charity another Liverpool slave trader, Foster Cunliffe,
contributed largely. He was a pioneer in the slave trade. He
and his two sons are listed as members of the Liverpool Committee of Merchants trading to Africa in 1752. Together they
had four ships capable of holding 1,120 slaves, the profits from
which were sufficient to stock twelve vessels on the homeward
journey with sugar and rum. An inscription to Foster Cunliffe
in St. Peter's Church describes him thus: "a Christian devout
and exemplary in the exercise of every private and publick duty,
friend to mercy, patron to distress, an enemy only to vice and
sloth, he lived esteemed by all who knew him ... and died
lamented by the wise and good. ..."[105] Thomas Leyland, one
of the largest slave traders of the same port, had, as mayor, no
mercy for the engrosser, the forestaller, the regrater, and was
a terror to evil doers.[106] The Heywoods were slave traders and
the first to import the slave-grown cotton of the United States.
Arthur Heywood was treasurer of the Manchester Academy

where his sons were educated. One son, Benjamin, was elected member of the Literary and Philosophical Society of Manchester, and was admitted to the Billiard Club, the most *recherché* club Manchester has ever possessed, which admitted only the very best men as regards manners, position and attainments. To be admitted to the charmed circle of the Forty meant unimpeachable recognition as a gentleman. Later Benjamin Heywood organized the first of the Manchester exhibitions of works of art and industry.[107]

These slave traders held high office in England. The Royal Adventurers trading to Africa in 1667, a list headed by royalty, included two aldermen, three dukes, eight earls, seven lords, one countess, and twenty-seven knights.[108] The signatures of the mayors of Liverpool and Bristol appear on a petition of the slave traders in 1739.[109] The Bristol Committee set up in 1789 to oppose abolition of the slave trade included five aldermen, one an ex-captain of a slaver.[110] Many a slave trader held Liverpool's highest municipal dignity.[111] The slave traders were firmly established in both houses of Parliament. Ellis Cunliffe represented Liverpool in Parliament from 1755 to 1767.[112] The Tarleton family, prominent in the slave trade, voiced Liverpool's opposition to abolition in Parliament.[113] The House of Lords, traditionally conservative, was confirmed in its instinctive opposition to abolition by the presence of many ennobled slave traders. It gave sympathetic hearing to the Earl of Westmorland's statement that many of them owed their seats in the Upper House to the slave trade,[114] and that abolition was Jacobinism.[115] No wonder Wilberforce feared the Upper Chamber.[116] Not without confidence did the Assembly of Jamaica state categorically in 1792 that "the safety of the West Indies not only depends on the slave trade not being abolished, but on a speedy declaration of the House of Lords that they will not suffer the trade to be abolished."[117]

Some protests were voiced by a few eighteenth century intellectuals and prelates. Defoe in his "Reformation of Manners," condemned the slave trade. The poet Thomson, in his "Summer," drew a lurid picture of the shark following in the wake of the slave ship. Cowper, after some hesitation, wrote his memorable lines in "The Task." Blake wrote his beautiful poem on the "Little Black Boy." Southey composed some poignant verses on the "Sailor who had served in the Slave Trade." But much of this eighteenth century literature, as Professor Sypher has shown in an exhaustive analysis,[118] concentrated on the "noble Negro," the prince unjustly made captive, superior even in bondage to his captors. This sentimentality, typical of the eighteenth century in general, more often than not carried the vicious implication that the slavery of the ignoble Negro was justified. Boswell on the other hand stated emphatically that to abolish the slave trade was to shut the gates of mercy on mankind, and dubbed Wilberforce a "dwarf with big resounding name."[119]

Two eighteenth century merchants, Bentley and Roscoe, opposed the slave trade before 1783; they were more than merchants, they were Liverpool merchants. Two eighteenth century economists condemned the expensiveness and inefficiency of slave labor—Dean Tucker and Adam Smith, the warning tocsin, the trumpeter of the new age. The discordant notes went unheeded. The eighteenth century endorsed the plea of Temple Luttrell: "Some gentlemen may, indeed, object to the slave trade as inhuman and impious; let us consider that if our colonies are to be maintained and cultivated, which can only be done by African negroes, it is surely better to supply ourselves with those labourers in British bottoms, than purchase them through the medium of French, Dutch, or Danish factors."[120]

On one occasion a Mauritius gentleman, eager to convince the abolitionist Buxton that "the blacks were the happiest people in the world," appealed to his wife to confirm his statement from her own impressions of the slaves she had seen. "Well, yes," replied the good spouse, "they were very happy, I'm sure, only I used to think it so odd to see the black cooks chained to the fireplace."[121] Only a few Englishmen before 1783, like the good spouse, had any doubts about the morality of the slave trade. Those who had realized that objections, as Postlethwayt put it, would be of little weight with statesmen who saw the great national emoluments which accrued from the slave trade. "We shall take things as they are, and reason from them in their present state, and not from that wherein we could hope them to be. . . . We cannot think of giving up the slave-trade, notwithstanding my good wishes that it could be done." Later, perhaps, some noble and benevolent Christian spirit might think of changing the system, "which, as things are now circumstanced, may not be so easily brought about."[122] Before the American Revolution English public opinion in general accepted the view of the slave trader: "Tho' to traffic in human creatures, may at first sight appear barbarous, inhuman, and unnatural; yet the traders herein have as much to plead in their own excuse, as can be said for some other branches of trade, namely, the *advantage* of it. . . . In a word, from this trade proceed benefits, far outweighing all, either real or pretended mischiefs and inconveniencies."[123]

· 3 ·

BRITISH COMMERCE

AND THE

TRIANGULAR TRADE

ACCORDING TO ADAM SMITH, the discovery of America and the Cape route to India are "the two greatest and most important events recorded in the history of mankind." The importance of the discovery of America lay not in the precious metals it provided but in the new and inexhaustible market it afforded for European commodities. One of its principal effects was to "raise the mercantile system to a degree of splendour and glory which it could never otherwise have attained to."[1] It gave rise to an enormous increase in world trade. The seventeenth and eighteenth centuries were the centuries of trade, as the nineteenth century was the century of production. For Britain that trade was primarily the triangular trade. In 1718 William Wood said that the slave trade was "the spring and parent whence the others flow."[2] A few years later Postlethwayt described the slave trade as "the first principle and foundation of all the rest, the mainspring of the machine which sets every wheel in motion."[3]

In this triangular trade England—France and Colonial America equally—supplied the exports and the ships; Africa the human merchandise; the plantations the colonial raw materials. The slave ship sailed from the home country with a cargo of manufactured goods. These were exchanged at a profit on the coast of Africa for Negroes, who were traded on the plantations, at another profit, in exchange for a cargo of colonial produce to be taken back to the home country. As the volume of trade increased, the triangular trade was supplemented, but never supplanted, by a direct trade between home country and the West Indies, exchanging home manufactures directly for colonial produce.

The triangular trade thereby gave a triple stimulus to British industry. The Negroes were purchased with British manufactures; transported to the plantations, they produced sugar, cotton, indigo, molasses and other tropical products, the processing of which created new industries in England; while the maintenance of the Negroes and their owners on the plantations provided another market for British industry, New England agriculture and the Newfoundland fisheries. By 1750 there was hardly a trading or a manufacturing town in England which was not in some way connected with the triangular or direct colonial trade.[4] The profits obtained provided one of the main streams of that accumulation of capital in England which financed the Industrial Revolution.

The West Indian islands became the hub of the British Empire, of immense importance to the grandeur and prosperity of England. It was the Negro slaves who made these sugar colonies the most precious colonies ever recorded in the whole annals of imperialism. To Postlethwayt they were "the fundamental prop and support" of the colonies, "valuable people" whose labor supplied Britain with all plantation produce. The British Empire was "a magnificent superstructure of American commerce and naval power on an African foundation."[5]

Sir Josiah Child estimated that every Englishman in the West Indies, "with the ten blacks that work with him, accounting what they eat, use and wear, would make employment for four men in England."[6] By Davenant's computation one person in the islands, white or Negro, was as profitable as seven in England.[7] Another writer considered that every family in the West Indies gave employment to five seamen and many more artificers, manufacturers and tradesmen, and that every white person in the islands brought in ten pounds annually clear profit to England, twenty times as much as a similar person in the home country.[8] William Wood reckoned that a profit of seven shillings per head per annum was sufficient to enrich a country; each white man in the colonies brought a profit of over seven pounds.[9] Sir Dalby Thomas went further—every person employed on the sugar plantations was 130 times more valuable to England than one at home.[10] Professor Pitman has estimated that in 1775 British West Indian plantations represented a valuation of fifty millions sterling,[11] and the sugar planters themselves put the figure at seventy millions in 1788.[12] In 1798 Pitt assessed the annual income from West Indian plantations at four million pounds as compared with one million from the rest of the world.[13] As Adam Smith wrote: "The profits of a sugar plantation in any of our West Indian colonies are generally much greater than those of any other cultivation that is known either in Europe or America."[14]

According to Davenant, Britain's total trade at the end of the seventeenth century brought in a profit of £2,000,000. The plantation trade accounted for £600,000; re-export of plantation goods £120,000; European, African and Levant trade £600,000; East India trade £500,000; re-export of East India goods £180,000.[15]

Sir Charles Whitworth, in 1776, made a complete compilation, from official records, of the import and export trade of Great Britain for the years 1697-1773. His book is invaluable for an appreciation of the relative importance of the Caribbean and mainland colonies in the British Empire of the eighteenth century. For the year 1697 the West Indian colonies supplied nine per cent of British imports, the mainland colonies eight per cent; four per cent of British exports went to the West Indies, slightly under four per cent to the mainland; the West Indies accounted for seven per cent of Britain's total trade, the mainland for six per cent. In 1773 the West Indies still maintained their lead, though as an export market they had become inferior to the mainland colonies with their larger white population. In that year nearly one-quarter of British imports came from all Caribbean areas, one-eighth from the entire mainland; the Caribbean consumed somewhat over eight per cent of British exports, the mainland sixteen per cent; fifteen per cent of Britain's total trade was with the West Indies, fourteen per cent with the mainland. Taking the totals for the years 1714-1773, and including in those totals trade with new acquisitions, foreign colonies temporarily occupied by British forces during the war, or foreign colonies in general, we get the following picture: One-fifth of British imports came from the Caribbean, one-ninth from the mainland; six per cent of British exports went to the Caribbean, nine per cent to the mainland; twelve per cent of Britain's total foreign commerce was accounted for by the Caribbean, ten per cent by the mainland. During these same years one-half per cent of British imports came from Africa, two per cent of British exports went to Africa, while African trade represented nearly one and a half per cent of total British trade. Leaving out of account, therefore, the plantation colonies on the mainland, Virginia, Maryland, Carolina, Georgia, the triangular and West Indian trades represented nearly one-seventh of total British trade during the years 1714-1773.

The amazing value of these West Indian colonies can more graphically be presented by comparing individual West Indian islands with individual mainland colonies. In 1697 British imports from Barbados were five times the combined imports from the bread colonies; the exports to Barbados were slightly larger. Little Barbados, with its 166 square miles, was worth more to British capitalism than New England, New York and Pennsylvania combined. In 1773 British imports from Jamaica were more than five times the combined imports from the bread colonies; British exports to Jamaica were nearly one-third larger than those to New England and only slightly less than those to New York and Pennsylvania combined. For the years 1714-1773 British imports from Montserrat were three times the imports from Pennsylvania, imports from Nevis were almost double those from New York, imports from Antigua were over three times those from New England. Imports from Barbados were more than twice as large as those from the bread colonies, imports from Jamaica nearly six times as large. For the same years Jamaica as an export market was as valuable as New England; Barbados and Antigua combined meant as much to British exporters as New York; Montserrat and Nevis combined were a better market than Pennsylvania. British exports to Africa during these years were only one-tenth less than those to New England, British imports from Africa one-quarter more than those from New York and more than double those from Pennsylvania.[16]

Mercantilists were enthusiastic. The triangular trade, and the associated trade with the sugar islands, because of the navigation they encouraged, were more valuable to England than her mines of tin or coal.[17] These were ideal colonies. But for them Britain would have no gold or silver, except what she received from illicit commerce with the Spanish colonies, and an unfavorable balance of trade.[18] Their tropical products, unlike those of the northern part of the mainland, did not compete with those of the home country. They showed little sign of that industrial development which was the constant fear where the mainland was concerned. Their large black population was an effective guarantee against aspirations to independence.[19] It all combined to spell one word, sugar. "The pleasure, glory and grandeur of England," wrote Sir Dalby Thomas, "has been advanced more by sugar than by any other commodity, wool not excepted."[20]

There was one qualification—monopoly. The economic philosophy of the age had no room for the open door, and colonial trade was a rigid monopoly of the home country. The mercantilists were adamant on this point. "Colonies," wrote Davenant, "are a strength to their mother kingdom, while they are under good discipline, while they are strictly made to observe the fundamental laws of their original country, and while they are kept dependent on it. But otherwise, they are worse than members lopped from the body politic, being indeed like offensive arms wrested from a nation to be turned against it as occasion shall serve."[21] The colonies, in return for their prosperity, owed the mother country, in Postlethwayt's view, gratitude and an indispensable duty—"to be immediately dependent on their original parent and to make their interest subservient thereunto."[22]

It was on these ideas that the mercantile system was erected. The colonies were obliged to send their valuable products to England only and use English ships. They could buy nothing but British unless the foreign commodities were first taken to England. And since, as dutiful children, they were to work for the greater glory of their parent, they were reduced to a state of permanent vassalage and confined solely to the exploitation of their agricultural resources. Not a nail, not a horseshoe, said Chatham, could be manufactured, nor hats, nor iron, nor refined sugar. In return for this, England made one concession— the colonial products were given a monopoly of the home market.

The keystone of this mercantilist arch was the Navigation Laws, "English measures designed for English ends."[23] The Navigation Laws were aimed at the Dutch, "the foster fathers," as Andrews calls them, of the early British colonies,[24] who supplied credit, delivered goods, purchased colonial produce and transported it to Europe, all at more attractive rates than the British could offer in open market. But the laws were aimed also at the Scotch and Irish[25] and Scotland's attempt to set up an independent African Company[26] aroused great fears in England and was largely responsible for the Act of Union in 1707. The sugar islands protested against this monopoly of their trade. Those who, in 1840, were loudest in their opposition to free trade, were, in 1660, the most fervent advocates of free trade. In 1666 the governor of Barbados begged "leave to be plain with His Majesty, for he is come to where it pinches. ... Free trade is the life of all colonies ... whoever he be that advised His Majesty to restrain and tie up his colonies is more a merchant than a good subject."[27] His successor repeated the warning: "Ye must make their port a free port for all people to trade with them that will come. The ordinary way thats taken for new plantations I humbly conceive is a little erroneous. My Lords the Act for Trade and Navigation in England will certainly in tyme bee the ruine of all his Maties forreigne plantations."[28] The Lords of Trade decided to "give him a cheque for upholding this maxim of free trade," and censured him severely for "these dangerous principles which he entertains contrary to the settled laws of the kingdom and the apparent advantage of it."[29]

Such subversive ideas could not possibly be tolerated in an age which heard demands that the Navigation Laws be stretched to confine the provision for "English built" ships to ships built of English timber and using British made canvas, and which passed legislation that the dead be buried in English wool and all servants and slaves on the plantations be made to wear English wool, to encourage England's foremost industry. Negroes, the most important export of Africa, and sugar, the most important export of the West Indies, were the principal commodities enumerated by the Navigation Laws. But the West Indian sugar planters never accepted this limitation on their trade. Ultimately in 1739 they were granted a modification of the Navigation Laws, but in so limited a form and only to such poor foreign markets in Europe—south of Cape Finisterre—that its advantages were nugatory. But even this concession, badly shorn though it was, aroused the wrath of English merchants. It would, said a Liverpool petition before the measure became a law, "be highly prejudicial in many instances to the interest and manufactures, to the trade and navigation of Great Britain in general and of this port in particular."[30] One hundred years later the same conflict was to be fought out, more bitterly, between monopoly and free trade, mercantilism and laissez faire. The antagonists were the same, British traders and industrialists on the one hand and West Indian sugar planters on the other. But British capitalism, now all for monopoly, was then all for free trade; the West Indian planters, on the other hand, forgot all their noble free trade sentiments and clung tenaciously to the principle of monopoly which they had formerly condemned, as making them "the merchants' slaves."[31]

B.   SHIPPING AND SHIPBUILDING

This external trade naturally drew in its wake a tremendous development of shipping and shipbuilding. Not the least of the advantages of the triangular trade was its contribution to the wooden walls of England. There was less distinction between a merchant ship and a man-of-war in those days than there is today. The "long voyage" was an admirable nursery for the seamen, the merchantmen invaluable aides to the navy in time of war; and advocates of the slave trade argued that its abolition would annihilate the marine by cutting off a great source of seamen.[32] As one Liverpool slave trader wrote: "It is a matter of two much importance to this kingdom—when ever it is *abolish'd* the naval importance of this kingdom is abolish'd with it, that moment our flagg will gradually cease to ride triumphant on the seas."[33]

In 1678 the Commissioners of Customs reported that the plantation trade was one of the great nurseries of the shipping and seamen of England and one of the greatest branches of its trade.[34] Here again the sugar colonies outdistanced the bread colonies. More English ships sailed to the sugar colonies than to all the mainland colonies combined. In 1690 the sugar colonies employed 114 ships, of 13,600 tons and 1,203 seamen; the mainland colonies 111 ships, of 14,320 tons and 1,271 seamen.[35] Between 1710 and 1714, 122,000 tons of British shipping sailed to the West Indies, 112,000 tons to the mainland.[36] The West Indian trade in 1709 employed one-tenth of British shipping engaged in foreign trade.[37] Between 1709 and 1787 British shipping engaged in foreign trade quadrupled;[38] ships clearing for Africa multiplied twelve times and the tonnage eleven times.[39]

Shipbuilding in England received a direct stimulus from the triangular trade. Vessels of a particular type were constructed for the slave trade, combining capacity with speed in an effort to reduce mortality. Many shipwrights in Liverpool were themselves slave traders. The outstanding firm was Baker and Dawson, one of the largest exporters of slaves to the West Indies, and engaged, after 1783, in the supplying of slaves to the Spanish colonies. John Gorell was one of the Liverpool members of the Company of Merchants trading to Africa. So was John Okill, one of Liverpool's most successful shipbuilders, but apparently he eschewed the slave trade. In a port whose prosperity was intimately connected with the slave trade, William Rathbone was a curiosity in his refusal to supply timber for the construction of vessels to be employed in the slave trade,[40] in which half of Liverpool's sailors were engaged.[41]

The shipping industry was divided, as industry in general, on the question of the organization of the slave trade. Some sections favored the Royal African Company, others the free traders.[42] But on the question of abolition the industry presented a united front, arguing that abolition would strike at the very roots of Britain's naval and imperial supremacy. The first reaction of Liverpool to the act of 1788 regulating the capacity of slavers was that it left 22 masters of slave ships, 47 mates and 350 seamen unemployed, with their families and the tradesmen dependent more indirectly on the trade with Africa.[43]

In addition to the seamen, there were the ancillary trades. Carpenters, painters and boat-builders; tradesmen and artisans connected with repairs, equipment and lading; commissions, wages, dock duties, insurances—all depended partly on the ships trading to Africa. To supply the ships, there were in 1774 fifteen roperies in Liverpool.[44] There were few people in the town, it was claimed, who would not be affected, directly or indirectly, by abolition.[45]

The sugar islands made yet another contribution to the growth of shipping. The peculiar economy developed in the West Indies concentrated on export crops while food was imported. Most important of all the food supplies was fish, an article dear to the heart of every mercantilist, because it provided employment for ships and training for seamen. Laws were passed in England to encourage the consumption of fish. Friday and Saturday were set apart as fish days. Fish was an important item of the diet of the slaves on the plantations, and the English herring trade found its chief market in the sugar plantations.[46] The Newfoundland fishery depended to a considerable extent on the annual export of dried fish to the West Indies, the refuse or "poor John" fish, "fit for no other consumption."[47] A West Indian tradition was thereby fostered. Imported salted cod is still today a normal and favorite dish in all but the well-to-do West Indian families; whether it is still "fit for no other consumption" is not known.

The increase in shipping subjected the eighteenth century docks of England to intolerable strain. The number of ships entering the port of London trebled between 1705 and 1795, the tonnage quadrupled, exclusive of the smaller vessels engaged in the coasting trade. The warehouses on the quays were inadequate for the imports. The colliers could not be discharged and the price of coals rose enormously. Sugar was piled six or eight hogsheads high on the quay, increasing the danger of fire and encouraging thefts. A great machine of organized crime was developed, involving some ten thousand people. The total annual depredations at the docks were estimated at half a million pounds, half this sum from vessels from the Caribbean.

The West Indian merchants set themselves to grapple with the problem. They organized a special force of constables to cope with the thefts, and set up a general register of laborers discharging West Indian ships. They lobbied in Parliament and eventually secured an act authorizing the construction of the West India Docks. For twenty-one years they were given a monopoly of loading and unloading vessels engaged in the West Indian trade. The first stone was laid in 1800, and the ceremony was followed by an elegant entertainment for the notables present, at which one toast was appropriately drunk to the prosperity of the West Indian colonies. The docks were publicly opened in 1802, the first ship being named after the Prime Minister, and the second laden with six hundred tons of sugar.[48]

C.   GROWTH OF THE GREAT BRITISH SEAPORT TOWNS

The development of the triangular trade and of shipping and shipbuilding led to the growth of the great seaport towns. Bristol, Liverpool and Glasgow occupied, as seaports and trading centers, the position in the age of trade that Manchester, Birmingham and Sheffield occupied later in the age of industry.

It was said in 1685 that there was scarcely a shopkeeper in Bristol who had not a venture on board some ship bound for Virginia or the Antilles. Even the parsons talked of nothing but trade, and it was satirically alleged that Bristol freights were owned not by merchants but by mechanics.[49] Customs duties rose from £10,000 in 1634 to £334,000 in 1785. Wharfage dues, payable on every vessel above sixty tons, doubled between 1745 and 1775.[50]

It was the slave and sugar trades which made Bristol the second city of England for the first three-quarters of the eighteenth century. "There is not," wrote a local annalist, "a brick in the city but what is cemented with the blood of a slave. Sumptuous mansions, luxurious living, liveried menials, were the produce of the wealth made from the sufferings and groans of the slaves bought and sold by the Bristol merchants. ... In their childlike simplicity they could not feel the iniquity of the merchandise, but they could feel it lucrative."[51] An analysis of a committee set up in 1789 to oppose the movement for abolition of the slave trade shows that among the members elected were nine merchants at some time mayors of Bristol, five who were sheriffs, seven had been or were to be Masters of the Society of Merchant Venturers.[52]

When Bristol was outstripped in the slave trade by Liverpool, it turned its attention from the triangular trade to the direct sugar trade. Fewer Bristol ships sailed to Africa, more went direct to the Caribbean. In 1700 the port had forty-six ships in the West Indian trade.[53] In 1787 there were thirty Bristol vessels engaged in the slave trade, seventy-two in the West Indian trade; the former averaged 140 tons each, the latter 240.[54] In 1788 Bristol had as many ships in the trade to the Leeward Islands, and almost as many in the trade to Jamaica, as in the trade to Africa.[55] Nearly one-third of the tonnage which entered, more than one-third of that which sailed from, the port was engaged in the trade with the sugar colonies;[56] and it was the amiable custom in Bristol to celebrate the arrival of the first sugar ship each year by a gift of wine at the expense of the fortunate owner.[57] The West Indian trade was worth to Bristol twice as much as all her other overseas commerce combined. As late as 1830 five-eighths of its trade was with the West Indies, and it was said in 1833 that without the West Indian trade Bristol would be a fishing port.[58]

Bristol had a West Indian Society of its own. The Town

Council distributed municipal funds for the relief of distress caused by fire in the sugar islands. It was customary for younger sons and junior members of West Indian firms to spend some years on the plantations before entering business at home. Bristol members of Parliament in the eighteenth century were frequently associated, in one way or another, with the sugar plantations, and so important did the islands become to Bristol that for the first half of the nineteenth century Bristol was always represented in Parliament by a West Indian—a Baillie, a Protheroe, or a Miles. James Evan Baillie exhorted his fellow citizens not to lay the axe at the root of their own prosperity by supporting the abolition of slavery in the islands.[59] His own prosperity was also at stake. The compensation paid to the family for their ownership of numerous slaves in Trinidad and British Guiana exceeded £62,000.[60] Bristol presented a determined opposition to the equalization of the sugar duties which gave the *coup de grace* to the West Indian monopoly. Thereafter Bristol's trade with the West Indies declined rapidly. In 1847 forty per cent of the port's tonnage was bound for the West Indies, and ships returning from the islands represented a mere eleven per cent. In 1871 no ship left Bristol for Jamaica, and the inward tonnage from the islands constituted less than two per cent of the arrivals. Bristol's trade with the islands did not revive until the end of the nineteenth century with the advent of the banana in the world market.[61]

What the West Indian trade did for Bristol the slave trade did for Liverpool. In 1565 Liverpool had 138 householders, seven streets only were inhabited, the port's merchant marine amounted to twelve ships of 223 tons. Until the end of the seventeenth century the only local event of importance was the siege of the town during the English Civil War.[62] In collecting ship money Strafford assessed Liverpool at fifteen pounds; Bristol paid two thousand.[63] The shipping entering Liverpool increased four and a half times between 1709 and 1771; the outward tonnage six and a half times. The number of ships owned by the port multiplied four times during the same period, the tonnage and sailors over six times.[64] Customs receipts soared from an average of £51,000 for the years 1750 to 1757 to £648,000 in 1785.[65] Dock duties increased two and a half times between 1752 and 1771.[66] The population rose from 5,000 in 1700 to 34,000 in 1773. By 1770 Liverpool had become too famous a town in the trading world for Arthur Young to pass it by on his travels over England.[67]

The abolitionist Clarkson argued that the rise of Liverpool was due to a variety of causes, among which were the salt trade, the prodigious increase of the population of Lancashire, and the rapid and great extension of the manufactures of Manchester.[68] This is a particularly flagrant case of putting the cart before the horse. It was only the capital accumulation of Liverpool which called the population of Lancashire into existence and stimulated the manufactures of Manchester. That capital accumulation came from the slave trade, whose importance was appreciated more by contemporaries than by later historians.

It was a common saying that several of the principal streets of Liverpool had been marked out by the chains, and the walls of the houses cemented by the blood, of the African slaves,[69] and one street was nicknamed "Negro Row."[70] The red brick Customs House was blazoned with Negro heads.[71] The story is told of an actor in the town, who, hissed by the audience for appearing before them, not for the first time, in a drunken condition, steadied himself and declared with offended majesty: "I have not come here to be insulted by a set of wretches, every brick in whose infernal town is cemented with an African's blood."[72]

It was estimated in 1790 that the 138 ships which sailed from Liverpool for Africa represented a capital of over a million pounds. Liverpool's own probable loss from the abolition of the slave trade was then computed at over seven and a half million pounds.[73] Abolition, it was said, would ruin the town. It would destroy the foundation of its commerce and the first cause of the national industry and wealth. "What vain pretence of liberty," it was asked in Liverpool, "can infatuate people to run into so much licentiousness as to assert a trade is unlawful which custom immemorial, and various Acts of Parliament, have ratified and given a sanction to?"[74]

This dependence on the slave trade has proved very awkward to sensitive and patriotic historians. A generation, argued a Bristol historian in 1939, which has seen the spoilation of Ethiopia, the brutal dismemberment of China and the rape of Czechoslovakia, cannot afford to condemn the slave trade.[75] In the opinion of a Liverpool town clerk, Liverpool has borne more than its share of the stigma attaching to the slave trade. The indomitable perseverance and energy of its people would have ensured an equal prosperity in other directions, as effectively if not as quickly, had the slave trade not existed, and the ultimate success of the port would perhaps have been retarded, though not prejudiced or impaired, without the slave trade.[76] According to yet another Liverpool writer, there was nothing derogatory in the fact that their ancestors had dealt in "niggers," and the horrors of the slave trade were exceeded by the horrors of the Liverpool drink traffic. But, after all, "it was the capital made in the African slave trade that built some of our docks. It was the price of human flesh and blood that gave us a start." Some of those who made their fortunes out of the slave trade had soft hearts under their waistcoats for the poor of Liverpool, while the profits from slave trading represented "an influx of wealth which, perhaps, no consideration would induce a commercial community to relinquish."[77]

Not until the Act of Union of 1707 was Scotland allowed to participate in colonial trade. That permission put Glasgow on the map. Sugar and tobacco underlay the prosperity of the town in the eighteenth century. Colonial commerce stimulated the growth of new industries. As Bishop Pococke wrote in 1760, after a visit to Glasgow: "the city has above all others felt the advantages of the Union, by the West India trade which they enjoy, which is very great, especially in tobacco, indigoes and sugar."[78] Sugar refining continued as an important industry in the Clyde Valley until the eclipse of the West Indian islands in the middle of the nineteenth century.

D.   THE GOODS IN THE TRIANGULAR TRADE

It is necessary now to trace the industrial development in England which was stimulated directly or indirectly by the goods for the triangular trade and the processing of colonial produce.

The widespread ramifications of the slave trade in English industry are illustrated by this cargo to Africa for the year 1787: cotton and linen goods, silk handkerchiefs, coarse blue and red woolen cloths, scarlet cloth in grain, coarse and fine hats, worsted caps, guns, powder, shot, sabers, lead bars, iron bars, pewter basons, copper kettles and pans, iron pots, hardware of various kinds, earthen and glass ware, hair and gilt leather trunks, beads of various kinds, silver and gold rings and ornaments, paper, coarse and fine checks, linen ruffled shirts and caps, British and foreign spirits and tobacco.[79]

This sundry assortment was typical of the slave trader's cargo. Finery for Africans, household utensils, cloths of all kinds, iron and other metals, together with guns, handcuffs and fetters: the production of these stimulated capitalism, provided employment for British labor, and brought great profits to England.

1. *Wool*

Until the tremendous development of the cotton industry in the Industrial Revolution, wool was the spoiled child of English manufactures. It figured largely in all considerations affecting the slave trade in the century after 1680. The cargo of a slave ship was in complete without some woolen manufactures—serges, says, perpetuanos, arrangoes and bays. Sometimes the cloth was called after the locality where it was first manufactured. Bridwaters represented Bridgewater's interest in the colonial market; Welsh Plaines, a woolen cloth of the simplest weave, was manufactured in western England and Wales.

A parliamentary committee of 1695 voiced the public sentiment that the trade to Africa was an encouragement to the woolen manufacture.[80] Among the arguments put forward to prove the importance of the slave trade, the exports of wool

which that trade encouraged were always given first place. A
pamphlet of 1680, illustrating the public utility and advantages of the African trade, begins with "the exportation of our
native woollen and other manufactures in great abundance, most
of which were imported formerly out of Holland ... whereby
the wooll of this nation is much more consumed and spent then
formerly; and many thousand of the poor people imployed."[81]
Similarly, the Royal African Company stated in a petition in
1696 that the slave trade should be supported by England,
because of the exports it encouraged of woolen and other English
manufactures.[82]

The woolen manufacturers of the kingdom took a prominent
part in the long and bitter controversy waged between the Royal
African Company and the separate traders. Those from whom
the company made its purchases argued that the interlopers
caused disturbances and dislocation of the trade, and that the
trade declined when the company's monopoly was modified. In
1694 the clothiers of Witney petitioned Parliament in favor
of the company's monopoly. The cloth workers of Shrewsbury
followed suit in 1696, and the weavers of Kidder-minster twice
in the same year. In 1709 the weavers of Exeter and the woolen
tradesmen of London, and in 1713 several tradesmen interested
in the woolen manufacture, also took the company's side.[83]

But the weight of the woolen interests was on the whole
thrown on the side of the free traders. The company's monopoly
enabled it to "screw up the tradesmen to a limited quantity
and price, length, breadth and weight."[84] Monopoly meant
one buyer and one seller only. A searcher in the custom house
testified that when the trade was open there was a greater
exportation of wool. According to the testimony of two London merchants in 1693, the monopoly had reduced the exports
of wool by nearly one-third. Suffolk exported 25,000 woolen
cloths a year; two years after the incorporation of the company, the number declined to 500.[85] In 1690 the clothiers of
Suffolk and Essex and the manufacturers of Exeter petitioned
against the company's monopoly. Exeter petitioned again in
1694, 1696, 1709, 1710 and 1711 in favor of free trade. The

woolen merchants of the kingdom complained in 1694 that restrictions had greatly lessened their sales. Similar petitions were presented against the monopoly by the woolen traders of London and the woolen merchants of Plymouth in 1710, the woolen dealers of Totnes and Ashburton, the woolen manufacturers of Kidderminster, the Merchant Adventurers of Minehead engaged in the woolen manufacture in 1711.[86]

Other petitions to Parliament emphasized the importance of the colonial market for the woolen industry. In 1690 the planters of Jamaica protested against the company's monopoly as a discouragement to trade, especially the woolen trade. A petition from Manchester in 1704 revealed that English wool was traded to Holland, Hamburg and the East for linen yarn and flax, which, when manufactured, were sent to the plantations. The merchants and traders of Liverpool in 1709, the merchants and inhabitants of Liverpool in 1715, contended that the company's monopoly was detrimental to the woolen industry. Petitions from the industrial North in 1735 disclosed that Wakefield, Halifax, Burnley, Colne and Kendal were all interested in the manufacture of woolen goods for Africa and the West Indies.[87]

That woolen goods should figure so prominently in tropical markets is to be attributed to the deliberate policy of mercantilist England. It was argued in 1732, on behalf of the mainland colonies, that Pennsylvania alone consumed more woolen exports from England than all the sugar islands combined, and New York more than any sugar island except Jamaica.[88] Woolen goods were more suited for these colder climates, and the Barbadian planters preferred light calicoes which could be easily washed.[89] But wool was England's staple, and climatic considerations were too great a refinement for the mercantilist mind. Any one familiar with British West Indian society today will appreciate the strength of the tradition thereby fostered. Woolen undergarments are still common in the islands today, though more among the older generation, and suits of blue serge are still a sign of the well-dressed man. Like the Englishman and unlike the North American in the colonies, the Caribbean colored middle class today still apes the fashions of the home country in its preference for the heavier materials which are so ridiculous and uncomfortable in a tropical environment.

But cotton later superseded wool in colonial markets as it did in domestic. Of a total export of four million pounds of woolen manufactures in 1772, less than three per cent went to the West Indies and less than four per cent to Africa.[90] The best customers were Europe and America. In 1783 the woolen industry was slowly beginning its belated imitation of the technological changes which had revolutionized the cotton industry. In its progress after 1783 the triangular trade and West Indian market played no appreciable part.

2.   Cotton Manufacture

What the building of ships for the transport of slaves did for eighteenth century Liverpool, the manufacture of cotton goods for the purchase of slaves did for eighteenth century Manchester. The first stimulus to the growth of Cottonopolis came from the African and West Indian markets.

The growth of Manchester was intimately associated with the growth of Liverpool, its outlet to the sea and the world market. The capital accumulated by Liverpool from the slave trade poured into the hinterland to fertilize the energies of Manchester; Manchester goods for Africa were taken to the coast in the Liverpool slave vessels. Lancashire's foreign market meant chiefly the West Indian plantations and Africa. The export trade was £14,000 in 1739; in 1759 it had increased nearly eight times; in 1779 it was £303,000. Up to 1770 one-third of this export went to the slave coast, one-half to the American and West Indian colonies.[91] It was this tremendous dependence on the triangular trade that made Manchester.

Light woolen goods were popular on the slave coast: so were silks, provided they were gaudy and had large flowers. But the most popular of all materials was cotton goods, as the African was already accustomed to coarse blue and white cotton cloths of his own manufacture, and from the beginning the striped loincloths called "annabasses" were a regular feature of every slave trader's cargo. Indian textiles, banned in England, soon established a monopoly of the African market. Brawls, tapsells, niccanees, cuttanees, buckshaws, nillias, salempores— these Indian cloths were highly prized, and yet another powerful vested interest was drawn into the orbit of the slave trade. Manchester tried to compete with the East India Company; bafts, for example, were cheap cotton fabrics from the East later copied in England for the African market. But the backwardness of the English dyeing process made it impossible for Manchester to get the fast red, green and yellow colors popular on the coast. Manchester proved unable to imitate the colors of these Indian cottons, and there is evidence to show that the French cotton manufacturers of Normandy were equally unsuccessful in learning the secrets of the East.

Manchester was more fortunate in its trade in cotton and linen checks, though figures for the first half of the eighteenth century are unreliable. The European and colonial wars of 1739-1748 and the reorganization which the African Company was undergoing up to 1750 caused a slump in the cotton trade to Africa, and when it revived after 1750 Indian exports were inadequate to satisfy the demand. English manufacturers made full use of this opportunity to push their own goods. In 1752 the export of cotton-linen checks alone from England was £57,000; in 1763, at the end of the Seven Years' War, it stood at the exceptionally high figure of £302,000, but after 1767 remained between £100,000 and £200,000, when Indian competition again proved formidable.

Available statistics make comparison between the value of English cotton checks and Indian cotton pieces exported to Africa impossible, as the former are given by value and the latter by quantity. But the growth of Indian and English cotton exports to Africa will give some indication of the importance of the African market. Total cotton exports stood at £214,600 in 1751; in 1763 they were more than double; in 1772 they were more than four times as great, but as a result of the American Revolution they declined to £195,900 in 1780. The effect of the war on the slave and plantation markets is at once apparent. By 1780 checks had ceased to be an important part of the cotton industry. But it was not the war alone that was to be blamed.

Manchester could satisfy the African market only when Indian cottons were scarce or dear. For the plantation market cheapness was essential, and by 1780 raw cotton was becoming increasingly expensive as the supply lagged behind the demand of the new inventions.[92]

But according to estimates given to the Privy Council in 1788, Manchester exported annually to Africa goods worth £200,000, £180,000 of this for Negroes only; the manufacture of these goods represented an investment of £300,000 and gave employment to 180,000 men, women and children.[93] The French manufacturers, impressed with the quality and cheapness of those special goods called Guinea cloths produced in Manchester, were sending agents over to get particulars, and extending open offers to Manchester manufacturers, should Britain abolish the slave trade, to set up in Rouen where they would be given every encouragement.[94] In addition, Manchester in 1788 furnished for the West Indian trade more than £300,000 annually in manufactures, which gave employment to many thousands.[95]

Between the cotton manufacturers of Manchester and the slave traders there were not the close connections that have already been noticed in the case of the shipbuilders of Liverpool. But two exceptional instances of such connections exist. Two well-known cotton manufacturers of Lancashire, Sir William Fazackerly and Samuel Touchet, were both members of the Company of Merchants trading to Africa. Fazackerly, a London dealer in fustians, presented the case of the separate traders of Bristol and Liverpool against the African Company in 1726.[96] Touchet, member of a great Manchester check-making house, represented Liverpool on the governing body of the company during the period 1753-1756. He was concerned in the equipping of the expedition which captured Senegal in 1758 and tried hard to get the contract for victualling the troops. A patron of Paul's unsuccessful spinning machine intended to revolutionize the cotton industry, accused openly of attempting to monopolize the import of raw cotton, Touchet added to his many interests a partnership, with his brothers, in about twenty ships in the West Indian trade. Touchet died, leaving a large fortune, and was described in his obituary notice as "the most considerable merchant and manufacturer in Manchester, remarkable for great abilities and strict integrity, and for universal benevolence and usefulness to mankind." Two modern writers have left us this description of the man: "Icarus-like soaring too high," he emerges as "the first considerable financier that the Manchester trade produced, and certainly as one of the earliest cases of a Manchester man who was concerned at once in manufacturing and in large scale financial and commercial ventures in the City and abroad."[97]

Other cases emphasize the significance of Touchet's career. Robert Diggles, African slave trader of Liverpool, was the son of a Manchester linen draper and brother of another. In 1747 a Manchester man was in partnership with two Liverpool men in a voyage to Jamaica. A leading Manchester firm, the Hibberts, owned sugar plantations in Jamaica, and at one time supplied checks and imitations of Indian goods to the African Company for the slave trade.[98]

Manchester received a double stimulus from the colonial trade. If it supplied the goods needed on the slave coast and on the plantations, its manufacturers depended in turn on the supply of the raw material. Manchester's interest in the islands was twofold.

The raw material came to England in the seventeenth and eighteenth centuries chiefly from two sources, the Levant and the West Indies. In the eighteenth century that Indian competition which proved too formidable for Manchester on the slave coast and which was threatening to swamp even the home market with Indian goods was effectively smashed, as far as England was concerned, by the prohibitive duties on Indian imports into England. The first step was thereby taken by which the motherland of cotton became in the nineteenth and twentieth centuries the chief market of Lancashire. In the eighteenth century the measure gave Manchester a monopoly of the home market, and private Indian traders began to import the raw cotton for the Lancashire factories. A competitor to the West Indian islands had arisen, to be followed later by Brazil, whose product by 1783 was recognized as clearly superior to all the other varieties.

But in the early eighteenth century England depended on the West Indian islands for between two-thirds and three-quarters of its raw cotton. Cotton, nevertheless, was essentially a secondary consideration in the West Indian planter's outlook, and however much the planters as a body looked with jealousy on its cultivation in India or Africa or Brazil, it remained a secondary consideration. In opposing the retention of Guadeloupe in 1763, the West India interest measured their arguments in terms of sugar, while, significantly, a contemporary pamphleteer pointed to its cotton exports to England as a reason for keeping the island.[99] But British consumption was small and the West Indian contribution welcome. In 1764 British imports of raw cotton amounted to nearly four million pounds; the West Indies supplied one-half. In 1780 Britain imported more than six and a half million pounds; the West Indies supplied two-thirds.[100]

In 1783, the West Indies, therefore, still dominated the cotton trade. But a new day was dawning. In the phenomenal expansion of an industry which was to clothe the world, a few tiny islands in the Caribbean could hardly hope to supply the necessary raw material. Their cotton was the long-staple, sea-island variety, easily cleaned by hand, limited to certain areas, and therefore expensive. When the cotton gin permitted the cultivation of the short-staple cotton by facilitating the task of cleaning, the center of gravity shifted from the islands to the mainland to meet the enormous demands of the new machinery in England. In 1784 a shipment of American cotton was seized by the Liverpool customs authorities on the ground that cotton, not being a bona fide product of the United States, could not legally be transported to England in an American vessel.

It was an evil omen for the West Indians, coinciding, as it did, with another significant development. During the American Revolution Manchester's cotton exports to Europe almost trebled.[101] The Revolution itself created another important market for Manchester, the independent United States, at a time when the cotton gin was just around the corner. For both its import and export markets, therefore, cotton was beginning to reach out to the world market. The sunny Caribbean sky was marred by a barely perceptible but portentous cloud, and the gentle West Indian breeze was rising ominously. It heralded the approaching political hurricane which, to alter Edmund Burke's description of those visitations of nature common in the West Indies, humbled the sugar planter's pride if it did not correct his vices.

3. *Sugar Refining.*

The processing of colonial raw materials gave rise to new industries in England, provided further employment for shipping, and contributed to a greater extension of the world market and international trade. Of these raw materials sugar was preeminent, and its manufacture gave birth to the sugar refining industry. The refining process transformed the crude brown sugar manufactured on the plantations into white sugar, which was durable and capable of preservation, and could be easily handled and distributed all over the world.

The earliest reference to sugar refining in England is an order of the Privy Council in 1615 prohibiting aliens from erecting sugar houses or practising the art of refining sugar.[102] The importance of the industry increased in proportion to its production on the plantations, and as sugar became, with the spread of tea and coffee, one of the necessities of life instead of the luxury of kings.

About the middle of the eighteenth century there were 120 refineries in England. Each refinery was estimated to provide employment for about nine men. In addition the distribution of the refined product called into existence a number of subsidiary trades and required ships and wagons for the coastal and inland trade.[103]

The sugar refining industry of Bristol was one of the most important of the kingdom. It was in Bristol in 1654 that the diarist, Evelyn, saw for the first time the method of manufacturing loaf sugar,[104] and in the annals of Bristol's history sugar figures frequently as a gift to distinguished visitors to the town—Richard, son of Oliver Cromwell, and King Charles II, in return for which the king knighted four of the town's merchants.[105]

In 1799, there were twenty refineries in Bristol, and the town did more refining than London in proportion to size and population. Bristol's sugar was considered superior in quality, its proximity to the coal supplies for fuel enabled it to sell cheaper than London, while it found in Ireland, the whole of South Wales and West England the markets for which it was destined by its geographical location.[106] Sugar refining long remained one of the staples of Bristol. The refiners of the city petitioned Parliament in 1789 against the abolition of the slave trade on which "the welfare and prosperity, if not the actual existence, of the West India Islands depend."[107] In 1811 there were sixteen refineries in the town, whose connection with this industry ceased only towards the end of the nineteenth century, when bananas replaced sugar.[108]

Some of Bristol's most prominent citizens were connected with the sugar refining business. Robert Aldworth, seventeenth century alderman, was closely identified with refining, while he was at the same time a merchant who built two docks to accommodate the increased shipping.[109] William Miles was the outstanding refiner of the eighteenth century. His career is typical of many other cases. Miles came to Bristol with three half-pence in his pocket, worked as a porter, apprenticed himself to a shipbuilder, saved fifteen pounds, and sailed to Jamaica as a ship's carpenter in a merchantman. He bought a cask or two of sugar which he sold in Bristol, at a huge profit, and with the proceeds bought articles in great demand in Jamaica and repeated his former investment. Miles soon became very wealthy and settled in Bristol as a refiner. This was the humble origin of one of the greatest fortunes made in the West Indian trade. Taking his son into partnership, Miles was wealthy enough to give him a check for £100,000 to enable him to marry the daughter of an aristocratic clergyman. The elder Miles became an alderman, and died rich and honored; the younger continued as a West Indian merchant dealing chiefly in sugar and slaves, and at his death in 1848 left property valued at more than a million.[110] In 1833 he was in possession of 663 slaves in

Trinidad and Jamaica, for which he received compensation to the amount of £17,850.[111]

The frequent association of Glasgow with the tobacco industry is only a part of the truth. The prosperity of the town in the eighteenth century was due at least as much to its sugar refining business. Sugar refining dated back to the second half of the seventeenth century. The Wester sugar-house was built in 1667, followed by the Easter in 1669, and shortly after the South sugar-house and another. Yet another followed in 1701. But Glasgow labored under the disadvantage that before 1707 direct trade relations with the colonies were illegal, and Glasgow's sugar refiners were forced to depend on Bristol for their raw material. By the Act of Union and a happy accident this unsatisfactory situation was brought to an end. Two Scotch officers, Colonel William Macdowall, cadet of an ancient family, and Major James Milliken, while quartered in St. Kitts, wooed and won two heiresses, the widow Tovie and her daughter, owners of great sugar plantations. The missing link had been found. The arrival of the heiresses and their husbands meant that Glasgow became one of the leading ports of entry for the cargoes of West Indian sugar. In the very year of the happy event a new refinery was set up.[112]

The majority of the refineries were located in and around the capital—eighty compared with Bristol's twenty. In 1774 there were eight refineries in Liverpool, one of them, the house of Branckers, a firm also engaged in the slave trade, being one of the most extensive in the whole kingdom.[113] There were others in Manchester, Chester, Lancashire, Whitehaven, Newcastle, Hull, Southampton and Warrington.

It may well be asked why the refining of the raw sugar was not done at the source, on the plantations. The division of labor, between the agricultural operations in the tropical climate, and the industrial operations in the temperate climate, has survived to this day. The original reason had nothing to do with the skill of labor or the presence of natural resources. It was the result of the deliberate policy of the mother country. The ban on sugar refining in the islands corresponded to the ban on iron and textile manufacture on the mainland. Should they have refiners in England or the plantations? asked Sir Thomas Clifford in 1671. "Five ships go for the blacks," was his answer, "and not above two if refined in the plantations; and so you destroy shipping, and all that belongs to it; and if you lose this advantage to England, you lose all." Hence the heavy duty placed on refined sugar imported into England, four times as much as upon the brown sugar. By this policy England was called upon for a larger number of casks for the raw sugar, more coals and victuals were consumed, and the national revenues increased.[114] Davenant's pleas for permission of colonial refining[115] fell on deaf ears.

It is significant that a similar struggle was taking place in France, resulting in a similar victory for the mercantilists. Colbert had permitted the refining of sugar in the French West Indies, and raw and refined sugar from the islands paid the same duty in France. But in 1682 the duty on refined sugar was doubled, while two years later, under penalty of a fine of 3,000 livres, it was forbidden to erect new refineries in the islands. A decree of 1698 was even more drastic. The duty on raw sugar from the West Indies was lowered from four to three livres per hundredweight, while the duty on refined sugar was increased from eight to twenty-two and a half livres. This latter figure was the same duty charged on refined sugar from foreign lands: "the drastic nature of the protection afforded the French refiners as against their compatriots in the colonies becomes apparent."[116]

The sugar refining interest of England was encouraged by such legislation. It did not always see eye to eye with the planting interest on whom it depended for supplies. Under the mercantile system the sugar planters had a monopoly of the home market, and foreign imports were prohibited. It was therefore the policy of the planters to restrict production in order to maintain a high price. Their legal monopoly of the home market was a powerful weapon in their hands, and they used it mercilessly, at the expense of the whole population of England. While the price of sugar was being naturally forced down in the world market by the increase of sugar cultivation in the French, Spanish and Portuguese colonies, the British planters were intent on maintaining a monopoly price in the home market.

The friends of the planters warned them of the "fatal and wretched error" they were making, for "if the British plantations cannot, or will not, afford sugar, etc., plenty and cheap enough the French, Dutch, and Portuguese do, and will."[117] There were not wanting writers, as early as 1730, who urged the government to "open the sluices of the laws, and let in even the French sugar upon them, till they would serve us at least as cheap as our neighbors are serv'd."[118] In 1739 Jamaica requested assistance from the mother country. The Council of Trade and Plantations issued a clear and unmistakable warning. Jamaica had twice as much land as all the Leeward Islands combined, yet the exports of the Leeward Islands exceeded those of Jamaica. "From whence it would naturally follow that not one half of your lands are at present cultivated, and that Great Britain does not reap half the benefit from your Colony, which she might do if it were fully settled."[119]

The planters would not listen. In the eighteenth century, they did not have to. The refiners of London, Westminster, Southwark and Bristol protested to Parliament in 1753 against the selfishness of the planters and the "most intolerable kind of a tax" represented by the higher price of British sugar. The refiners urged Parliament to make it the interest of the sugar planters to produce more raw sugar by increasing the area under cultivation. They were careful, however, not to pretend to "set ourselves in competition with the inhabitants of all the sugar colonies, either for numbers, wealth, or consequence to the public." Parliament sidetracked the issue by passing resolutions about the encouragement of white settlers in Jamaica.[120]

Another crisis in relations between producers and processors developed during the American Revolution. Imports of sugar declined by one-third between 1774 and 1780. Prices were high, and the refiners, in distress, petitioned Parliament for relief in the form of the admission of prize sugar. Reading between the lines of the evidence taken by the parliamentary committee on the subject, we see the conflict of interests between refiner and planter. High prices benefited the planter, while the refiners wanted an increased supply which the planters would not, or could not, give. If they would not, make them; the refiners of Bristol recommended "a salutary law," which would "make it the interest of the British sugar colonies, to extend the cultivation of their lands, in order to enable them to raise a larger produce, and to send greater quantities of sugar to Great Britain, and thereby become more useful to their mother country, its trade, navigation, and revenue."[121] If they could not, buy elsewhere—the French colonies, for example. "Was I a refiner," said one witness, a wholesale grocer, "I should certainly prefer St. Domingo sugars to any other."[122] The chasm was yawning at the feet of the sugar planter, but, head held proudly in the air, he went his way mumbling the lesson he had been taught by the mercantilists and which he had learned not wisely but too well.

4. *Rum Distillation*

Yet another colonial raw material gave birth to yet another English industry. One of the important by-products of sugar is molasses, from which rum may be distilled. But rum never attained the importance of cotton, far less of sugar, as a contribution to British industry, partly, perhaps, because much rum was imported direct from the islands in its finished state. Imports from the islands increased from 58,000 gallons in 1721 to 320,000 in 1730. In 1763 the figure stood at one and a quarter million gallons and was steadily over two million between 1765 and 1779.[123]

Rum was indispensable in the fisheries and the fur trade, and as a naval ration. But its connection with the triangular trade was more direct still. Rum was an essential part of the cargo of the slave ship, particularly the colonial American slave ship. No slave trader could afford to dispense with a cargo of rum. It was profitable to spread a taste for liquor on the coast. The Negro dealers were plied with it, were induced to drink till they lost their reason, and then the bargain was struck.[124] One slave dealer, his bag full of the gold paid him for his slaves, stupidly accepted the slave captain's invitation to dinner. He was made drunk and awoke next morning to find his money gone and himself stripped, branded and enslaved with his own victims, to the great mirth of the sailors.[125] In 1765 two distilleries were established at Liverpool for the express purpose of supplying ships bound for Africa.[126] Of equal importance to the mercantilist was the fact that from molasses could be obtained, in addition to rum, brandy and low wines imported from France. The distilleries were an important evidence of Bristol's interest in the sugar plantations, and many were the jeremiads which they sent to Parliament in defence of their interests and in opposition to the importation of French brandies. Bishop Berkeley voiced the prevailing feeling when he asked acidly, in strict mercantilist language, "whether if drunkenness be a necessary evil, men may not as well get drunk with the growth of their own country?"

The eighteenth century in England was notorious for its alcoholism. The popular drink was gin, immortalized by Hogarth in his *Gin Lane*. A classic advertisement of a gin shop in Southwark read: "Drunk for a penny, dead drunk for two-pence, clean straw for nothing." Gin and rum contended for pride of place.

The West Indian planters argued that the rum they produced was equal to one-fourth of the value of all their other products. To prohibit the sale of rum would therefore be to ruin them, and drive the people to foreign substitutes. The planters expressed the hope that the suppression of the evils occasioned by the excessive use of spirituous liquors would not entail the destruction of the sugar trade.[127] As they saw it, the question was not whether people should drink, but what they should drink. Gin, argued an anonymous writer, was "vastly more destructive to the human frame" than rum. "Gin is a spirit too fiery, acrid, and inflameing for inward use—but. . . . Rum is a spirit so mild, balsamic and benign, that if its properly used and attempered it may be made highly useful, both for the relief and regalement of human nature."[128] This was a strange description of the spirit which the Barbadians more appropriately nicknamed "Kill-Devill."

Against the planters it was contended that the West Indian rum trade was too unimportant to permit the continuance of a glaring enormity which tended to destroy the health and morals of the people of Great Britain.[129] It is not unlikely that other considerations were involved. Rum competed with spirits made from corn. The West India interest was therefore at odds with the English agricultural interest. The sugar planters charged that distilling from corn tended to raise the price of bread. This concern for the poor consumer of bread was touching, coming as it did from extortionists who wanted the poor to spend more money on their sugar, and it antedated by a hundred years a similar but more significant conflict between English farmers and English industralists, over cheaper bread or lower wages for the working classes. "Molasses" embittered the relations between West Indian sugar planter and English landlord as it embittered relations between planter and mainland colonist, and the West India interest was always quick to recommend its substitution in England whenever there was a grain shortage, they said, but in reality whenever there was a glut of sugar. "Sweet gentlemen!" wrote an anonymous champion of the barley counties in 1807. "They have sought a very far fetched argument in support of their saccharine cause";[130] and Michael Sadler, in 1831, opposed the idea: "A wholesome beverage might be made from that article, but the people of England did not like it."[131]

The real enemy, however, of the West Indian distiller was not the English farmer but the New England distiller. The New England traders refused to purchase West Indian rum and insisted on molasses, which they themselves distilled, and sent to Newfoundland, the Indian tribes, and above all Africa. The rum trade on the slave coast became a virtual monopoly of New England. In 1770 New England exports of rum to Africa represented over four-fifths of the total colonial export of that year,[132] and yet another important vested interest drew its sustenance from the triangular trade. But here, too, lay the seed of future disruption. French West Indian molasses was cheaper than British, because French distilling was not permitted to compete with the brandies of the home country. Rather than feed their molasses to their horses, they preferred to sell it to the mainland colonists. The latter therefore turned

to the French planters, and molasses was one of the principal items in that trade between mainland and the foreign
sugar colonies which, as the sequel showed, had far-reaching
consequences for the British sugar planters.

5. *Pacotille*

The slave cargoes were in complete without the "pacotille," the
sundry items and gewgaws which appealed to the Africans' love
of bright colors and for which, after having sold their fellows,
they would, late in the nineteenth century, part with their land
and grant mining concessions. Articles of glass and beads were
always in demand on the slave coast, and on the plantations there
was a great demand for bottles. Most of these articles were manufactured in Bristol.[133] One slave dealer received a fine Negro
from a prince in return for thirteen beads of coral, half a string of
amber, twenty-eight silver bells, and three pairs of bracelets for
his women; in acknowledgment of this liberality, he presented
to the prince's favorite a present of some rows of glass beads and
about four ounces of scarlet wool.[134] Individually these items
were of negligible value; in the aggregate they constituted a
trade of great importance, so essential a part of the slave transactions that the word "pacotille" is still commonly used in the
West Indies today to denote a cheap and tawdry bauble given
as compensation for objects of great value.

6. *The Metallurgical Industries*

Slave trading demanded goods more gruesome though not a
whit less useful than woolen and cotton manufacturers. Fetters
and chains and padlocks were needed to fasten the Negroes more
securely on the slave ships and thus prevent both mutiny and
suicide. The practice of branding the slaves to identify them
required red-hot irons. Legal regulations prescribed that on any
ship designed for Africa, the East Indies, or the West Indies,
"three-fourths of their proportion of beer was to be put in iron
bound cask, hooped with iron hoops of good substance, and
well wrought iron."[135] Iron bars were the trading medium on
a large part of the African coast and were equivalent to four

copper bars.[136] Iron bars constituted nearly three-quarters of the value of the cargo of the *Swallow* in 1679, nearly one-quarter of the cargo of the *Mary* in 1690, nearly one-fifth of a slave cargo in 1733.[137] In 1682 the Royal African Company was exporting about 10,000 bars of iron a year.[138] The ironmasters, too, found a useful market in Africa.

Guns formed a regular part of every African cargo. Birmingham became the center of the gun trade as Manchester was of the cotton trade. The struggle between Birmingham and London over the gun trade was merely another angle to the struggle for free trade or monopoly which we have already noticed for the slave trade in general between the capital and the outports. In 1709 and 1710 the gun makers of London petitioned in favor of the Royal African Company's monopoly. The Birmingham gun makers and iron makers threw their weight and influence against the company and the London interests. Three times, in 1708, 1709, and 1711, they petitioned against a renewal of the company's monopoly which had been modified in 1698.[139] Their trade had increased since then and they feared a renewal of the monopoly, which would subject their manufactures "to one buyer, or to anyone monopolizing society, exclusive of all others."[140]

In the nineteenth century Birmingham guns were exchanged for African palm-oil, but the eighteenth century saw a less innocent exchange. The Birmingham guns of the eighteenth century were exchanged for men, and it was a common saying that the price of a Negro was one Birmingham gun. The African musket was an important Birmingham export, reaching a total of 100,000 to 150,000 annually. With the British government and the East India Company, Africa ranked as the most important customer of the Birmingham gunmakers.[141]

The needs of the plantations too were not to be despised. In the late seventeenth century the ironmasters, Sitwells, of Derbyshire were producing among their items sugar stoves and rollers for crushing cane in Barbados, and Birmingham, too, was interested in the plantations.[142] Exports of wrought iron and nails went to the plantations, though these exports tended to fluctuate according to the condition of the sugar trade. As one ironmaster said in 1737: "The bad state of some of our sugar islands has been ... some prejudice to the iron-trade; for the consumption of iron ware, in those islands, is more or less, as their trade for sugar is better or worse."[143] An old historian of the city has left us a picture of Birmingham's interest in the colonial system: "axes for India, and tomahawks for the natives of North America; and to Cuba and the Brazils chains, handcuffs, and iron collars for the poor slaves.... In the primeval forests of America the Birmingham axe struck down the old trees; the cattle pastures of Australia rang with the sound of Birmingham bells; in East India and the West they tended the fields of sugar cane with Birmingham hoes."[144]

Along with iron went brass, copper and lead. The exports of brass pans and kettles to Africa dated back before 1660 but increased with free trade after 1698. Thereafter Birmingham began to export large quantities of cutlery and brass goods, and throughout the eighteenth century British goods effectively sustained competition with foreign in colonial markets. The Cheadle Company, founded in North Staffordshire in 1719, soon became one of the leading brass and copper concerns in England. It extended the scope of its operations to include the brass wire, "the Guinea rods" and the "manelloes" (metal rings worn by the African tribes) used in the African trade. The company's capital increased eleven times between 1734 and 1780 when the company was reorganized. "Starting from small beginnings ..., it became one of the most important, if not the most important, of the brass and copper concerns of the eighteenth century." According to tradition, ships sailed to Africa with the holds full of idols and "manelloes," while the cabins were occupied by missionaries—"an edifying example of a material good in competition with an immaterial one."[145] The Baptist Mills of Bristol produced a prodigious quantity of brass which, drawn into wire and formed into "battery," was extensively used in the African trade.[146] The Holywell works, in addition to producing copper sheathing for the Liverpool ships, manufactured brass pans for the West Indian sugar and East India tea merchants, and all varieties of cheap and gaudy brass instruments for the African trade.[147] Brass pans and kettles were exported to Africa and the plantations, and in one list, after the heading "brass pans," we read "ditto large to wash their bodies in."[148] These "bath pans," made now of galvanized tin, are still a normal feature of West Indian life today.

The needs of shipbuilding gave a further stimulus to heavy industry. The iron chain and anchor foundries, of which there were many in Liverpool, lived off the building of ships. Copper sheathing for the vessels gave rise to local industries in the town and adjacent districts to supply the demand. Between thirty and forty vessels were employed in transporting the copper, smelted in Lancashire and Cheshire, from the works at Holywell to the warehouses in Liverpool.[149]

The ironmaster's interest in the slave trade continued throughout the century. When the question of abolition came before Parliament, the manufacturers of and dealers in iron, copper, brass and lead in Liverpool petitioned against the project, which would affect employment in the town and send forth thousands as "solitary wanderers into the world, to seek employment in foreign climes."[150] In the same year Birmingham declared that it was dependent on the slave trade to a considerable extent for a large part of its various manufactures. Abolition would ruin the town and impoverish many of its inhabitants.[151]

These apprehensions were exaggerated. The munitions demand for the commercial wars of the eighteenth century had prepared the ironmasters for the still greater demands to come during the Revolutionary and Napoleonic Wars. The colonial markets, moreover, were inadequate to absorb the increased production which resulted from the technological innovations. Between 1710 and 1735 iron exports almost trebled. In 1710 the British West Indies took over one-fifth of the exports, in 1735 less than one-sixth. In 1710, over one-third of the exports to the plantations went to the sugar islands, in 1735 over one-quarter. The peak was reached in 1729, when the West Indies took nearly one-quarter of the total exports, and nearly one-half of the exports to all the plantations.[152] Expansion at home, contraction in the sugar islands. In 1783 the ironmasters, too, were beginning to look the other way. But Cinderella, decked out temporarily in her fancy clothes, was enjoying herself too much at the ball to pay any attention to the hands of the clock.

· 4 ·

THE WEST INDIA INTEREST

"OUR TOBACCO COLONIES," wrote Adam Smith, "send us home no such wealthy planters as we see frequently arrive from our sugar islands."[1] The sugar planter ranked among the biggest capitalists of the mercantilist epoch. A very popular play, "The West Indian," was produced in London in 1771. It opens with a tremendous reception being prepared for a planter coming to England, as if it were the Lord Mayor who was expected. The servant philosophized: "He's very rich, and that's sufficient. They say he has rum and sugar enough belonging to him, to make all the water in the Thames into punch."[2]

The West Indian planter was a familiar figure in English society in the eighteenth century. The explanation lies in the absentee landlordism which has always been the curse of the Caribbean and is still one of its major problems today.

One absentee planter once argued that "the climate of our sugar colonies is so inconvenient for an English constitution, that no man will chuse to live there, much less will any man chuse to settle there, without the hopes at least of supporting his family in a more handsome manner, or saving more money, than he can do by any business he can expect in England, or in our plantations upon the continent of America."[3] But the West Indian climate is not disagreeable, and, his fortune once made, the slave owner returned to Britain. Writing in 1689 the agent for Barbados stated that "by a kind of magnetic force England draws to it all that is good in the plantations. It is the center to which all things tend. Nothing but England can we relish or fancy: our hearts are here, wherever our bodies be. . . . All that we can rap and rend is brought to England."[4] In 1698 the West Indies were sending back annually to England about three hundred children to be educated, the difference being, according to Davenant, that the fathers went out poor and the children came back rich.[5] "Well," says Mr. Belcour, the planter, in the comedy "The West Indian," "for the first time in my life here am I in England, at the fountain-head of pleasure, in the land of beauty, of arts, of elegancies. My happy stars have given me a good estate, and the conspiring winds have blown me hither to spend it."[6] Returned to England, the planters' fondest wish was to acquire an estate, blend with the aristocracy, and remove the marks of their origin. Their presence in England, as Brougham pointed out, had a frequently deleterious effect on English character and morals; where they were numerous and had acquired land, they commonly introduced a bad state of manners into the locality.[7] Their colossal wealth permitted lavish expenditures which smacked of vulgarity and excited the envy and disapproval of the less opulent English aristocracy.

The political economist, Merivale, later in the nineteenth century argued that the change from residence to absenteeism was a credit rather than a disgrace to the English character, as evincing a distaste for the deep-rooted hard-heartedness and profligacy of life in the slave colonies. But that peculiar fastidiousness which shrank from contact with slavery whilst it had no objection to enjoying the profits of slavery, Merivale could explain only by "the general apology of the inconsistency of human nature."[8]

Absenteeism, however, had serious consequences in the islands. Plantations were left to be mismanaged by overseers and attorneys. On occasions governors found it difficult to obtain a quorum for the councils. Many offices were held by a single individual, and the disproportion between white and black population was increased, aggravating the danger of slave rebellions. The Deficiency Laws failed to restrain the practice of absenteeism, so the local assemblies tried to confiscate the large tracts of land lying idle and owned by absentees, and proposed their redivision among small farms. Both measures were opposed by the British government at the insistence of the absentee planters.[9]

Of the sugar planters resident in England the most prominent were the Beckfords, an old Gloucestershire family dating back to the twelfth century. One died fighting for his king on Bosworth Field in 1483, another found in the English conquest of Jamaica a means of retrieving the family fortunes. In 1670 Alderman Sir Thomas Beckford, one of the first of absentee proprietors, was getting £2,000 per annum from his Jamaican property clear of all charges. Peter Beckford became the most distinguished of the new colonists. He held in the course of time all the most important military and civil positions in the island, became President of the Council and later Lieutenant-Governor and Commander-in-Chief. At his death in 1710 he "was in possesion of the largest property real and personal of any subject in Europe." In 1737 his grandson, William, inherited the family wealth and became the most powerful West Indian planter in England.[10]

Beckford, on his Wiltshire estate, built Fonthill Mansion, long regarded as the most attractive and splendid seat in the West of England.

"It was a handsome, uniform edifice, consisting of a centre of four stories, and two wings of two stories, connected by corridors, built of fine stone, and adorned with a bold portico, resting on a rustic basement, with two sweeping flights of steps: its apartments were numerous, and splendidly furnished. They displayed the riches and luxury of the east; and on particular occasions were superbly brilliant and dazzling. Whilst its walls were adorned with the most costly works of art, its sideboards and cabinets presented a gorgeous combination of gold, silver, precious metals, and precious stones, arranged and worked by the most tasteful artists and artisans. Added to these splendours, these dazzling objects, apparently augmented and multiplied by large costly mirrors, was a vast, choice, and valuable library. . . . Some idea may be formed of the extent, etc., of the house by the measurement of its great entrance hall, in the basement story, which was eighty-five feet ten inches in length, by thirty-eight feet six inches in breadth. Its roof was vaulted, and supported by large stone piers. One apartment was fitted up in the Turkish style, with large mirrors, ottomans, etc., whilst others were enriched with fine sculptured marble chimney-pieces."[11]

Beckford, Junior, was not to be outdone. Possessed of a vivid fancy and a vast fortune which, according to the family historian, could not be satisfied with anything commonplace, he desired novelty, grandeur, complexity and even sublimity. The result was Fonthill Abbey, the construction of which provided employment for a vast number of mechanics and laborers, even a new village being built to accomodate some of the settlers. The abbey grounds were in one section planted with every species of American flowering shrub and tree, growing in all their native wildness.[12] In 1837 Beckford was awarded £15,160 by way of compensation for 770 slaves he owned in Jamaica.[13]

The Hibberts were West Indian planters as well as merchants, who, as we have seen, supplied cotton and linen checks for Africa and the plantations. Robert Hibbert lived in Bedfordshire off the income from his West Indian property. His plantation was one of the finest in Jamaica; "though he was always an eminently kind master," his biographer assures us, "he had no repugnance to this kind of property on moral grounds." On his death he left in trust a fund yielding about one thousand pounds per annum for three or more divinity scholarships to encourage the spread of Christianity in its simplest and most intelligible form and the unfettered exercise of private judgment in matters of religion.[14] A relative, George, was partner in an opulent trading firm in London, and was for many years agent of Jamaica in England. George Hibbert took the lead in the construction of the West India Docks. He was elected first chairman of the board of directors, and today his portrait, painted by Lawrence, hangs in the board room of the Port of London Authority. A great collector of books, the sale of his library lasted forty-two days.[15] The Hibberts received £31,120 in compensation for their 1,618 slaves.[16] The family mansion in Kingston, one of the oldest houses in Jamaica, still stands today, while the family name is perpetuated in the Hibbert Journal, the celebrated quarterly journal devoted to religion, theology and philosophy. First published in October, 1902, the Journal had "the sanction and support of the Hibbert Trustees," who, however, disclaimed responsibility for the opinions expressed in its pages.[17]

Also connected with Jamaica were the Longs. Charles Long, at his death, left property in Suffolk, a house in Bloomsbury, London, and total property in Jamaica comprising 14,000 acres. He enjoyed a very great income, by far the largest of any Jamaican proprietor of that period, and was accordingly entitled to live in splendor.[18] His grandson, a Jamaican planter, wrote a well-known history of the island. A relative, Beeston Long, Jr., was chairman of the London Dock Company and a Bank director, and his family mansion in Bishopsgate Street, London, was justly famous.[19] Another member of the family, Lord Farnborough, built Bromley Hill Place in Kent, one of the most famous mansions of England, noted for its wonderful ornamental gardens.[20]

Not content with his partnership in the Liverpool business house of Corrie and Company engaged in the grain trade, John Gladstone was indirectly concerned in the slave traffic as a slave owner in the West Indies. "Like many more merchants of reputed probity and honesty, (he) was able to satisfy his conscience by arguing it to be a necessity." Gladstone, through foreclosures, acquired large plantations in British Guiana and Jamaica, while at the same time he was extensively engaged in the West Indian trade. The sugar and other produce which he sold on the Liverpool Exchange were grown on his own plantations and imported in his own ships. The fortune amassed by this means permitted him to open up trade connections with Russia, India and China and to make large and fortunate investments in land and house property in Liverpool. He contributed largely to the charities of Liverpool, built and endowed churches, and was an eloquent champion in the town of the Greeks in their struggle for independence. When his famous son, William Ewart, was electioneering in Newark in 1832, a public journal, accurately if not in good taste, reminded the electors that the candidate was "the son of Gladstone of Liverpool, a person who had amassed a large fortune by West India dealings. In other words, a great part of his gold has sprung from the blood of black slaves."[21] During the greater part of the agitation for emancipation John Gladstone was chairman of the West India Association, and on one occasion conducted a memorable controversy in one of the Liverpool journals with James Cropper, a Liverpool abolitionist, on the question of West Indian slavery.[22] The compensation paid to Gladstone in 1837, in accordance with the Act of 1833, amounted to £85,600 for 2,183 slaves.[23]

The Codringtons were another well-known family which owed its wealth and status to its slave and sugar plantations. Christopher Codrington was governor of Barbados during the seventeenth century, and his plantations in Barbados and Barbuda were worth £100,000 in modern money. He founded a college there which still bears his name, and on his death left £10,000, most of it for a library, and his valuable collection of books worth £6,000 to All Souls College, Oxford, where they formed the nucleus of the famous Codrington Library. One of his descendants was hero of the naval victory of Navarino in the cause of Greek Independence in the nineteenth century.[24]

The Warner family was dispersed over the Leeward Islands, some in Antigua, some in Dominica, some in St. Vincent, some in Trinidad. Thomas Warner was a pioneer among British colonists in the Caribbean. Joseph, one of the family, rose to be one of the three leading surgeons of his day, surgeon at Guy's Hospital, and first member of the College of Surgeons founded in 1750. His picture by Samuel Medley is in the possession of the Royal College of Surgeons. In the nineteenth century another Warner was President of the Council of Antigua, while yet another, as Attorney-General of Trinidad, was the great advocate of East Indian immigration. Perhaps the best known of this West Indian family is Pelham Warner, famous English cricketer and acknowledged authority on the great English game.[25]

Other names, less spectacular, recall the glory that was sugar. Bryan Edwards, historian of the British West Indies at the end of the eighteenth century, would, by his own confession, have lived and died in oblivion on the small paternal estate in the decayed town of Westbury in Wiltshire, but for his two opulent uncles engaged in sugar cultivation in the West Indies.[26] The Pinneys, well-known in Bristol, owned sugar plantations in Nevis.[27] Joseph Marryat's son was Captain Frederick Marryat, the famous novelist of sea life, and the inventor of a code of signals for the merchant marine not abandoned until 1857.[28] Colonel William Macdowall was the most notable figure in Glasgow. "Owner of a noble mansion in the country and a rich estate in the West-Indies, with ships on the seas and cargoes of sugar and rum constantly coming home, he had also the social prestige of his army rank and his long family descent, and must have held the regard of everyone as he stepped, with his tall goldheaded cane, along the causeway."[29]

Bryan Edwards indignantly denied the charge that his fellow planters were remarkable for gigantic opulence or an ostentatious display of it. The available evidence points to the contrary. The wealth of the West Indians became proverbial. Communities of opulent West Indians were to be found in London and Bristol, and the memorial plaques in All Saints' Church, Southampton, speak eloquently of the social position they once enjoyed.[30] The public schools of Eton, Westminster, Harrow, and Winchester, were full of the sons of West Indians.[31] The carriages of the planters were so numerous, that, when they gathered, Londoners complained that the streets were for some distance blocked. The story is told of how, on a visit to Weymouth, George III and Pitt encountered a wealthy Jamaican with an imposing equipage, including out-riders and livery. George III, much displeased, is reported to have said, "Sugar, sugar, eh? all *that* sugar! How are the duties, eh, Pitt, how are the duties?"[32] West Indian planters were familiar visitors at the resorts of Epsom and Cheltenham;[33] their children mingled on terms of equality with the elegant throngs at the Assembly Rooms and the Hot Wells of Bristol.[34] A West Indian heiress was a desirable plum, and Charles James Fox almost decided that the £80,000 fortune of Miss Phipps was the solution to his heavy gambling debts.[35] One might speculate on what effect such a marriage would have had on Fox's career as an abolitionist.

Many a humble individual in England rose to wealth and affluence from some chance legacy of a West Indian plantation. The time came when such a legacy was considered gall and wormwood,[36] but it was not so in the eighteenth century. George Colman's play, "Africans," portrays in Young Mr. Marrowbone, the butcher, a situation that must have been very familiar to the audience. The butcher was left a West Indian plantation, and "now barters for blacks, instead of bargaining for bullocks."[37]

The strength of the planters was increased, too, by the large number of West Indian merchants who drew vast profits from the West Indian trade. According to Professor Namier, "there were comparatively few big merchants in Great Britain in 1761 who, in one connection or another, did not trade with the West Indies, and a considerable number of gentry families had interests in the Sugar Islands, just as vast numbers of Englishmen now hold shares in Asiatic rubber or tea plantations or oil fields."[38] The two groups did not always see eye to eye. At the outset planters and merchants represented distinct organizations, and the bond between them—credit—did not always make for harmony. But this in itself would not have been a basic cause for conflict, as the merchant could always have recourse to foreclosure. More important than the factor of debt was the planters' determination to maintain monopoly prices, and in the struggle for the grant of a direct trade to Europe in 1739 ill-feeling between the two groups increased considerably.[39] But by and large the identity of interests was greater and more important than the clash, and planters and merchants finally coalesced about 1780, when all the strength they could jointly muster was soon to be needed to strengthen the dykes of monopoly against the gathering torrent of free trade.

The combination of these two forces, planters and merchants, coupled with colonial agents in England, constituted the powerful West India interest of the eighteenth century. In the classic age of parliamentary corruption and electoral venality, their money talked. They bought votes and rotten boroughs and so got into Parliament. Their competition forced up the price of seats. The Earl of Chesterfield was laughed to scorn in 1767 when he offered £2,500 for a seat for which a West Indian would offer double.[40] No private hereditary English fortune could resist this torrent of colonial gold and corruption. The English landed aristocracy were indignant, "vexed, put to great expenses, and even baffled" by the West Indians at elections.[41] There is an unmistakable note of this concern in the warning issued by Cumberland in his drama to the West Indian ostentatiously flaunting his wealth and boasting of his plans to spend it. "To use it, not to waste it, I should hope; to treat it, Mr. Belcour, not as a vassal, over whom you have a wanton and a despotic power; but as a subject, which you are bound to govern with a temperate and restrained authority."[42] In the elections of 1830 a West Indian planter successfully spent £18,000 getting himself elected in Bristol.[43] The election expenses of the unsuccessful West Indian candidate in Liverpool in the same year cost nearly £50,000, of which a rich West Indian merchant, slave trader and slaveowner, John Bolton, supplied one-fifth.[44]

The Beckford dynasty was fittingly represented in Parliament in accordance with its wealth. King William was M.P. for Shaftesbury from 1747-1754, and for the metropolis from 1754-1770. Another brother represented Bristol, a third Salisbury, while a fourth was intended for a Wiltshire borough.[45] Richard Pennant at one time represented Liverpool.[46] One of the Codringtons was a member of Parliament in 1737.[47] George Hibbert represented Seaford from 1806 to 1812.[48] Edward Colston, the Cunard of the seventeenth century, sat for Bristol from 1710 to 1713.[49] The West India interest established a monopoly, in all but name, of one Bristol seat. John Gladstone sat first for Woodstock and then for Lancaster; it was his pleasure to listen in May, 1833, to the maiden speech of his son, M.P. for Newark, in defence of slavery on the family estates in Guiana.[50] The great statesman found all his filial feelings involved in the question of slavery, and his family connections with West Indian sugar plantations brought out all his eloquence.[51] One of the Lascelles sat in Parliament in 1757.[52] To the bitter end Henry Goulburn fought the West Indian battle.

In 1833 he was still asking Parliament to mark the impulse given to trade and agriculture, and to look at the hamlets that had sprung into towns, in consequence of the connection with the colonies.[53] Parliament paid no heed, and Goulburn had to be content with nearly £5,000 compensation for his 242 slaves.[54] Joseph Marryat of Trinidad, Henry Bright of Bristol, Keith Douglas, Charles Ellis, all were West Indians. Ten out of fifteen members of one of the most important committees of the Society of Planters and Merchants held seats in the English Parliament.[55]

To make assurance doubly sure the West Indians, like the slave traders, were entrenched not only in the lower house but also in the House of Lords, to defend their plantations and the social structure on which they rested. Passage from one house to another was easy, peerages were readily conferred in return for political support. There are few, if any, noble houses in England, according to a modern writer, without a West Indian strain.[56] Richard Pennant became Lord Penrhyn. The Lascelles, an old Barbadian family, were ennobled and became Harewoods; one of their descendants is at present married to the sister of the reigning King of England. The Marquis of Chandos, sponsor of the "Chandos Clause" in the Reform Bill of 1832, owned West Indian plantations and was a spokesman of the West India interest, though he lived to see the day when it was almost hopeless to advocate the cause of the West Indies.[57] The Earl of Balcarres possessed sugar plantations in Jamaica. Emancipation found him owner of 640 slaves, for whom he received nearly £12,300 compensation.[58] This explains his hysterical opposition, as governor of the island, to the convention made by General Maitland with the slave leader, Toussaint L'Ouverture, for the evacuation of Saint Domingue after Britain's abortive effort to conquer the French colony. "It would be thought somewhat odd," he wrote home, "if the City of London should send over an immense quantity of provisions and clothing for the use of the *sans culotte* army assembled for the purpose of invading England!"[59] Lord Hawkesbury, né Jenkinson, was a West Indian proprietor,[60] and, as President of the Privy Council for Trade, he lent consistent support to the cause of the slave owners and slave traders. For this devotion tracts in favor of the slave trade were dedicated to him,[61] and Liverpool conferred on him the freedom of the city in gratitude for the essential services rendered to the town by his exertions in Parliament in support of the slave trade.[62] Hawkesbury symbolized the connection by assuming the title Earl of Liverpool when raised to the peerage and accepting the Corporation's offer to quarter its arms with his own.[63]

It was not only the mother of parliaments that the slaveowners dominated. Like their allies, the sugar merchants and slave traders, they were in evidence everywhere, as aldermen, mayors and councillors. William Beckford was alderman of the city of London and twice Lord Mayor. Contemporaries laughed at his faulty Latin and loud voice; they were forced to respect his wealth, position and political influence. As mayor his civic entertainments were magnificent. On one occasion, at a sumptuous banquet, six dukes, two marquises, twenty-three earls, four viscounts, and fourteen barons of the Upper House joined the members of the Commons and went in procession to the city to honor him. He remains famous, this slaveowner, for his defence of Wilkes and liberty of speech, indifferent to royal displeasure.[64] In the London Guildhall there stands a splendid monument erected in his honor, with the famous speech, graven in letters of gold on the pedestal, which made George III blush.[65] His brother Richard was also an alderman of the city of London. William Miles lived to become an alderman of Bristol. George Hibbert became an alderman of London.[66]

The West India interest had powerful friends. Chatham was the consistent defender of West Indian claims, right or wrong, and was a close friend of Beckford. "He should ever consider the sugar colonies as the landed interest of this kingdom, and it was a barbarism to consider them otherwise."[67] John Gladstone and John Bolton were vigorous supporters of Canning, who always harped on the fearfulness and delicacy and "most awful importance" of the West Indian question.[68] Huskisson and Wellington were very cordially disposed to the planters, the latter refusing to "plunder the proprietors in the West Indies in order to acquire for themselves a little popularity in

England,"[69] the former considering emancipation unattainable by legislative interposition or statutory enactment.[70] But the recalcitrance of the planters and their wilful refusal to make concessions to the anti-slavery sentiment of England later alienated these friends. Canning found West Indian slavery an unpalatable topic;[71] slave questions nearly drove Huskisson mad and the planters seemed to him insane;[72] Wellington, before the final word was said on British slavery, subjected a West Indian deputation in London to some rough treatment.[73]

Allied with the other great monopolists of the eighteenth century, the landed aristocracy, and the commercial bourgeoisie of the seaport towns, this powerful West India interest exerted in the unreformed Parliament an influence sufficient to make every statesman pause, and represented a solid phalanx "of whose support in emergency every administration in turn has experienced the value."[74] They put up a determined resistance to abolition, emancipation, and the abrogation of their monopoly. They were always on the warpath to oppose any increase of the duties on sugar, which Beckford once described as "a *coup-de-grace* to our sugar colonies and sugar trade."[75] The West India interest was the *enfant terrible* of English politics until American Independence struck the first great blow at mercantilism and monopoly.

In 1685 the governor of Jamaica protested that any additional duty proposed on sugar would discourage planting, throw new plantations out of cultivation and prevent the enlargement of others. By the proposal "Virginia receives a mortal stab, Barbados and the Islands fall into a hectic fever, and Jamaica into a consumption."[76] In 1744 the planters sent their case to every member of Parliament in an attempt to encourage popular clamor against another proposal to increase the sugar duties. The proposal was carried by a majority of twenty-three. "Nor was the smallness of it matter of surprize to those who considered how many were either by themselves or their friends, deeply concerned in one part or another of the sugar trade, and that the cause itself was always popular in the House of Commons."[77] The West Indians, however, succeeded in transferring the extra duty proposed on sugar to foreign linens. The whole episode merely illustrated "the difficulties which attended the laying a further duty upon sugar from the number and influence of those concerned directly or indirectly in that extensive branch of trade."[78]

The issue came up again when it was necessary to finance the Seven Years' War. The landed aristocrat of England was usually the supporter of his brother in the colonies, but when it came to choosing between himself and his distant relative he took the view that "his shirt was near him but his skin was nearer." Beckford, in defence of his fellows, was interrupted by horse-laughs every time he uttered the word "sugar."[79] The magic finger was writing. The agent for Massachusetts reported in 1764 that there were fifty or sixty West Indian voters who could turn the balance any side they pleased.[80] It was the heyday of the power of the West India sugar interest. But in the new century and in the Reformed Parliament there appeared another combination of fifty or sixty voters. It was the Lancashire cotton interest, and its slogan was not monopoly but laissez faire.

BRITISH INDUSTRY

AND THE

TRIANGULAR TRADE

BRITAIN WAS ACCUMULATING great wealth from the triangular trade. The increase of consumption goods called forth by that trade inevitably drew in its train the development of the productive power of the country. This industrial expansion required finance. What man in the first three-quarters of the eighteenth century was better able to afford the ready capital than a West Indian sugar planter or a Liverpool slave trader? We have already noticed the readiness with which absentee planters purchased land in England, where they were able to use their wealth to finance the great developments associated with the Agricultural Revolution. We must now trace the investment of profits from the triangular trade in British industry, where they supplied part of the huge outlay for the construction of the vast plants to meet the needs of the new productive process and the new markets.

A. THE INVESTMENT OF PROFITS FROM THE TRIANGULAR TRADE

1. *Banking*

Many of the eighteenth century banks established in Liverpool and Manchester, the slaving metropolis and the cotton capital respectively, were directly associated with the triangular trade. Here large sums were needed for the cotton factories and for the canals which improved the means of communication between the two towns.

Typical of the eighteenth century banker is the transition from tradesman to merchant and then the further progression from merchant to banker. The term "merchant," in the eighteenth century context, not infrequently involved the gradations of slaver captain, privateer captain, privateer owner, before settling down on shore to the respectable business of commerce. The varied activities of a Liverpool businessman include: brewer, liquor merchant, grocer, spirit dealer, bill-broker, banker, etc. Writes the historian: "One wonders what was covered by that 'etc.'"[1] Like the song the sirens sang, that "etc." is not beyond all conjecture. It included, at some time or other, some one or more aspects of the triangular trade.

The Heywood Bank was founded in Liverpool in 1773 and endured as a private bank until 1883, when it was purchased by the Bank of Liverpool. Its founders were successful merchants later elected to the Chamber of Commerce. "They had their experience," the historian writes, "of the African trade," besides privateering. Both appear in the list of merchants trading to Africa in 1752 and their African interests survived up to 1807. The senior partner of one of the branches of the firm was Thomas Parke, of the banking firm of William Gregson, Sons, Parke and Morland, whose grandfather was a successful captain in the West Indian trade. Typical of the commercial interrelationships of the period, the daughter of one of the partners of the Heywoods later married Robertson, son of John Gladstone, and their son, Robertson Gladstone, obtained a partnership in the bank. In 1788 the firm set up a branch in Manchester, at the suggestion of some of the town's leading merchants. The Manchester branch, called the "Manchester Bank," was well known for many years. Eleven of fourteen Heywood descendants up to 1815 became merchants or bankers.[2]

The emergence of Thomas Leyland on the banking scene was delayed until the early years of the nineteenth century, but his investments in the African slave trade dated back to the last quarter of the eighteenth. Leyland, with his partners, was one of the most active slave traders in Liverpool and his profits were immense. In 1802 he became senior partner in the banking firm of Clarkes and Roscoe. Leyland and Roscoe: curious combination! Strange union of the successful slaver and the consistent opponent of slavery! Leyland struck off on his own in 1807, in a more consistent partnership with his slave partner Bullins, and the title of Leyland and Bullins was borne proudly and unsmirched for ninety-four years until the amalgamation of the bank, in 1901, with the North and South Wales Bank Limited.[3]

The Heywoods and Leylands are only the outstanding examples of the general rule in the banking history of eighteenth century Liverpool. William Gregson, banker, was also slave trader, shipowner, privateer, underwriter, and owner of a ropewalk. Francis Ingram was a slave trader, member of the African Company in 1777, while he also had a share in a ropery business, and embarked on a privateering enterprise in partnership with Thomas Leyland and the Earles. The latter themselves had amassed a huge fortune in the slave trade, and remained slave traders right up to 1807. The founder of Hanly's bank was Captain Richard Hanly, slave trader, whose sister was herself married to a slave trader. Hanly was a prominent member of the "Liverpool Fireside," a society composed almost entirely of captains of vessels, slavers, and privateers, with a sprinkling of superior tradesmen. Robert Fairweather, like Hanly, was slave trader, member of the Liverpool Fireside, merchant and banker.

Jonas Bold combined both slave and West Indian trades. One of the Company of Merchants trading to Africa from 1777 up to 1807, Bold was a sugar refiner, and became a partner in Ingram's bank. Thomas Fletcher began his career as apprentice to a merchant banker who carried on an extensive trade with Jamaica. Raised to a partnership, Fletcher later became successively Vice-Chairman and Chairman of the Liverpool West India Association, and at his death his assets included interests in mortgages on a coffee and sugar plantation, with the slaves thereon, in Jamaica. Charles Caldwell, of the banking firm of

Charles Caldwell and Co., was a partner in Oldham, Caldwell, and Co., whose transactions were principally in sugar.
Isaac Hartman, another banker, owned West Indian plantations; while James Moss, banker and prominent citizen in the
eighteenth century, had some very large sugar plantations in
British Guiana.[4]

What has been said of Liverpool is equally true of Bristol,
London and Glasgow. Presiding over the meeting of the influential committee set up in Bristol in 1789 to oppose abolition
was William Miles. Among the members of the committee were
Alderman Daubeny, Richard Bright, Richard Vaughan, John
Cave and Philip Protheroe. All six were bankers in Bristol. Cave,
Bright and Daubeny were partners in the "New Bank" established in 1786. Protheroe was partner in the Bristol City Bank.
William Miles bought a leading partnership in the old banking
house of Vaughan, Barker and Company; two of his sons were
mentioned in 1794, and "Miles's Bank," as it was popularly
called, had a lengthy and prosperous career.[5]

For London only one name need be mentioned, when that
name is Barclay. Two members of this Quaker family, David
and Alexander, were engaged in the slave trade in 1756. David
began his career in American and West Indian commerce and
became one of the most influential merchants of his day. His
father's house in Cheapside was one of the finest in the city of
London, and was often visited by royalty. He was not merely
a slave trader but actually owned a great plantation in Jamaica
where, we are told, he freed his slaves, and lived to find that "the
black skin enclosed hearts full of gratitude and minds as capable
of improvement as the proudest white." The Barclays married
into the banking families of Gurney and Freame, like so many
other intermarriages in other branches of industry which kept
Quaker wealth in Quaker hands. From the combination sprang
Barclay's Bank whose expansion and progress are beyond the
scope of this study.[6]

The rise of banking in Glasgow was intimately connected
with the triangular trade. The first regular bank began business in 1750. Known as the Ship Bank, one of the original
partners was Andrew Buchanan, a tobacco lord of the city.

Another was the same William Macdowall whose meeting with the sugar heiresses of St. Kitts had established both the fortunes of his house and those of the city. A third was Alexander Houston, one of the greatest West Indian merchants of the city, whose firm, Alexander Houston and Company, was one of the leading West Indian houses in the kingdom. This firm itself only grew out of the return of the two Scotch officers and their island brides to the city. For three-quarters of the century the firm carried on an immense trade, owning many ships and vast sugar plantations. Anticipating the abolition of the slave trade, it speculated on a grand scale in the purchase of slaves. The bill, however, failed to pass. The slaves had to be fed and clothed, their price fell heavily, disease carried them off by the hundreds. The firm consequently crashed in 1795, and this was the greatest financial disaster Glasgow had ever seen.

The success of the Ship Bank stimulated the formation of other banks. The Arms Bank was founded in the same year, with one of the leading partners Andrew Cochrane, another tobacco lord. The Thistle Bank followed in 1761, an aristocratic bank, whose business lay largely among the rich West Indian merchants. One of the chief partners was John Glassford, who carried on business on a large scale. At one time he owned twenty-five ships and their cargoes on the sea, and his annual turnover was more than half a million sterling.[7]

2.   *Heavy Industry*

Heavy industry played an important role in the progress of the Industrial Revolution and the development of the triangular trade. Some of the capital which financed the growth of the metallurgical industries was supplied directly by the triangular trade.

It was the capital accumulated from the West Indian trade that financed James Watt and the steam engine. Boulton and Watt received advances from Lowe, Vere, Williams and Jennings—later the Williams Deacons Bank. Watt had some anxious moments in 1778 during the American Revolution when the West Indian fleet was threatened with capture by the French. "Even in this emergency," wrote Boulton to him hopefully, "Lowe, Vere and Company may yet be saved, if ye West Indian fleet arrives safe from ye French fleet . . . as many of their securities depend on it."[8]

The bank pulled through and the precious invention was safe. The sugar planters were among the first to realize its importance. Boulton wrote to Watt in 1783: ". . . Mr. Pennant, who is a very amiable man, with ten or twelve thousand pounds a year, has the largest estate in Jamaica; there was also Mr. Gale and Mr. Beeston Long, who have some very large sugar plantations there, who wish to see steam answer in lieu of horses."[9]

One of the leading ironmongers of the eighteenth century, Antony Bacon, was intimately connected with the triangular trade. His partner was Gilbert Francklyn, a West Indian planter, who later wrote many letters to the Lord President of the Committee of Privy Council emphasizing the importance of taking over the French sugar colony of Saint Domingue in the war with revolutionary France.[10] Bacon, like so many others, ventured into the African trade. He began a lucrative commerce in first victualling troops on the coast and then supplying seasoned and able Negroes for government contracts in the West Indies. During the years 1768-1776 he received almost £67,000 under this latter heading. In 1765 he set up his iron works at Merthyr Tydfill which expanded rapidly owing to government contracts during the American war; in 1776 he set up another furnace at Cyfartha. The iron ore for his furnaces was exported from Whitehaven, and as early as 1740 Bacon took a part in improving its harbor.

Bacon made a fortune out of his artillery contracts with the British government. He retired in 1782 having acquired a veritable mineral kingdom. His ironworks at Cyfartha he leased to Crawshay, reserving for himself a clear annuity of £10,000, and out of Cyfartha Crawshay himself made a fortune. He sold Penydaren to Homfray, the man who perfected the puddling process; Dowlais went to Lewis and the Plymouth works to Hill. The ordinance contract had already been transferred to Carron, Roebuck's successor. No wonder that it was stated that Bacon considered himself as "moving in a superior orbit."[11]

William Beckford became a master ironmonger in 1753.[12] Part of the capital supplied for the Thorncliffe ironworks, begun in 1792, came from a razor-maker, Henry Longden, who received a bequest of some fifteen thousand pounds from a wealthy uncle, a West Indian merchant of Sheffield.[13]

3.   *Insurance*

In the eighteenth century, when the slave trade was the most valuable trade and West Indian property among the most valuable property in the British Empire, the triangular trade occupied an important position in the eyes of the rising insurance companies. In the early years, when Lloyd's was a coffee house and nothing more, many advertisements in the London Gazette about runaway slaves listed Lloyd's as the place where they should be returned.[14]

The earliest extant advertisement referring to Lloyd's, dated 1692, deals with the sale of three ships by auction. The ships were cleared for Barbados and Virginia. The only project listed at Lloyd's in the bubbles of 1720 concerned trade to Barbary and Africa. Relton, the historian of fire insurance, states that insurance against fires in the West Indies had been done at Lloyd's "from a very early date." Lloyd's, like other insurance companies, insured slaves and slave ships, and was vitally interested in legal decisions as to what constituted "natural death" and "perils of the sea." Among their subscriptions to public heroes and merchant captains is one of 1804 to a Liverpool captain who, on passage from Africa to British Guiana, successfully beat off a French corvette and saved his valuable cargo. The third son of their first secretary, John Bennett, was agent for Lloyd's in Antigua in 1833, and the only known portrait of his father was recently discovered in the West Indies. One of the most distinguished chairmen of Lloyd's in its long history was Joseph Marryat, a West Indian planter, who successfully and brilliantly fought to maintain Lloyd's monopoly of marine insurance against a rival company in the House of Commons in 1810, where he was opposed by another West

Indian, father of the famous Cardinal Manning.[15] Marryat
was awarded £15,000 compensation in 1837 for 391 slaves in
Trinidad and Jamaica.[16]

In 1782 the West Indian sugar interest took the lead in
starting another insurance company, the Phoenix, one of the
first companies to establish a branch overseas—in the West
Indies.[17] The Liverpool Underwriters' Association was formed
in 1802. Chairman of the meeting was the prominent West
Indian merchant, John Gladstone.[18]

B.   THE DEVELOPMENT OF BRITISH INDUSTRY TO 1783

Thus it was that the Abbé Raynal, one of the most progress-
ive spirits of his day, a man of wide learning in close touch with
the French bourgeoisie, was able to see that the labors of the
people in the West Indies "may be considered as the principal
cause of the rapid motion which now agitates the universe."[19]
The triangular trade made an enormous contribution to Britain's
industrial development. The profits from this trade fertilized the
entire productive system of the country. Three instances must
suffice. The slate industry in Wales, which provided material
for roofing, was revolutionized by the new methods adopted on
his Carnarvonshire estate by Lord Penrhyn,[20] who, as we have
seen, owned sugar plantations in Jamaica and was chairman of
the West India Committee at the end of the eighteenth century.
The leading figure in the first great railway project in England,
which linked Liverpool and Manchester, was Joseph Sandars, of
whom little is known. But his withdrawal in 1824 from the
Liverpool Anti-Slavery Society is of great importance, as at least
showing a reluctance to press the sugar planters.[21] Three other
men prominently identified with the undertaking had close
connections with the triangular trade—General Gascoyne of
Liverpool, a stalwart champion of the West India interest, John
Gladstone and John Moss.[22] The Bristol West India interest
also played a prominent part in the construction of the Great
Western Railway.[23]

But it must not be inferred that the triangular trade was

solely and entirely responsible for the economic development. The growth of the internal market in England, the ploughing-in of the profits from industry to generate still further capital and achieve still greater expansion, played a large part. But this industrial development, stimulated by mercantilism, later outgrew mercantilism and destroyed it.

In 1783 the shape of things to come was clearly visible. The steam engine's potentialities were not an academic question. Sixty-six engines were in operation, two-thirds of these in mines and foundries.[24] Improved methods of coal mining, combined with the influence of steam, resulted in a great expansion of the iron industry. Production increased four times between 1740 and 1788, the number of furnaces rose by one-half.[25] The iron bridge and the iron railroad had appeared; the Carron Works had been founded; and Wilkinson was already famous as "the father of the iron trade." Cotton, the queen of the Industrial Revolution, responded readily to the new inventions, unhampered as it was by the traditions and guild restrictions which impeded its older rival, wool. Laissez faire became a practice in the new industry long before it penetrated the text books as orthodox economic theory. The spinning jenny, the water frame, the mule, revolutionized the industry, which, as a result, showed a continuous upward trend. Between 1700 and 1780 imports of raw cotton increased more than three times, exports of cotton goods fifteen times.[26] The population of Manchester increased by nearly one-half between 1757 and 1773,[27] the numbers engaged in the cotton industry quadrupled between 1750 and 1785.[28] Not only heavy industry, cotton, too—the two industries that were to dominate the period 1783–1850—was gathering strength for the assault on the system of monopoly which had for so long been deemed essential to the existence and prosperity of both.

The entire economy of England was stimulated by this beneficent breath of increased production. The output of the Staffordshire potteries increased fivefold in value between 1725 and 1777.[29] The tonnage of shipping leaving English ports more than doubled between 1700 and 1781. English imports increased fourfold between 1715 and 1775, exports trebled between 1700 and 1771.[30] English industry in 1783 was like Gulliver, tied down by the Lilliputian restrictions of mercantilism.

Two outstanding figures of the eighteenth century saw and, what was more, appreciated the irrepressible conflict: Adam Smith from his professorial chair, Thomas Jefferson on his plantation.

Adam Smith denounced the folly and injustice which had first directed the project of establishing colonies in the New World. He opposed the whole system of monopoly, the keystone of the colonial arch, on the ground that it restricted the productive power of England as well as the colonies. If British industry had advanced, it had done so not because of the monopoly but in spite of it, and the monopoly represented nothing but the sacrifice of the general good to the interests of a few, the sacrifice of the interest of the home consumer to that of the colonial producer. In the colonies themselves the ban on colonial manufactures seemed to him "a manifest violation of the most sacred rights of mankind . . . impertinent badges of slavery imposed upon them, without any sufficient reason, by the groundless jealousy of the merchants and manufacturers of the mother country." British capital had been forced from trade with neighboring countries to trade with more distant countries; money that could have been used to improve the lands, increase the manufactures, and extend the commerce of Great Britain had been expended in fostering a trade with distant areas from which Britain derived nothing but loss (!) and frequent wars. It was a fit system for a nation whose government was influenced by shopkeepers.[31]

The *Wealth of Nations* was the philosophical antecedent of the American Revolution. Both were twin products of the same cause, the brake applied by the mercantile system on the development of the productive power of England and her colonies. Adam Smith's role was to berate intellectually "the mean and malignant expedients"[32] of a system which the armies of George Washington dealt a mortal wound on the battlefields of America.

· 6 ·

THE AMERICAN REVOLUTION

IN 1770 the continental colonies sent to the West Indies nearly one-third of their exports of dried fish and almost all their pickled fish; seven-eighths of their oats, seven-tenths of their corn, almost all their peas and beans, half of their flour, all their butter and cheese, over one-quarter of their rice, almost all their onions; five-sixths of their pine, oak and cedar boards, over half their staves, nearly all their hoops; all their horses, sheep, hogs and poultry; almost all their soap and candles.[1] As Professor Pitman has told us, "It was the wealth accumulated from West Indian trade which more than anything else underlay the prosperity and civilization of New England and the Middle Colonies."[2]

But in the imperial scheme of the eighteenth century the mainland colonies ran a bad second. Sugar was king, and the West Indian islands the sugar bowl of Europe. The acquisition of Jamaica made Cromwell so happy that he refused to transact any further business on the day when the glad tidings was announced. He would have taken a week's holiday if he had captured Hispaniola, the French part of which, Saint Domingue, later became the pearl of the Antilles and the bane of the British planters. Barbados was the "fair jewell" of His Majesty's Crown, a little pearl more precious and rare than any the kings of Europe possessed,[3] and in 1661 Charles II showed its importance by creating thirteen baronets among its planters in a single day[4] The governorship of Jamaica ranked next in colonial appointments to the lord-lieutenancy of Ireland, and the postal system made better provision for the islands than for the mainland.

Mercantilists looked askance at the northern colonies in particular. They were full of farmers, merchants, fishermen, seamen—but no planters. They were, with the exception of their yet undeveloped manufactures, in a very literal sense New England.[5] Rivalry with Old England was inevitable. They competed with the home country in the fisheries, which became a nursery for the seamen of New England. In their agricultural products they were enabled, by virtue of their situation, to undersell their English rivals in island markets. By this competition England was losing, in sales and freights, two and a half millions sterling a year. "Can any one think from hence," asked an anonymous writer, "that the *trade* and *navigation* of our colonies are worth one groat to this nation?"[6] Sir Josiah Child pointed out that ten men in Massachusetts did not provide employment for a single Englishman at home. "New England," he concluded, "is the most prejudicial plantation to this kingdom."[7] Chichester would have preferred to labor with his hands in Ireland than "dance and sing in Virginia."[8] Petty said bluntly that the inhabitants of New England should be repatriated or sent to Ireland.[9] Four separate efforts were made to persuade the New Englanders to remove—to the Bahamas, to Trinidad, to Maryland, and to Virginia. Cromwell looked on New England "only with an eye of pity, as poor, cold and useless."[10] Orders of the Council of State were sent in 1655 to the governors and inhabitants holding out tempting offers to go to Jamaica "to enlighten those parts . . . by people who know and fear the Lord; that those of New England, driven from the land of their nativity into that desert and barren wilderness, for conscience' sake may remove to a land of plenty."[11]

These views were too extreme. If the Northern colonies were squeezed out of the provisions trade, they would be unable to pay for British manufactures, the export of which was more valuable to England than the export of agricultural commodities and salted meat. What was much worse, the colonists might thereby be tempted to develop their own industries. Better then, Davenant concluded, that they should have the food trade.[12]

For the West Indian colonies needed food. If they were to concentrate on the sugar to which the economic specialization of the mercantile epoch confined them, they had no back country where staples could not be raised, and their cash crop was too profitable for them to afford the luxury of diverting land and labor to cattle grazing and food crops. "Men are so intent upon planting sugar," a correspondent wrote to Governor Winthrop in 1647 about the West Indies, "that they had rather buy foode at very deare rates than produce it by labour, so infinite is the profitt of sugar workes after once accomplished."[13] The tradition was thereby established by which sugar became "the wheat or bread" of the West Indies.[14] Only the possession of the mainland colonies permitted this sugar monopoly of the West Indian soil. "To subsist a colony in America," wrote the Abbé Raynal, "it is necessary to cultivate a province in Europe."[15] Britain voluntarily abdicated this privilege, as the lesser of two evils, to the mainland colonists. Mercantilism was ultimately destroyed as a bad system, but it is absurd not to recognize that it was a system, and that there was method in its badness.

Thus did the North American colonies come to have a recognized place in imperial economy, as purveyors of the supplies needed by the sugar planters and their slaves, and the New Englanders came to be regarded as the Dutchmen of America. The mixed husbandry of the Northern and Middle colonies supplemented the specialized agriculture of the West Indies, as in the nineteenth century it fed the cotton and rice regions of the American South. As early as 1650 the New England colonies were feeding their "elder sisters," Virginia and Barbados.[16] Winthrop assigned the credit to Providence,[17] but mercantilism had much to do with the arrangement. "His ma[tys] collonys in these parts," wrote Governor Willoughby of Barbados in 1667, "cannot in tyme of peace prosper, nor in tyme of war subsist, without a correspondence with the people of Newe England."[18] Not only food, but horses to supply the motive power of the tread-mills used in sugar manufacture, and lumber for buildings, were the articles most in demand in the islands. "There is no island the Brittish possess in the West Indies," wrote Samuel Vetch in 1708, "that is capable of subsisting without the assistance of the Continent, for to them we transport their bread, drink and all the necessaryes of humane life, their cattle and horses for cultivating their plantations, lumber and staves of all sorts to make casks for their rumm, sugar and molasses, without which they could have none, ships to transport their goods to the European markets, nay, in short, the very houses they inhabitt are carryed over in frames, together with shingles that cover them, in so much that their being, much more their well being, depends almost entirely upon the Continent."[19] The West Indian planters entertained no illusions about the importance of mainland provisions and horses. The Barbadians, wrote a Boston factor in 1674, are "all sensable of the greate prejudis which will accrue to them yf they loose the benefitt of those two commodyties, which are vendable in noe part of ye world but New England and Virginia."[20]

This was deliberate policy on the part of statesmen in England and the planters in the colonies. Many of the articles exported by New England to the islands could have been produced in the islands themselves. But, as a Jamaican planter asked, "If this island were able to maintain itself with diet and other necessaries what would become of the New England trade?"[21] The answer is that without the sugar islands the mainland colonies would have received a serious setback. They became "the key to the Indies,"[22] without which the islands would have been unable to feed themselves except by a diversion of profitable sugar land to food crops, to the detriment not only of New England farmers but British shipping, British sugar refining, and the customs revenue, glory and grandeur of England. In 1698 Parliament rejected a proposal to prohibit the export of corn, meal, flour, bread and biscuit from England to the sugar islands. The prohibition "may put the inhabitants there upon planting provisions themselves, instead of sugarcanes, cotton, ginger, and indico; which will be greatly prejudicial to England, in respect of its navigation and riches."[23]

Economic relations between islands and mainland were strengthened by individual contacts. West Indians owned property on the mainland, North Americans owned plantations in the islands. South Carolina was settled from Barbados. The Middletons, Bulls and Colletons of South Carolina owned plantations in Jamaica and Barbados. Aaron Lopez, Rhode Island slave trader, was owner of a sugar plantation in Antigua. Alexander Hamilton was born in Nevis. The Gedney Clarkes of Salem are the outstanding example of North American success in the islands. The father owned extensive plantations in Barbados and Guiana. His son became surveyor general of customs in Barbados, member of the House of Assembly and subsequently of the Council. North Americans soon discovered the value of West Indian sunshine, West Indians sought in North America the recovery of broken constitutions. "I would advise Adam Chart," wrote an American to friends in Philadelphia, "to begin another house directly and call it the Barbados Hotel, putting up for a sign, the worn-out West Indian, dying of a dropsy from intemperate living." West Indian heiresses, it is said, were as desirable in North America as they were in England.[24]

In exchange for their provisions the mainland colonists took West Indian sugar, rum and molasses, in such quantities that as early as 1676 the English merchants complained that New England was becoming the great mart and staple of colonial produce.[25] It was a mutual interdependence between the two units. The maintenance of harmony imperatively demanded two things: island production of sugar and molasses must be sufficient to satisfy mainland consumption; island consumption of mainland staples must keep pace with mainland production.

At best this would have been difficult, because of the relative size of the two interdependent areas. But the impending conflict could have been postponed in one of two ways or both. In the first place the British sugar planter could have extended his cultivation. More land would have required more slaves who would have produced more sugar and called for greater supplies of food. Jamaica could have done this more easily than Barbados, which in the eighteenth century was already suffering from the inevitable consequences of slave labor and quick extraction of profit from the soil. There was fresh land in abundance in Jamaica. The second remedy was the acquisition of more sugar colonies. This would have appeased, partially, the legitimate grievances of the mainland. But these, the only possible solutions without resort to force, the British sugar planters resolutely opposed. The cultivation of fresh lands and the acquisition of more sugar colonies meant a greater supply of sugar in the British market and a consequent reduction of price. The Barbadians had very early in their history looked apprehensively at the extension of British sugar conquests. They opposed British settlement of Surinam;[26] they resented the drain of their white servants to the Leeward Islands, and when asked by the governor of Jamaica to contribute to an expedition to put down piracy in the Leeward Islands, they replied that they would not spend twenty shillings to save the Leeward Islands and Jamaica.[27] In 1772 it was proposed in Parliament that adequate security be offered to foreigners willing to advance money for the development of the sugar islands annexed after the Seven Years' War. The proposal was warmly opposed, as an "impolitic innovation," by the West Indian planters.[28] It was the old division, in the words of Professor Namier, between "saturated planters" and "planters on the make."[29]

The foreign sugar islands, too, were already illustrating the law of slave production. Less exhausted than the longer-settled English islands, cultivation in the French islands was easier and the cost of production less. As early as 1663, a mere twenty years after the rise of the sugar industry, Barbados was "decaying fast,"[30] and the complaints of soil exhaustion grew more numerous and more plaintive. In 1717 Barbados, according to a representation to the Board of Trade, needed five times the number of Negroes and many more head of cattle and horses than the French islands to cultivate a given acreage; one slave in French Saint Domingue was equivalent to four in Jamaica.[31] In 1737 the Barbadian owner of a plantation of one thousand acres, which required a capital investment of fifty thousand pounds, was making a profit of two per cent; a similar plantation in the French islands cost one-sixth as much, and yielded a profit of eighteen per cent.[32] There was some exaggeration in these figures, but the fundamental superiority of the French sugar planter, as a result of large tracts of fertile, unexhausted soil, was notorious. French sugar was invading the European markets and selling at half the price it was sold at in England.[33] Acquisition of such islands would have meant the eclipse of the older British planters. The latter, therefore, demanded their destruction rather than their acquisition. The governor of Jamaica wrote in 1748 that unless French Saint Domingue was destroyed during the war, it would, on the return of peace, ruin the British sugar colonies by the quality and cheapness of its production.[34] During the Seven Years' War, Britain captured Cuba from Spain and Guadeloupe from France. Both islands were restored to their owners in 1763, Britain taking in return Florida and Canada.

To rationalize this decision in the light of the importance of the different areas today misses the whole point. Cuba was still an ugly duckling in 1763, but any fool could have guessed what a beautiful swan it would eventually turn out to be. There was no excuse where Guadeloupe was concerned. The "few acres of snow," as Voltaire derisively described Canada, could boast only of furs; Guadeloupe had sugar. "What does a few hats signify," asked a shrewd anonymous writer in 1763, "compared with that article of luxury, sugar?" He pointed out, too, that the way to keep North America dependent was to leave the French in Canada.[35]

It is inconceivable that the British ministry of the day was ignorant of what was public knowledge, in England, France and America. Between 1759 and 1762 British imports from "Quebec" totalled £48,000, exports to Quebec £426,400. British imports from Guadeloupe amounted to £2,004,933 between 1759 and 1765, exports to Guadeloupe to £475,237. British imports from Havana were £263,084 between 1762 and 1766, exports to Havana £123,421. Compare Canada and Florida with Grenada and Dominica, two of the West Indian conquests that were retained in 1763. Up to 1773 British imports from Grenada amounted to eight times the imports from Canada, British exports to Canada were double those to Grenada. Imports from

Dominica were more than eighteen times the imports from Florida; exports to Dominica were only one-seventh less than those to Florida.[36] Clearly Canada and Florida were retained not because they were more valuable than Cuba or Guadeloupe, but precisely because they were less valuable.

Thus the peace treaty of 1763 simply makes no sense unless it is regarded as another victory for the powerful West India interest. It proved ultimately to be a Pyrrhic victory, but in 1763 it was none the less a victory. The two most strenuous advocates of the return of Guadeloupe were two West Indian planters, Beckford and Fuller,[37] and Beckford's influence with Chatham was notorious. "Thus Guadeloupe, one of the greatest acquisitions Britain ever made, acquires many powerful enemies from private views, and has nothing to plead but her public utility an advantage often found too feeble an opponent to the private interest of a few."[38] The West Indians had two aims in view. They wished to prevent the French from making Canada a North America, a source of supplies for their sugar colonies— a baseless fear, as the British sugar planter realized after 1783 when Canada proved a poor substitute for the lost Northern colonies; and, more important, they were determined to keep a dreaded rival out of the British sugar market. So Chatham conquered in the islands to annex on the continent, conquered sugar to annex furs. The question aroused great controversy in England, and Chatham once asked whether he should be hanged for returning Canada or returning Guadeloupe.[39] If there was any hanging to be done, Beckford had the best claim.

It all amounted to this—the whole empire was to be brow-beaten into paying tribute to the sugar planters and accepting sugar at a monopoly price because it was British grown. The mainland colonists turned naturally, if unpatriotically, to the foreign sugar colonies. "Forgetting all ties of duty to his Majesty," so ran a petition of London merchants in 1750, "the interest of their mother-country, and the reverence due to its laws,"[40] the mainland colonists saw only that increased trade was demanded by their increased production. If they could not trade with foreign sugar colonies become British, they would

trade with those colonies outside the imperial framework—
even in wartime. Their existence was at stake. The tug-of-war
between islands and mainland had begun, and thereafter the
West Indians and North Americans were always "jarring."[41]

Naturally the mainland colonist did not boycott the British
sugar islands. It would have been cutting off his own nose to
spite the sugar planter's face. Instead the mainland continued
to supply the British islands. But in return they insisted on
cash, which drained the islands of specie and raised the specter
of inflation. In 1753 the total value of the trade between Northern colonies and Jamaica was estimated at £75,000 sterling.
The Northern colonists took in return products to the value of
£25,000; the rest was carried away in cash.[42] With the cash
they went to the French islands where they bought sugar at
cheaper rates and the molasses which the French planter was not
allowed to distil into rum because it would compete with French
brandies. The British sugar planters lost a market for their sugar
and rum. Their French rivals stole this market from them, while
in addition they received the supplies they needed to enable
them to compete on more advantageous terms with the British.

This complicated triangular trade of the mainland was a
complete violation of the British imperial scheme. The sugar
planters thought it reprehensible. The smallest sugar island, in
their view, was ten times more valuable to England than New
England.[43] It was a contest, they argued, not between colony
and colony but between England and France for the control of
the sugar trade.[44]

Strict mercantilists endorsed this view. The French government, it was alleged, not only connived at the trade,
but encouraged it, in order to depress the British sugar
colonies.[45] Postlethwayt called it a licentious and pernicious
commerce, and was quick to see that it had "too much contributed to loosen the dependency of our colonies upon their
mother-country, and have produced such connection of interests
between them and those of France, as have tended to alienate
them from Great Britain, and to make it too indifferent to
them whether they were under a French or a British govern-

ment."[46] Chatham echoed Postlethwayt. It was "an illegal and most pernicious trade . . . flagitious practices, so utterly subversive of all laws, and so highly repugnant to the well-being of this kingdom."[47] It is not clear, however, why this American trade should have been singled out for condemnation. It was no different from the trade carried on from Jamaica with the Spanish colonies, by which much Spanish colonial sugar was smuggled into England as British colonial produce. The North American policy of supplying the French planters with provisions was at least no more reprehensible than the British policy of supplying them with slaves.

The mainland colonists countered that "the one great end always aimed at by the sugar planters, (was) that they may raise what further prices they shall think fit upon their fellow-subjects, more especially those in North America, for the necessaries of life."[48] It was absurd for the planters to attempt to maintain monopoly prices in England when the laws of supply and demand were operating all over Europe to reduce the price of sugar in response to an increasing supply; it would be as sensible for them "to pray for an Act of Parliament to enable them to wash their blackamoors white."[49] These "overgrown West Indians"[50] who were pleading distress and throwing themselves on the mercy of Parliament were not poor and indigent. They were wealthy planters who wished to roll in their gilded equipages through the streets of London at the expense of the North Americans.[51] "What would we say to a man who should ask our charity in an embroider'd coat?"[52] If the interests of the mainland colonies as well as those of the English consumers were to be sacrificed to a handful of pampered sugar barons in tiny Barbados, then it would be better if that island were sunk in the sea.[53] "It appears to me," wrote John Dickinson, "no paradox to say that the public would be as great a gainer, if estates here (in the West Indies) were so moderate that not a tenth part of the *West Indian* gentlemen who now sit in the House of Commons could obtain that frequently expensive honour."[54] Pennsylvania produced a curious argument: the islands were less useful to England than the mainland; their slaves were naked, they had few white residents, the great heat of their climate destroyed a number of useful British sailors.[55] English exports, particularly woolen, would suffer considerably if the Northern colonies were injured.[56] The British West Indies could neither consume all the produce of New England nor provide supplies of molasses at sufficiently low rates for the Northern colonies. It was a dog-in-the-manger attitude, "to prevent their fellow-subjects receiving from others what they themselves do not furnish."[57] In 1763 all but three per cent of Massachusetts' imports of molasses came from the French West Indies; the British West Indies supplied barely one-tenth of the imports of Rhode Island and Massachusetts. The distilling business occupied an important position in colonial economy. Massachusetts had sixty distilleries in 1763, Rhode Island thirty. In addition, it was only by this trade with the French West Indies that Rhode Island was able to make remittances to England of £40,000 a year. "Without this trade," the colony protested, "it would have been and always will be, utterly impossible for the inhabitants of this colony to subsist themselves, or to pay for any considerable quantity of British goods."[58] The more trade they had with the foreign colonies, pleaded Colden, the greater would be their consumption of British manufactures.[59]

If any argument could soften the mercantilist heart, that was the one. It was the plea of an important mercantilist, William Wood. Writing as early as 1718, he was prepared to permit the trade between the mainland and the foreign plantations in the West Indies. He argued that by this trade English manufactures would be smuggled into the French islands; in return the North Americans might not get gold and silver, but they would get what was just as valuable, the products of those countries. "This may not perhaps be relished by our planters; but if they will not allow it to be for their interest in particular, I am sure they can't dispute its being for the interest of Great Britain in general. For by this means we render foreign colonies and plantations, to be in effect, the colonies and plantations of Great Britain." The trade would increase shipping and seamen; it would increase the supply of colonial produce for re-export by England. One condition only must be respected: in return for their supplies, the Americans must not take foreign manufactures.[60]

This was a curious argument for a mercantilist and it anticipated the policy of the nineteenth century in many respects. It would have antagonized the sugar planters, but it would have retained the allegiance of the mainland. But it was rank heresy against the mercantilist faith. The friends of the mainland pleaded instead for caution. They ought not, said Oglethorpe, "to encourage or raise one colony upon the destruction or detriment of another."[61] If the relief or encouragement asked for by the planters appeared to be an injury to the empire as a whole, or if it appeared that it would do more harm to other parts of the empire than good to the West Indies, the relief should be refused.[62] Sir John Barnard warned that not the whole army of excise officers could prevent the smuggling of a commodity essential to mainland prosperity.[63] Heathcote cautioned that to prohibit the trade would be to encourage the French to develop Canada.[64]

Parliament remained loyal to King Sugar and the West India interest. "It was laid down as a fundamentall that the Islands were the only usefull colonies we had and that the continent was rather a nusance."[65] The Molasses Act of 1733 was a triumph for the sugar planters. It prohibited American exports to the foreign islands, and imposed high duties on foreign sugar and molasses. It was, Pitman writes, "a challenge to the future progress of the whole region from Portland to Baltimore."[66]

It was one thing, however, to pass the Act, another thing to enforce it. As James Otis boasted, not even the King of England, encamped on Boston Common at the head of 20,000 men, could have enforced obedience to the Act.[67] Lawlessness was erected into a cardinal virtue of American economic practice, the customs officers made a lucrative job of shutting their eyes, or at least of opening them no further than their private interest required. As the Pennsylvania petition of 1751 put it, "every community may afford a few bad men."[68] The Sugar Duties Act of 1764 repeated the injunctions of the former measure; to discourage smuggling, however, the duties were lowered, but they were to be collected. The act caused, in the words of Governor Bernard, a greater alarm in America than did the capture of Fort William Henry in 1757,[69] and it has been rightly said that it was a greater blow to rising colonial consciousness than the Stamp Act. The North Americans began to chafe under the inconvenience of being British subjects. The attempt to render the Act effective and stamp out smuggling led directly to the American Revolution. It was this that John Adams had in mind when he stated that he did not know why the Americans "should blush to confess that molasses was an essential ingredient in American independence."[70]

"When in the course of human events, it becomes necessary for one people to dissolve the political bands which have connected them with another. . . ." Jefferson wrote only part of the truth. It was economic, not political, bands that were being dissolved. A new age had begun. The year 1776 marked the Declaration of Independence and the publication of the *Wealth of Nations*. Far from accentuating the value of the sugar islands, American independence marked the beginning of their uninterrupted decline, and it was a current saying at the time that the British ministry had lost not only thirteen colonies but eight islands as well.

American independence destroyed the mercantile system and discredited the old regime. Coinciding with the early stages of the Industrial Revolution, it stimulated that growing feeling of disgust with the colonial system which Adam Smith was voicing and which rose to a veritable crescendo of denunciation at the height of the free trade era. Reared in the same school as Adam Smith, Arthur Young, the champion of the agricultural revolution in England, drew important lessons from the American revolt and called the colonies nuisances. "That great lesson of modern politicks," he wrote with asperity, "the independancy of North America ought to enlarge the horizon of our commercial policy." It was not that the sugar islands were not of consequence; "they have been mischievously made of great consequence: but they are not of the importance their advocates falsely contend for."[71]

The sugar planters were fully aware of the implications of

American secession. The Stamp Act was as unpopular with the merchants of the islands as it was on the mainland; the stamps were publicly burnt, to the accompaniment of shouts of liberty.[72] "God only knows," wrote Pinney from Nevis as soon as hostilities broke out, "what will become of us. We must either starve or be ruined."[73] It was worse. They did both. Fifteen thousand slaves died of famine in Jamaica alone between 1780 and 1787,[74] and American independence was the first stage in the decline of the sugar colonies.

After the independence of the mainland was recognized, the economic interest of the sugar planters led them to make the revolutionary suggestion that the Navigation Law "must adapt itself to every material alteration of circumstances or its provisions will be no longer wise or salutary."[75] The Americans were equally alive to this interdependence. "The commerce of the West India Islands," wrote Adams, "is a part of the American system of commerce. They can neither do without us, nor we without them. The Creator has placed us upon the globe in such a situation that we have occasion for each other."[76] In England Adam Smith and Pitt pleaded in vain that the old economic relations be allowed to continue. But, as Chalmers put it, a community of 72,000 masters and 400,000 slaves was too unimportant to permit the sacrifice of vital English interests.[77] "The Navigation Act," wrote Lord Sheffield, "the basis of our great power at sea, gave us the trade of the world. If we alter that Act, by permitting any state to trade with our islands ... we desert the Navigation Act, and sacrifice the marine of England."[78] Lord North's opinion embodied the quintessence of British imperialism: "The Americans had refused to trade with Great Britain, it was but just that they be not suffered to trade with any other nation."[79]

The Americans became foreigners, subject to all the provisions of the Navigation Laws, and the islands were deflected from their natural market in accordance with the world historical situation of that time. Nova Scotia would be made into another New England. But Nova Scotia could not be built up overnight, and nothing could compensate for the loss of America. The demand for American products was not diminished by independence, only the supply was made more difficult. The West Indian islands begged for the creation of free ports,[80] American supplies continued to penetrate the British islands by devious routes which resulted merely in increasing the prices to the British planter, while in time of war serious relaxations on the prohibition of American trade had to be permitted to relieve embarrassment and distress in the islands. In 1796 American exports to the British West Indies were three times the figure for 1793; British exports declined by one-half.[81] In 1801 American exports to the West Indies were nearly five times what they were in 1792. Five-sixths of the exports in 1819 came through Canada and the Swedish and Danish islands.[82]

Denied the British West Indian market, the Americans turned increasingly to the foreign islands, where the outbreak of war between England and France and the destruction of the French navy and marine made the United States the great carrier of French and Spanish produce. American transport of foreign West Indian produce to Europe increased from less than one million pounds of coffee and seventy-five thousand pounds of sugar in 1791 to forty-seven million pounds of coffee and one hundred and forty-five million pounds of sugar in 1806.[83] Despite the wars at the end of the eighteenth century foreign plantation produce continued its competition with British in the markets of Europe.

But the greatest disaster for the British sugar planters was that the revolt of America left them face to face with their French rivals. The superiority of the French sugar colonies was for the British planters the chief among the many ills which flew out of the Pandora's box that was the American Revolution. Between 1783 and 1789 the progress of the French sugar islands, of Saint Domingue especially, was the most amazing phenomenon in colonial development. The fertility of the French soil was decisive. French sugar cost one-fifth less than British, the average yield in Saint Domingue and Jamaica was five to one.[84] During the years 1771 to 1781 the plantations of the Long family in Jamaica earned on an average a profit of nine and a half per cent, the profit in 1774 being as high as sixteen per cent.[85] In 1788 the net profit in Jamaica was four per cent as compared with an average of eight to twelve per cent in Saint Domingue.[86] In 1775 Jamaica had 775 plantations; by 1791, out of every hundred twenty-three had been sold for debt, twelve were in the hands of receivers, while seven had been abandoned;[87] and the West Indian planters, indebted to the enormous sum of twenty millions, could be challenged "on any principle to prove that any new system would involve them so deep as that on which they had hitherto proceeded."[88] Saint Domingue's exports in 1788 were double those of Jamaica; in 1789 they were valued at over one-third more than those of all the British West Indies combined. In the period of ten years before 1789 the Negro population and total production of Saint Domingue almost doubled.[89] All the English sugar colonies, boasted Hilliard d'Auberteuil, were not equal to French Saint Domingue;[90] and the British planters admitted that they could no longer continue to "retain in the European market that ascendancy which, we now fear, is irretrievably lost to Britain."[91] French colonial exports, over eight million pounds, and imports, over four millions, employed 164,000 tons of shipping and 33,000 sailors; British colonial exports, five million pounds, and imports, less than two millions, employed 148,000 tons of shipping and 14,000 seamen.[92] In every respect the sugar colonies had become vastly more essential to France than they were to England.

The Caribbean ceased to be a British lake when the American colonies won their independence. The center of gravity in the British Empire shifted from the Caribbean Sea to the Indian Ocean, from the West Indies to India. In 1783, momentous year, Prime Minister Pitt began to take an abnormally great interest in the British dominions in the East.[93] In 1787 Wilberforce was encouraged by Pitt to sponsor the proposal for abolition of the slave trade.[94] In the same year the East India Company turned its attention to the cultivation of sugar in India,[95] and in 1789 a committee of the company formally recommended its cultivation to the court of directors.[96]

Prior to 1783 the British government was uniformly consistent in its policy towards the slave trade. The withdrawal of the thirteen colonies considerably diminished the number of slaves in the empire and made abolition easier than it would have been had the thirteen colonies been English when the cotton gin revivified a moribund slave economy in the South. "As long as America was our own," wrote Clarkson in 1788, "there was no chance that a minister would have attended to the groans of the sons and daughters of Africa, however he might feel for their distress. From the same spot, which was once thus the means of creating an insuperable impediment to the relief of these unfortunate people, our affection, by a wonderful concatenation of events, has been taken off and a prospect presented to our view, which shows it to be a policy to remove their pain."[97]

The old colonial system had been based on the idea that, without a monopoly of the colonial market, British manufactures would not be sold. The other aspect of the monopolistic picture, the colonial monopoly of the home market, was based on the same assumption. The old colonial system, in other words, was a denial of the principle that trade will find its natural outlets. American independence exploded these fallacies. In July 1783 an Order in Council decreed free trade between Britain and the United States. British imports from the former colonies increased fifty per cent between 1784 and 1790; when the invention of the cotton gin entered the picture, British imports increased from nine million dollars in 1792 to nearly thirty-one million in 1801.[98] "The commerce between the mother country and the colony," as Merivale put it in 1839, "was but a peddling traffic, compared to that vast international intercourse, the greatest the world has ever known, which grew up between them when they had exchanged the tie of subjection for that of equality."[99] These facts impressed the capitalist class which was beginning to regard the Empire from the standpoint of profit and loss, and contributed to the success of Adam Smith's book in undermining the mercantilist philosophy. In 1825 Huskisson, the first of the free traders, asked pointedly "whether the disseverance of the United States from the British Empire, viewed as a mere question of commerce, has been an injury to this country? Whether their emancipation from the commercial thraldom of the colonial system has really been prejudicial to the trade and industry of Great Britain? ... Is there no useful admonition to be derived from this example?"[100] There was, but Rip Van Winkle, drugged by the potion of mercantilism, had gone to sleep for a hundred years on his sugar plantation.

· 7 ·

THE DEVELOPMENT

OF BRITISH CAPITALISM

1783-1833

FAR FROM BEING A NATIONAL DISASTER, as it was generally regarded in England and the world at the time, American independence in reality marked the end of an outworn age and the emergence of a new. In this new age there was no room for the West Indian monopoly. We must now trace the expansion of the productive forces of England, stimulated and brought to the eve of maturity by the colonial system, and see how that colonial system in the new age acted as a brake which had to be removed.

In June, 1783, the Prime Minister, Lord North, complimented the Quaker opponents of the slave trade on their humanity, but regretted that its abolition was an impossibility, as the trade had become necessary to almost every nation in Europe.[1] Slave traders and sugar planters rubbed their hands in glee. The West Indian colonies were still the darlings of the empire, the most precious jewels in the British diadem.

But the rumblings of the inevitable storm were audible for those who had ears to hear. The year of Yorktown was the year of Watt's second patent, that for the rotary motion, which converted the steam engine into a source of motive power and made industrial England, in Matthew Boulton's phrase, "steam-mill mad."[2] Rodney's victory over the French, which saved the sugar colonies, coincided with Watt's utilization of the expansive power of steam to obtain the double stroke for his pistons. The peace treaty of 1783 was being signed while Henry Cort was working on his puddling process which revolutionized the iron industry. The stage was set for that gigantic development of British capitalism which upset the political structure of the country in 1832 and thereby made possible the attack on monopoly in general and West Indian monopoly in particular.

By 1833 no single British industry had achieved a complete technical revolution; the ancient types of organization survived everywhere, and not merely as fossils or curiosities. Wool was still given out to be spun, yarn to be woven, nail-rod to be made up into nails, leather to be returned as shoes. Looms were generally hand worked, wooden spinning jennies were legion, and the word "spinster" connoted a category based on production and not yet on matrimony.[3]

But if household production still survived, it had ceased to be typical. The early phase of the Industrial Revolution was tied up with water power, the later with steam power. The application of steam was, however, a gradual process. At the beginning of the nineteenth century its use in industry was neither universal nor extensive. The total number of engines in existence in the United Kingdom was 321, the total horse power amounted to 5210.[4] According to Clapham, writing in the twenties, the total horse power of Glasgow and the Clyde in 1831 would have driven one modern cruiser.[5] But, in Mantoux's words, "there was more difference between a spinning mill and a domestic workshop as they existed side by side between 1780 and 1800, than between a factory of that date and a modern one."[6]

The cotton industry was the capitalist industry par excellence. A calculation in 1835 gave an average employment figure of 175 for all cotton mills, 125 for silk, 93 for linen, 44 for wool. The size of the average cotton mill was something unprecedented in British economic history. Forty-three important mills in Manchester had an average labor force of 300 in 1815;

in 1832 the figure had risen to 401.[7] The first steam spinning mill was set up in England in 1785, the first in Manchester in 1789. Between 1785 and 1800, eighty-two steam engines were constructed for cotton mills, fifty-five of these in Lancashire alone.[8] The first steam loom factory was built in Manchester in 1806. In 1835 there were 116,800 power looms in all Great Britain, all but six per cent in the cotton industry.[9]

In 1785 the exports of British cotton manufactures exceeded one million pounds in value;[10] they were thirty-one million in 1830.[11] The cloth printed in Great Britain increased from 20 million yards in 1796 to 347 million in 1830.[12] The population employed by the industry rose from 350,000 in 1788[13] to 800,000 in 1806.[14] There were 66 cotton mills in Manchester and Salford in 1820, 96 in 1832.[15] Cotton was "raising men like mushrooms."[16] Oldham in 1760 was a village of 400 inhabitants; in 1801 it had 20,000. In 1753 Bolton had a single, rough, illpaved street; in 1801 the population was 17,000.[17] Manchester's population increased sixfold between 1773 and 1824.[18] Cotton weavers and manufacturers, unrepresented in the Manchester procession of trades in 1763 on the occasion of the coronation of George III, were the most prominent feature of the coronation procession of George IV in 1820.[19] In a larger sense it was the coronation of King Cotton.

The Manchester capitalist from his mountain, like Moses on Pisgah, beheld the promised land. British cotton imports rose from 11 million pounds in 1784[20] to 283 million in 1832.[21] The New World, thanks to Eli Whitney, had come, not for the last time, to the rescue of the Old. The United States supplied less than one-hundredth part of British cotton imports in the five years 1786-1790, three-quarters in the years 1826-1830, four-fifths in 1846-1850. The British West Indian planter, faithful to his first love, sugar, could not keep pace with Manchester's requirements. The sugar islands provided seven-tenths of British cotton imports in 1786-1790, one-fiftieth in 1826-1830, less than one-hundredth part in 1846-1850.[22] The West Indies had built up Manchester in the eighteenth century. But they had become a tiny speck on Manchester's limitless horizon in the year her parvenu magnates sent their first delegates to Westminster, and this was full of portent for those who persisted in their delusion that the bonds of empire, like those of matrimony, were indissoluble.

Less spectacular, perhaps, but no less significant was the progress made in the metallurgical industries, without which the reign of machinery would have been impossible. Britain's production of pig iron increased ten times between 1788 and 1830.[23] There were three times as many furnaces in operation in 1830 as in 1788.[24] The iron sent down the Glamorganshire and Monmouthshire Canals increased two and a half times between the years 1820 and 1833; from Cyfartha the export doubled, from Dowlais it trebled during the same period.[25] In 1800 the proportion of home make to the foreign import was four to one; in 1828, fifty to one.[26] "Britain after Waterloo," Clapham writes, "clanged with iron like a smithy."[27]

Iron smelting required coal. The coal mines worked in Northumberland and Durham almost doubled in number between 1800 and 1836, production increased from six million tons in 1780 to thirty million in 1836.[28] An enormous saving was effected when in 1829 the invention of the hot blast in smelting reduced the coal fuel required by more than two-thirds.[29]

Iron was being put to a variety of new uses—pillars, rails, gas and water mains, bridges, ships. Wilkinson built a "cast iron chapel" for the Methodists at Bradley,[30] and London even experimented with iron paving. But the greatest victory was in the construction of machinery. The early textile machinery was made of wood, by the manufacturers themselves or to their order. The decade of the twenties saw the emergence of the professional purveyor of machines made with the help of other machines, and the beginning of the manufacture of interchangeable parts which was facilitated by the invention of new tools and the discovery of the technique of cutting accurate screws. In 1834 the firm of William Fairbairn offered to turn out an equipped mill for any price, trade, site or motive power.[31]

In 1832 the average iron master ranked, as capitalist and entrepreneur, on equal terms with the cotton spinner.[32] In the

Reformed Parliament not only cotton, iron, too, was ready to discard monopoly as a suit it had outgrown. Bar iron exports more than doubled between 1815 and 1833, and in 1825 Britain permitted—what turned out to be a fatal decision—a partial relaxation of the ban on the export of machinery. British rails covered the railroads of France and the United States. The sugar colonies took one-tenth of British iron exports in 1815, one-thirty-third in 1833; the United States one-quarter in 1815, one-third in 1833.[33] The sugar planters, who had for so long enjoyed an unquestioned right to a box seat, could now barely find standing room.

"In my humble opinion," wrote a manufacturer in 1804, "the woollen cannot too closely follow the steps of the cotton trade."[34] Imitation, however, was slow, and the persistence of the ancient forms more pronounced in the woolen industry. The flying shuttle was not in general use in the West Riding till 1800, power weaving remained experimental down to 1830. The domestic clothier was still a powerful element in woolen production, and as late as 1856 only half the number of people employed in the industry worked in factories. The average woolen or worsted mill in 1835 contained, as we have seen, only one-fourth of the number of workers in cotton mills.[35]

In 1817 the production of woolen pieces in the West Riding, the chief center of the industry, was six times the figure for 1738.[36] In 1800 the imports of wool were 4,000 tons; in the late thirties they were five times as large.[37] The value of woolen fabrics exported rose from four million pounds in 1772 to seven million in 1801. In 1802, for the first time, they were exceeded by the exports of cotton manufactures; in 1830 they were five million pounds, one-sixth of the value of the cotton exports.[38] Population increased rapidly, as in the cotton centers. Leeds had a population of 17,000 on the eve of the American Revolution, seven times as many in 1831. Halifax more than doubled its population between 1760 and 1831; Bradford's increased two and a half times between 1801 and 1831; Huddersfield's doubled. During these thirty years the population of the whole West Riding rose from 564,000 to 980,000.[39]

Up to 1815 Britain depended for her supplies of wool chiefly on Spain, Portugal and Germany. Captain John Macarthur, on his way to New South Wales, bought some merino sheep at the Cape. In 1806 the first shipment of Australian wool, 246 pounds, reached England. Twenty-four years later, the import was 3,564,532 pounds.[40] In 1828 Australian wool was described as of extraordinary softness and more highly prized than any other variety, and it was predicted that in fifteen or twenty years Britain would be getting from Australia as much of the finer wool as she needed.[41] The prediction was justified. Australia enjoyed in the nineteenth century in regard to wool "something approaching to the kind of monopoly," as Merivale put it, "which Mexico enjoyed, in the days of her prosperity, in the production of the precious metals."[42] In the new anti-imperialist world which began in the forties, emphasis shifted, where empire had to be maintained, from islands to continents, from tropical to temperate climates, from plantations of blacks to settlements of whites.

Britain's mechanized might was making the whole world her footstool. She was clothing the world, exporting men and machines, and had become the world's banker. With the exception of India and Singapore—the key to the China trade—acquired in 1819, the British Empire was a geographical expression. "It would not be worth my while," wrote Boulton in 1769 of his steam engines, "to make for three counties only, but I find it very well worth my while to make for all the world."[43] British capital, like British production, was thinking in world terms. "Between 1815 and 1830," writes Leland Jenks, "at least fifty million pounds had been invested more or less permanently in the securities of the most stable European governments, more than twenty million had been invested in one form or another in Latin America, and five or six millions had very quietly found their way to the United States."[44] But no one would advance a shilling on West Indian plantations.[45]

Between 1820 and 1830 over one-third of United States exports went to Britain, and the United States took one-sixth of British exports, which constituted over two-fifths of her total imports.[46] In 1821 the United States took one-seventh of British exports, in 1832 one-ninth; the exports increased in value by one-tenth.[47] British purchases of Southern cotton stimulated the expansion of the cotton kingdom; private and state-owned banks in the South sought loans in London.[48]

The revolutions in Latin America opened up a wide vista to British trade, once the barriers of Spanish mercantilism had been broken down, while Britain's ancient alliance with Portugal gave her a privileged position in Brazil. "The nail is driven," wrote Canning in exultation, "Spanish America is free, and if we do not mismanage our affairs sadly she is English."[49] Brazil took one-twentieth of total British exports in 1821, one-twelfth in 1832; the exports increased two and a half times.[50] Foreign colonies in North and South America, which accounted for one-thirteenth of the total British export trade in 1821, took more than one-seventh in 1832; the exports trebled in value during these years.[51] The new Latin American governments found willing lenders in English financial circles. "The more a country borrowed," says Jenks, "the better its credit, it seemed."[52] Liverpool forgot Jamaica, Grenada and Barbados; it traded and thought now in terms of Valparaiso, Antofagasta, Callao and Guayaquil.

In 1821 British exports to the world amounted to forty-three million pounds; in 1832 they were sixty-five million, an increase of one-half.[53] In both years Europe took nearly half of the total.[54] The East Indies and China took one-twelfth in 1821, one-tenth in 1832; the exports increased by three-quarters.[55]

What, then, of the British West Indies? Exports to all the islands declined by one-fifth, to Jamaica by one-third. In 1821 the British West Indies took one-ninth of the total, in 1832 one-seventeenth; in 1821 Jamaica took one-thirteenth, in 1831 one-thirty-third.[56] The British West Indies were thus becoming increasingly negligible to British capitalism, and this was of profound importance to an age in which the doctrine of increasing returns was finding its way into the body of economic thought. As Burn writes: "judged by the standards of economic imperialism, the British West India colonies, a considerable success about 1750, were a failure eighty years later."[57]

In 1825, moreover, the Navigation Laws had been modified, and the colonies were given permission to trade directly with any part of the world. The first salient in the monopolistic front had been driven. It was enlarged in the same year, when the sugar of Mauritius, an Eastern possession acquired in 1815, was admitted on the same footing as British West Indian sugar. The colonial monopoly of the home market remained. This was vital to the West Indian. As far as the British capitalist was concerned, no special legislation was required to make the West Indian sugar planter buy goods which the whole world was buying because they were cheapest and best. If Manchester still thrived on "shirts for black men," the British West Indies had no monopoly of blacks, and the larger slave populations of the United States and Brazil offered attractive markets. The West Indian planter did not pay a farthing more than his Brazilian rival for calicoes. Of what use, then, asked Manchester in wrath, was the system of monopoly to the British manufacturer?[58] Its original purpose was now, as Merivale put it, "pursued by means of sacrifices on our part, made absolutely without any consideration from theirs".[59] If, to alter somewhat the words of a modern writer, the British West Indies in 1832 were, socially, an inferno; they were, economically, what was much worse, an anachronism.[60]

Mercantilism had run its course. It was necessary only to give political expression to the new economic situation. The agitation for the Reform Bill was most powerful in the industrial centers and their commercial satellites. In this political struggle the West Indian slave owners were vitally interested. "God forbid," said Lord Wynford, "that there should be anything like a forcing of the master to abandon his property in the slave! Once adopt that principle and there was an end to all property."[61] West Indian slavery depended upon the rotten boroughs, and Cobbett realized only belatedly that "the fruit of the labour of these slaves has long been converted into the means of making us slaves at home."[62]

When the Reform Bill was rejected by the House of Lords, the London reformist press appeared in black-edged editions, and nightly in every church in the land the bells were rung. Nottingham Castle, owned by the Duke of Newcastle, prince of rotten-borough-owners, was burned to the ground by an angry crowd. Bristol's representative, who had opposed Reform in the House of Commons, was in danger of his life. The town hall was sacked, the jails and bishop's palace burned. Attwood formed the Political Union in Birmingham and threatened revolution. The tricolor was raised at Bethnal Green, London; revolutionary manifestoes appeared and placards were displayed bearing the inscription, "no taxes paid here." The Common Council called upon the House of Commons not to pass to the budget until the Reform Bill had become law. The Royal Family were caricatured and insulted and advised to leave London. A revolutionary device was proposed—a run on the banks: "to stop the Duke (Wellington), go for gold." Revolution was around the corner.[63]

The opponents of the measure, however, backed down after the King's reluctant promise to create sufficient new peers, and the Reform Bill became law. The political structure of England was brought into accord with the economic revolution which had taken place. In the new Parliament the capitalists, their needs and aspirations were paramount. Once the colonial trade had meant everything. In the new capitalist society the colonies had little place. "The exportation of a piece of British broadcloth," wrote Eden in 1802, "is more beneficial to us than the re-exportation of a quantity of Bengal muslin or of West India coffee of equal value."[64] In 1832 an official of the East India Company explained to a parliamentary committee that woolens were exported to China, even when the market was not good, as a matter of tradition and duty: "it was considered a moral obligation."[65] Trade by "moral obligation" was one of the deadly sins in the gospel according to Manchester.

· 8 ·

THE NEW INDUSTRIAL ORDER

IT WAS THIS TREMENDOUS INDUSTRIAL EXPANSION that the West Indian monopolists had to face. They had the advantages of prestige, custom, their great contributions to British economy in the past, and a strongly entrenched position. We can see today that they were doomed, that the Lilliputians could not hold down Gulliver nor their barbs hurt him. Lecturing to Oxford undergraduates in 1839, Merivale warned that "the rapid tide of sublunary events is carrying us inevitably past that point at which the maintenance of colonial systems and navigation laws was practicable, whether it were desirable or not. We are borne helplessly along with the current; we may struggle and protest, and marvel why the barriers which ancient forethought had raised against the stream now bend like reeds before its violence, but we cannot change our destiny. The monopoly of the West Indian islands cannot stand. . . ."[1] The West Indians, however, could not see this and acted as all vested interests do. They put up a desperate fight, "struggling by the aid of their accumulated wealth against the encroaching principle of decay,"[2] blind to all considerations and consequences except the maintenance of their diseased system.

The attack on the West Indians was more than an attack on slavery. It was an attack on monopoly. Their opponents were not only the humanitarians but the capitalists. The reason for the attack was not only that the West Indian economic system was vicious but that it was also so unprofitable that for this reason alone its destruction was inevitable.[3] The agent for

Jamaica complained in 1827 that "the cause of the colonies altogether, but more especially that part of it which touches upon property in slaves, is so unattractive to florid orators and so unpopular with the public, that we have and must have very little protection from Parliamentary speaking."[4] Hibbert was only half right. If West Indian slavery was detestable, West Indian monopoly was unpopular, and the united odium of both was more than the colonies could bear.[5]

The attack falls into three phases: the attack on the slave trade, the attack on slavery, the attack on the preferential sugar duties. The slave trade was abolished in 1807, slavery in 1833, the sugar preference in 1846. The three events are inseparable. The very vested interests which had been built up by the slave system now turned and destroyed that system. The humanitarians, in attacking the system in its weakest and most indefensible spot, spoke a language that the masses could understand. They could never have succeeded a hundred years before when every important capitalist interest was on the side of the colonial system. "It was an arduous hill to climb," sang Wordsworth in praise of Clarkson. The top would never have been reached but for the defection of the capitalists from the ranks of the slaveowners and slave traders. The West Indians, pampered and petted and spoiled for a century and a half, made the mistake of elevating into a law of nature what was actually only a law of mercantilism. They thought themselves indispensable and carried over to an age of anti-imperialism the lessons they had been taught in an age of commercial imperialism. When, to their surprise, the "invisible hand" of Adam Smith turned against them, they could turn only to the invisible hand of God.[6] The rise and fall of mercantilism is the rise and fall of slavery.

A.   PROTECTION OR LAISSEZ FAIRE?

Queen Victoria once sent a famous message to two African chiefs: "England has become great and happy by the knowledge of the true God and Jesus Christ."[7] To the Manchester capitalist, "Jesus Christ was Free Trade, and Free Trade was Jesus Christ."[8]

If Corn was the king of monopolies, Sugar was his queen. The attack on the preferential sugar duties of the West Indies was a part of that general philosophy which in 1812 destroyed the East India Company's monopoly and in 1846 the Corn Laws of England. The Anti-Corn Law League, said its treasurer, was "established on the same righteous principle as the Anti-Slavery Society. The object of that society was to obtain the free right for the Negroes to possess their own flesh and blood—the object of this was to obtain the free right of the people to exchange their labor for as much food as could be got for it."[9] In the delirium of free trade sentiments the brunt of the advance on the anti-monopolistic front had to be borne by the West Indian monopoly which was not only iniquitous but expensive.

The advocates of East India sugar persistently attacked the West Indian monopoly. They called the islands "sterile rocks," whose insatiable calls for money represented "an eternal sponge on the capitals of this country, both national and commercial." Even before the end of the eighteenth century Britain was "ripe for an abolition of monopolies." A general hardship could not be inflicted on the community at large for the sake of affording a partial and unreasonable benefit to a small number of its members.[10]

The East Indian opposition was more virulent in the eighteen twenties. They wanted, at least so they alleged, no exclusive favor, preference or protection. All they asked for was equality with the West Indies.[11] Were the West Indians entitled to the enjoyment of the monopoly merely because they had enjoyed it for a length of time? "It would be to contend, that because a great many people who used to be employed in the manufacture of cotton, or other articles, by hand, are thrown out of employment by the invention of machinery, a tax upon machinery should therefore be levied. ... It would be to say that because the conveyance by canal has been found much more cheap and convenient than the old mode of conveyance by wagon, a tax should therefore be laid upon canal conveyance."[12] The claim of the West Indians that they were entitled to a continuance of protection because they had invested their capital in sugar cultivation was "a claim which might be urged with equal force in the case of *every* improvident speculation."[13] They could not depart from the ordinary principles of commerce in order to benefit the West Indians.[14] Hume trusted that the good sense, the honest feeling and the patriotism of the British people would never allow the continuance of such a monopoly, for all restraints and monopolies were bad.[15]

As early as 1815 a protest was entered in the Journals of the House of Lords against the Corn Laws, threatening the very keystone of the arch of protection. In 1820 the merchants of London presented a petition to Parliament in which it was stated that "freedom from restraint is calculated to give the utmost extension to foreign trade and the best direction to the capital and industry of the country."[16] In the same year Mr. Finlay, of Glasgow, made an impassioned speech in support of a petition from the Chamber of Commerce of Glasgow praying for free trade and the removal of all restrictions upon commercial imports and exports. "If it should be found," said Finlay, "that the history of our commercial policy has been a tissue of mistakes and false notions, it surely was not too much to express a hope that the policy should be given up."[17] All monopolies, declared the merchants of Liverpool, which prohibited trade with any other country, and in particular the East India Company's monopoly, were injurious to the general interests of the country. The Corporation of the town declared that British subjects possessed "an inherent right" to a free intercourse with any part of the world. Not without reason had Pitt complimented Adam Smith some thirty years before at a dinner party, "We are all your scholars."[18]

The West Indian monopoly was not only unsound in theory, it was unprofitable in practice. In 1828 it was estimated that it cost the British people annually more than one and a half million pounds.[19] In 1844 it was costing the country £70,000 a week and London £6,000.[20] England was paying for its sugar five millions more a year than the Continent.[21] Three and a half million pounds of British exports to the West Indies in 1838, said Merivale, purchased less than half as much sugar and coffee as they would have purchased if carried to Cuba and Brazil. Goods to the value of one and three-quarter million pounds "were therefore as completely thrown away, without remuneration, as far as Britain is concerned, as if the vessels which conveyed them had perished on the voyage."[22] Two-fifths of the price of every pound of sugar consumed in England represented the cost of production, two-fifths went in revenue to the government, one-fifth in tribute to the West Indian planter.[23]

It was high time to revise this "beetle-eyed" policy which bolstered up "the rotten cause" of the West Indian slaveholder.[24] Huskisson pleaded for caution. "That the West Indian was an owner of slaves was not his fault but his misfortune; and if it was true that the production of slavery was more costly than that of free labour, that would be an additional reason for not depriving him of the advantage of his protecting duty."[25] But the West Indians were not to misunderstand this. "The time must come, and could not be far distant, when the subject would be ripe for consideration, and when it would be the imperative duty of Parliament to enter into a full investigation of all the circumstances connected with it."[26]

The capitalists, eager to lower wages, advocated the policy of "the free breakfast table." It was injustice and folly to impose protective duties on food.[27] Monopoly was unsound, costly to all, and had destroyed the great colonial empires of the past.[28] The West India interest was doomed. "There can be no prosperity for the West India colonies by any arrangement or juggling of duties in this house. No majorities here will give prosperity to the West Indies; and no dancing attendance at the Colonial Office will accomplish any such end."[29] The protective system was compared to many monkeys in different cages, each stealing from his neighbor's pan, and each losing as much as he had stolen.[30] Ricardo advised the planters to yield gracefully; "the ball was rolling, and nothing that they could do would suffice to stop it."[31]

Time was when the leading statesmen were on the West Indian side. Now Palmerston lined up with the opponents of the planters. The word "protection" should be erased from every commercial dictionary,[32] as "a principle of fatal injury to the country and inimical to the prosperity of every country to whose affairs it may be applied."[33]

The protectionists were on the side of the West Indians. The landed aristocracy of the corn bushels joined hands with the landed aristocracy of the sugar hogsheads. Peel, free trader in cotton and silk, was protectionist in corn and sugar. The West Indian cause was ably championed by Bentinck, Stanley and Disraeli. If the West Indian interest was made, as Disraeli criticized, "the harridan of party,"[34] he too was instrumental in so making it. The debates on the repeal of the corn laws and the equalization of the sugar duties gave him an audience for his matchless oratory and mordant wit, but it is doubtful whether any serious personal convictions or economic philosophy motivated his diatribes. For when the West Indians, after 1846, were trying to postpone the evil day of actual enforcement of the principle of free trade in sugar, Disraeli, too, turned against them. "After the immense revolution that has been carried into effect, we cannot cling to the rags and tatters of a protective system";[35] and in *Sybil* he wrote with detachment that in a commercial country like England every half century developed some new source of public wealth and brought into public notice some new and powerful class—the Levant merchant, the West Indian planter, the East Indian nabob.[36] Mercantilism was not only dead but damned.

The West Indians tried to stem the free trade torrent. The colonial system was "an implicit compact ... for a mutual monopoly."[37] It was theirs, they claimed, not of grace but of right. Their exclusive possession of the home market was their just reward for the restrictions imposed on them by the colonial system.[38] At other times they were not indisposed to plead for charity. The superior advantages of their rivals made competition impossible and the protecting duty indispensable to their preservation. In the case of India they pointed to the cheapness of labor, the abundance of food and unlimited extent of the richest soil, capable of irrigation and intersected with navigable rivers.[39] In the case of Brazil they blamed the facility with which the Brazilians could acquire laborers for their fertile soil. Whatever the state of these colonies their refrain was always the same—protection. "Ruin" was ever the first word in their vocabulary—a word used to designate "not the poverty of the people, not the want of food or raiment, not even the absence of riches or luxury, but simply the decrease of sugar cultivation."[40] Where they had, as slaveowners before 1833, demanded protection against the free-grown sugar of India, now, as employers of free labor after 1833, they demanded it against the slave-grown sugar of Brazil and Cuba. Where formerly they had extenuated the evils of sugar cultivation by slaves, now they exaggerated those evils. As slave owners they had apologised for the evils of slavery; as employers of free men they exalted the blessings of freedom. Inconsistent in all things, they were yet consistent in one—the maintenance of their monopoly.

To the very end the West Indians continued to suffer from their myopia and to demand a seventeenth century position in a nineteenth century empire. Read their manifestoes, pamphlets and speeches—instead of Saint Domingue there is India or Mauritius or Brazil or Cuba. The dates have changed, freedom has replaced slavery. But their claims are the same, their fallacies identical. They keep "crying out for more monopoly, in order to redress those evils which monopoly itself inflicted."[41] They are greeted with sneers and contempt[42] but pay no heed. Occasionally they talk free trade, as when a West Indian, opposing the renewal of the charter of the West India Dock Company, lectured Parliament on "the impolicy as well as injustice of continuing, in an enlightened age as this, such monopolies, which were at once injurious to commerce and to the revenue of the country."[43] In general, however, they remain oblivious of the new order and the beam in their own eyes.

Protection and Labor—these were their slogans in 1846 as they had been in 1746. Protection was simply justice.[44] To refuse it was un-English.[45] The protecting duty was necessary to safeguard the experiment of free labor.[46] Sugar cultivation requires labor. Give us indentured Africans, indentured East Indians, convicts, now that you have emancipated the Negroes and made them lazy; and some, in desperation, even advocated the renewal of the slave trade.[47]

Their outstanding champion was Gladstone. But Gladstone

was more than a West Indian; he was an imperial statesman as well, who never lost sight of the wood for the trees. With all the casuistry and eloquence at his disposal—and he had much of both—Gladstone tried to justify the West Indian monopoly on the ground that it was protection for free-grown sugar against slave-grown sugar. But he was forced to admit that the distinction was not so clear that it could be drawn with uniform and absolute precision.[48] Nor could he ignore the fact that the West Indian claim for protection was weakened after 1836 when the protecting duty was extended to East Indian sugar which could plead no such difficulties and disadvantages as faced the West Indians.[49] And Gladstone knew that the course had been run. Protection could not be permanent, and even if continued for twenty years, would not bring West Indian cultivation to a sound and healthy state.[50]

B.   THE GROWTH OF ANTI-IMPERIALISM

The colonial system was the spinal cord of the commercial capitalism of the mercantile epoch. In the era of free trade the industrial capitalists wanted no colonies at all, least of all the West Indies.

The trend dated back, as we have seen, to the early years of the Industrial Revolution. Its development paralleled the development of the free trade movement. The whole world row became a British colony and the West Indies were doomed. The leader of the movement was Cobden. Cobden referred approvingly to Adam Smith's chapters in his "immortal work" on the expense of colonies.[51] To him the colonial question was a pecuniary question.[52] The colonies were expensive encumbrances, making dazzling appeals to the passions of the people, serving only as "gorgeous and ponderous appendages to swell our ostensible grandeur, but, in reality, to complicate and magnify our government expenditure, without improving our balance of trade." He could see nothing but a "monstrous impolicy" in "sacrificing our trade with a new continent, of almost boundless extent of rich territory, in favour of a few small islands, with comparatively exhausted soils."[53] In 1852 the British declared war on Burma and annexed Lower Burma. Cobden protested. He wrote an article entitled "How wars are got up in India," suggesting that Britain ought "to advertise in the *Times* for a governor-general who can collect a debt of a thousand pounds without annexing a territory which will be ruinous to our finances."[54]

To Molesworth, one of the outstanding colonial reformers, Britain's colonial policy was motivated by "an insane desire of worthless empire," as on the frontier of the Cape Colony in South Africa, where "the loss of one axe and two goats . . . has cost this country a couple of millions sterling." Australia was a collection of "communities, the offspring of convict emigration." New Zealand was a constant headache with its "imbecile governors, discreditable functionaries, and unnecessary wars with the natives." South Africa was "a huge worthless and costly empire, extending over nearly 300,000 square miles, chiefly rugged mountains, and arid deserts, and barren plains, without water, without herbage, without navigable rivers, without harbours, in short, without everything except the elements of great and increasing expense to this country." In charge of this diverse and heterogeneous collection of colonies was the Colonial Secretary, "traversing and retraversing, in his imagination, the terraqueous globe—flying from the Arctic to the Antarctic pole—hurrying from the snows of North America to the burning regions of the Tropics—rushing across from the fertile islands of the West Indies to the arid deserts of South Africa and Australia—like nothing on earth, or in romance, save the Wandering Jew."[55] The cost of protecting this empire was one-third of Britain's export trade to the colonies. Colonial independence was cheaper. The colonies should be freed from the "ever-changing, frequently well-intentioned, but invariably weak and ignorant despotism" of the Colonial Office.[56]

Hume, another radical politician, joined in the attack on "Mr. Mother Country." Remove the iron chains which fettered the best exertions of the colonies,[57] let them manage their own affairs instead of being kept in leading strings and subjected to the fluctuating management of Downing Street.[58] The Colonial Office "is" a nuisance and should be locked up.[59]

Trusteeship was out of fashion. Roebuck, a free-lance Radical, opposed as cant the humanitarian refusal to surrender the colonies to local self-government. History taught that the savage must disappear in the face of the relentless advance of a superior race; justice and humanity must yield to the iron law of an unjust necessity.[60] James Stephen, the famous Permanent Under-Secretary of the Colonial Office, never wavered in his determination not to lay down the "wretched burdens which in an evil hour we assumed." But the capitalists, like Taylor, also of the Colonial Office, could see in the colonies nothing but "furious assemblies, foolish governors, missionaries and slaves,"[61] which, in the words of Merivale, were to be retained for the mere "pleasure of governing them."[62] Nothing was true but what went to West Indian condemnation, nothing was just but what went to West Indian ruin.[63] It seemed to the desperate planters as if a coalition had been formed to destroy the colonies.[64] The assemblies of Jamaica and British Guiana went on strike in 1838 and 1840 and refused to vote supplies. Jamaica preferred "Yankee Doodle" to "God save the Queen."[65] Who cared? Members of Parliament were prepared to barter the West Indies to America for a slight compensation.[66] "Jamaica to the bottom of the sea," thundered Roebuck, "and all the Antilles after it." These "barren colonies" had been a source of nothing but war and expenditure.[67] They had ever been the "most fatal appendages" of the British empire, and if they were to be blotted out from the face of the earth Britain would lose not "one jot of her strength, one penny of her wealth, one instrument of her power."[68]

It was an epidemic. Even Disraeli, the arch imperialist of later decades, was infected. In 1846 the "forlorn Antilles" were still to him "a fragment, but a fragment which I value, of the colonial system of England."[69] Six years later Canada had become a diplomatic embarrassment, and the wretched colonies a "damnosa hereditas," millstones round Britain's neck.[70] In nine cases out of ten, according to Gladstone, it was impossible to secure parliamentary attention to colonial concerns and in the tenth case it was only obtained by the casual operations of party spirit.[71] The age of empire was dead; that of free traders, economists, and calculators had succeeded, and the glory of the West Indies was extinguished for ever. Only another thirty years, however, the tune would change. But the West Indian Humpty Dumpty had had a great fall, and all the King's horses and all the King's men could not put Humpty Dumpty together again.

C. THE GROWTH OF WORLD SUGAR PRODUCTION

The strength of the British sugar islands before 1783 lay in the fact that as sugar producers they had few competitors. In so far as they could, they would permit none. They resisted the attempt to introduce the cultivation of sugar (and cotton) into Sierra Leone on the ground that it would be a precedent to "foreign nations, who have as yet no colonies anywhere,"[72] and might prove detrimental to those who possessed West Indian colonies;[73] just as a century previously they had opposed the cultivation of indigo in Africa.[74] Their chief competitors in the sugar trade were Brazil and the French islands, Cuba being hampered by the extreme exclusiveness of Spanish mercantilism. This situation was radically altered when Saint Domingue forged ahead in the years immediately following the secession of the mainland colonies.

The cultivation of Barbados and Jamaica had transferred the sugar trade of Europe from Portugal to England. The progress of Saint Domingue gave control of the European sugar market to France. Between 1715 and 1789 French imports from the colonies multiplied eleven times, French colonial products re-exported abroad ten times.[75] In 1789 two-thirds of French exports to the Baltic, over one-third of the exports to the Levant, were colonial produce. It was "by it, and by it alone, that she turned the balance of the trade with all the world to a favourable result.".[76]

It was the old law of slave production at work. Saint Domingue was larger than any British colony, its soil was more fertile and less exhausted, hence its costs of production were lower. This difference in costs of production became an object of particular inquiry with the Privy Council Committee of 1788.

From the standpoint of the British Prime Minister, William Pitt, this was the decisive factor. The age of the British sugar islands was over. The West Indian system was unprofitable, and the slave trade on which it rested, "instead of being very advantageous to Great Britain ... is the most destructive that can well be imagined to her interests."[77] For a Prime Minister whose father had been consistently on the West Indian side of the fence, and whose predecessor a mere ten years previously had blandly turned down a petition for abolition, this was a momentous conversion. Pitt turned to India.

Pitt's plan was twofold: to recapture the European market with the aid of sugar from India,[78] and to secure an international abolition of the slave trade[79] which would ruin Saint Domingue. If not international abolition, then British abolition. The French were so dependent on British slave traders that even a unilateral abolition by England would seriously dislocate the economy of the French colonies.

Pitt's plan failed, for two reasons. The importation of East India sugar, on the scale planned, was impossible owing to the high duties imposed on all sugar not the produce of the British West Indies.[80] Lord Hawkesbury, for the West Indian monopolists, opposed the alteration of the existing law "in favour of a monopolising company" which was exceeding the bounds of its charter.[81] But Hawkesbury was more than a West Indian. He was in close touch with British commerce and industry, especially Liverpool. He therefore recommended, instead, the importation of all foreign sugar provided it was done in British ships and solely for refining and re-export. "The commerce and shipping of France will be more diminished, and the commerce and shipping of Great Britain more augmented, than by any single measure that has been pursued for the last century."[82] By this very simple regulation Britain would recover the sugar trade she had enjoyed from 1660 to 1713 but which thereafter she lost to France.[83]

Secondly, the French, Dutch and Spaniards refused, with what Lord Liverpool called thirty years later "sheer perverseness,"[84] to abolish the slave trade.[85] It was not difficult to see the political motives behind Pitt's cloak of humanitarianism. Gaston-Martin, the well-known French historian of the slave trade and the Caribbean colonies, accuses Pitt of aiming by propaganda to free the slaves, "in the name no doubt of humanity, but also to ruin French commerce," and concludes that in this philanthropic propaganda there were economic motives which explain the liberality with which Britain put funds at the disposal of the French abolitionists, and the way in which France was swamped with translations of the anti-slavery works of the British abolitionist, Clarkson.[86] As Ramsay had admitted: "We may confidently conclude that the African trade is more confined in its utility than is generally imagined and that of late years it has contributed more to the aggrandisement of our rivals than of our national wealth."[87]

At this juncture the French Revolution came to the aid of Pitt. Fearful that the idealism of the revolutionary movement would destroy the slave trade and slavery, the French planters of Saint Domingue in 1791 offered the island to England,[88] and were soon followed by those of the Windward Islands.[89] Pitt accepted the offer, when war broke out with France in 1793. Expedition after expedition was sent unsuccessfully to capture the precious colony, first from the French, then from the Negroes. It was not, Parliament was assured, "a war for riches or local aggrandisement but a war for security."[90] The allied cause in Europe was weakened in the interests of British imperialism. "The secret of England's impotence for the first six years of the war," writes Fortescue, historian of the British army, "may be said to lie in the two fatal words, St. Domingo."[91] Britain lost thousands of men and spent thousands of pounds in the attempt to capture Saint Domingue. She failed, but the world's sugar bowl was destroyed in the process and French colonial superiority smashed forever. "For this," writes Fortescue, "England's soldiers had been sacrificed, her treasure squandered, her influence weakened, her arm for six fateful years fettered, numbed and paralysed."[92]

This is of more than academic interest. Pitt could not have had Saint Domingue and abolition as well. Without its 40,000 slave imports a year, Saint Domingue might as well have been at the bottom of the sea. The very acceptance of the island meant logically the end of Pitt's interest in abolition. Naturally he did not say so. He had already committed himself too far in the eyes of the public. He continued to speak in favor of abolition, even while giving every practical encouragement to the slave trade. But it was not the old Pitt of 1789-1791, the Pitt of Latin tags, brilliant oratory and infectious humanitarianism. The change can be followed in the debates in Parliament and in Wilberforce's diary. In 1792 Wilberforce's diary struck the first ominous note: "Pitt threw out against slave motion on St. Domingo account."[93] Thereafter Pitt's support of Wilberforce's annual motions became nothing short of perfunctory. On one occasion he supported the West Indians, on another he put off the motion, on another he "stood stiffly" by Wilberforce, on yet another he simply stayed away.[94] Under Pitt's administration the British slave trade alone more than doubled,[95] and Britain conquered two more sugar colonies, Trinidad and British Guiana. As the abolitionist Stephen wrote with bitterness: "Mr. Pitt, unhappily for himself, his country and mankind, is not zealous enough in the cause of the negroes, to contend for them as decisively as he ought, in the cabinet any more than in parliament."[96]

Liberal historians plead Pitt's fear of Jacobinism. The real reason is more simple. It can be taken as axiomatic that no man occupying so important a position as Prime Minister of England would have taken so important a step as abolishing the slave trade purely for humanitarian reasons. A Prime Minister is more than a man, he is a statesman. Pitt's reasons were political and only secondarily personal. He was interested in the sugar trade. Either he must ruin Saint Domingue by flooding Europe with cheaper Indian sugar or by abolishing the slave trade; or he must get Saint Domingue for himself. If he could get Saint Domingue, the balance in the Caribbean would be restored. Saint Domingue would be "a noble compensation" for the loss of America, and "a glorious addition to the dominion, navigation, trade and manufactures of Britain."[97] It would give Britain a monopoly of sugar, indigo, cotton and coffee: "This island, for ages, would give such aid and force to industry as would be most happily felt in every part of the kingdom." Followed by an offensive and defensive alliance between Britain and Spain, "such friendship for ages might preclude France and America from the New World, and effectually secure the invaluable possessions of Spain."[98] But if Pitt captured Saint Domingue, the slave trade must continue. When Saint Domingue was lost to France, the slave trade became merely a humanitarian question.

The destruction of Saint Domingue meant the end of the French sugar trade. Not all the decrees of consuls, black or white, wrote Eden with complacency, could fill up the gaps in the population of the island.[99] But the ruin of Saint Domingue did not mean the salvation of the British West Indies. Two new enemies appeared on the scene. Cuba forged ahead to fill the gap left in the world market by the disappearance of Saint Domingue. Bonaparte, defeated in his attempts to recapture the lost colony and determined to conquer England by strangulation of her trade, gave the first impetus to beet sugar, and the war of the two sugars began. Whilst, under the American flag, Cuban and other neutral sugar still found a market in Europe, British West Indian surpluses piled up in England. Bankruptcies were the order of the day. Between 1799 and 1807, 65 plantations in Jamaica were abandoned, 32 were sold for debts, and in 1807 suits were pending against 115 others. Debt, disease and death were the only topics of conversation in the island.[100] A parliamentary committee set up in 1807 discovered that the British West Indian planter was producing at a loss. In 1800 his profit was 2 1/2 per cent, in 1807 nothing. In 1787 the planter got 19/6d profit per hundredweight; in 1799, 10/9d; in 1803, 18/6d; in 1805, 12/-; in 1806, nothing. The committee attributed the main evil to the unfavorable state of the foreign market.[101] In 1806 the surplus of sugar in England amounted to six thousand tons.[102] Production had to be curtailed. To restrict production, the slave trade must be abolished. The "saturated" colonies needed only seven thousand slaves a year.[103] It was the new colonies, crying out for labor, full of possibilities, that had to be restrained, and they were permanently crippled by abolition. That explains the support of the abolition bill by so many West

Indian planters of the older islands. Ellis had stated categorically in 1804 that the slave trade should be continued, but only to the older colonies.[104] It was the same old conflict between "saturated planters" and "planters on the make."

The war and Bonaparte's continental blockade made abolition imperative if the older colonies were to survive. "Are they not now," asked Prime Minister Grenville, "distressed by the accumulation of produce on their hands, for which they cannot find a market; and will it not therefore be adding to their distress, and leading the planters on to their ruin, if you suffer the continuation of fresh importations?"[105] Wilberforce rejoiced: West Indian distress could not be imputed to abolition.[106] Actually, abolition was the direct result of that distress.

If abolition of the slave trade was the solution of the planter's problems, it was only a temporary solution. For, as Merivale argued soundly, without imports to replace their slaves, the West Indies, and especially the newer colonies, could not hope to sustain the still fiercer competition of the nineteenth century. "Slavery without the slave trade . . . was rather a loss than a gain."[107] At the end of the Napoleonic Wars in 1815, the sugar planters were no better off than they had been before. India was still a rival to be feared. The one devil of Saint Domingue was replaced by three, Mauritius, Cuba, Brazil. Sugar cultivation was later extended to Louisiana, Australia, Hawaii, Java. Beet continued its progress until its major victory in 1848 when it freed the slaves on the cane sugar plantations of the French colonies, while it became later a permanent European and even an American feature in the interest of autarchy.

Between 1793 and 1833 the imports of sugar into Britain more than doubled. Complete records for the same period for the West Indies are lacking, but between 1815 and 1833 West Indian production was stationary—3,381,700 hogsheads in 1815, 3,351,800 in 1833, with a maximum of 4,068,000 in 1828. It is significant that this level of production was maintained only at the expense of the older islands with their exhausted soil. Between 1813 and 1833 Jamaica's production declined by nearly one-sixth; the exports of Antigua, Nevis and Tobago by more than one-quarter, St. Kitts by nearly one-half, St. Lucia's by two-thirds, St. Vincent's by one-sixth, Grenada's by almost one-eighth. Dominica's exports showed a slight increase, while Barbados almost doubled its exports. On the other hand, the output of the newer colonies increased, British Guiana's by two and a half times, Trinidad's by one-third.[108]

Mauritius lends further confirmation to this law of slave production. Its exports to Britain, less than Antigua's in 1820, were over four times Antigua's in 1833.[109] East India sugar sold in England increased twenty-eight times between 1791 and 1833.[110] Foreign sources were arising as suppliers of the raw material Britain needed for refining, consumption and export. Singapore's exports in 1833 were six times those of 1827; imports from the Philippines quadrupled, from Java increased more than twenty times.[111] Cuban sugar production increased more than forty times between 1775 and 1865.[112] British imports from Brazil increased sevenfold between 1817 and 1831, from Cuba sixfold between 1817 and 1832.[113]

Sugar production, as we have seen, is more efficient on a large plantation than on a smaller one. But the size of the plantation is limited by one factor—transportation. The cane, within a specified time after it has been cut, must be taken to the factory. More than any other British island, Jamaica in the eighteenth century was the land of large planters. But in 1753 there were only three plantations in the 2,000-acre class in Jamaica which had about one-tenth of the land in cane. The largest, belonging to Philip Pinnock, and called by Pitman "the show place" of Jamaica of that day, contained 2,872 acres of which 242 were in cane, employed 280 slaves, and produced 184 tons of sugar a year.[114] After emancipation Jamaica was faced with the shortage of labor and wages rose. The island was unable to compete with the more extensive and more fertile soil of Cuba with its slave population. The development of the railroad— the first was constructed in Cuba in 1837—enabled the Cuban planter to enlarge his plantation, increase his output and reduce his costs of production, while the Jamaican planter was still asking for protection and labor. The competition thereby became more unequal. By 1860 we read of "monster" plantations in Cuba, the largest comprising 11,000 acres, of which over one-tenth was in cane, employing 866 slaves, and producing 2,670 tons of sugar a year.[115]

The British West Indies had clearly lost their monopoly of sugar cultivation. In 1789 they could not compete with Saint Domingue; nor in 1820 with Mauritius; nor in 1830 with Brazil; nor in 1840 with Cuba. Their day had passed. Limited in extent, slave or free, they could not compete with larger areas, more fertile, less exhausted, where slavery was still profitable. Cuba could contain all the British islands of the Caribbean, Jamaica included. One of Brazil's mighty rivers could hold all the West Indian islands without its navigation being obstructed.[116] India could produce enough rum to drown the West Indies.[117]

The West Indian situation was aggravated by the fact that production was in excess of the home consumption. This surplus, estimated at twenty-five per cent,[118] had to be sold in European markets in competition with cheaper Brazilian or Cuban sugar. This could be done only by subsidies and bounties. The West Indian planters were being paid, in fact, to enable them to compete with people who, as we have seen, were some of Britain's best customers. Between 1824 and 1829 the imports of Cuban and Brazilian sugar into Hamburg increased by ten per cent while those into Prussia doubled; Cuban sugar imported by Russia increased by fifty per cent and Brazilian by twenty-five per cent in the same period.[119] To the capitalists this was intolerable. Overproduction in 1807 demanded abolition; overproduction in 1833 demanded emancipation. "As far as the amount of the production of sugar is concerned," stated Stanley, sponsor of the emancipation measure, "I am not quite certain that to some extent a diminution of that production would be a matter of regret—I am not quite certain that it might not be for the benefit of the planters and of the colonies themselves, in the end, if that production were to be diminished."[120] A century before the British had complained of West Indian underproduction, now they were complaining of West Indian overproduction. Common sense alone would show that the emancipated Negroes would remain on the plantations only where they had no choice. In fact, comparing the years 1839-1842 with the years 1831-1834, the production of Jamaica and Grenada declined by one-half, British Guiana's by three-fifths, St. Vincent's by two-fifths, Trinidad's by one-fifth, and the other islands proportionately.[121]

In justification of emancipation, it was argued that the restriction of production would give the planters a "real" monopoly of the home market by equating production with home consumption. This was parliamentary strategy. Every effort was being made to make West Indian cultivation as expensive as possible. In 1832 the Trinidad Council petitioned for the abolition of the slave tax of one pound island currency per head. The Colonial Office refused: it was "of very great importance that this tax should be continued; instead of rendering slave labour cheaper it is desirable to render it dearer."[122] The issue at stake was the monopoly itself. It was only the West Indian monopoly which restricted the full development of British trade in sugar with all the world. The monopoly therefore must be destroyed. In 1836 the monopoly was modified by admitting East India sugar on equal terms. In 1846, the year of the repeal of the Corn Laws, the sugar duties were equalized. The British West Indian colonies were thereafter forgotten, until the Panama Canal reminded the world of their existence and revolts of their underpaid free workers made them front-page news.

· 9 ·

BRITISH CAPITALISM

AND THE

WEST INDIES

WHEREAS BEFORE, in the eighteenth century, every important vested interest in England was lined up on the side of
monopoly and the colonial system; after 1783, one by one,
every one of those interests came out against monopoly and the
West Indian slave system. British exports to the world were
in manufactured goods which could be paid for only in raw
materials—the cotton of the United States, the cotton, coffee
and sugar of Brazil, the sugar of Cuba, the sugar and cotton
of India. The expansion of British exports depended on the
capacity of Britain to absorb the raw material as payment. The
British West Indian monopoly, prohibiting the importation of
non-British-plantation sugar for home consumption, stood in
the way. Every important vested interest—the cotton manufacturers, the shipowners, the sugar refiners; every important
industrial and commercial town—London, Manchester, Liverpool, Birmingham, Sheffield, the West Riding of Yorkshire,
joined in the attack on West Indian slavery and West Indian
monopoly. The abolitionists, significantly, concentrated their
attack on the industrial centers.[1]

A. THE COTTON MANUFACTURERS

The West Indian planters in the eighteenth century were
both exporters of raw cotton and importers of cotton manu-

154

factures. In both respects, as we have seen, they had become increasingly negligible. The steam engine and the cotton gin changed Manchester's indifference into downright hostility. As early as 1788 Wilberforce exulted at the fact that a liberal subscription towards abolition had been raised at Manchester, "deeply interested in the African trade."[2]

Manchester was unrepresented in the House of Commons before 1832, so its parliamentary denunciation of the West Indian system comes only after that date. But the seat of the cotton industry was interested in the problem before 1832. In 1830 Cobbett, the workers' champion, presented himself as a candidate for the constituency of Manchester. His opposition to the landed interest would have endeared him to the later seat of the Anti-Corn Law League. The test came on his attitude to West Indian slavery. Cobbett hated Wilberforce and the Methodists. When he fled to the United States in 1818 he wrote a letter to Orator Hunt, in which he stated that America had "No Wilberforces. Think of *that!* No Wilberforces."[3] The Methodists were "the vilest crew God ever suffered to infest the earth," and he encouraged the people to pelt them with rotten eggs. In his opinion the slaves were "fat and lazy niggers," laughing from morning till night, and the slave-owners men as gentle, as generous and as good as ever breathed.[4] The West Indian monopoly cost the English people nothing.[5] Manchester turned him down, and his conversion to the cause came too late.

Manchester was openly in favor of the campaign on behalf of East India sugar. On May 4, 1821, the Manchester Chamber of Commerce presented a petition to the House of Commons deprecating a preference to one colony over another, and particularly a preference to a settlement of slaves over a nation of free men.[6] In 1833 Manchester advocated the admission of Brazilian sugar for refining. Mark Philips, its representative in Parliament, spoke briefly but tersely on the vast importance of the subject to the great seat of the cotton manufacture which he represented. He emphasized the hardships imposed on ships having to return from Brazil without cargoes, and argued that the encouragement of sugar refining would increase employment for the industrious laboring classes.[7]

In this single name Philips is summed up the whole evolution of Manchester and its cotton industry. In 1749 the firm of J. N. Philips and Company was deeply engaged in the West Indian trade. In 1832 Mark Philips was elected as one of the two members to represent Manchester, for the first time, in the Reformed Parliament.[8] Philips' West Indian connections still persisted. A relative of Robert Hibbert, he was selected by the latter as one of the first board of trustees to administer the Robert Hibbert Trust.[9] But economically his connections with the West Indies were over. He was opposed to the foul blot of slavery, a sentiment which aroused cheers at a dinner given in the town to celebrate his election. Mr. Hadfield's eloquent humanitarianism on the same occasion evoked loud applause. "I appeal to you . . . if liberty could possibly be enjoyed by any rational men without the desire to communicate it to others? . . . Shall the mere distinction of black and white for ever cause one race to be slaves while another is free? Shall it always be that one man should be a slave because he is black, and another be free because he is white? . . . I tell you, that until we wash out this foul pollution from the institutions of our country, liberty itself is not safe anywhere."[10] The foul pollution was not slavery but monopoly. Manchester was interested not in the Holy Scriptures but in the census returns.

After 1833 the Manchester capitalists were all for free trade in sugar, which meant slave-grown sugar. Philips supported the equalization of the East Indian sugar duties. The planters had had their compensation and should not get a farthing more.[11] In 1839 he was for the equalization of the duties on all foreign sugar, for it was the duty of Parliament to lower the prices of all the necessities of life and afford every encouragement to the valuable trade with Brazil.[12] John Bright and Milner Gibson, who at one time was Vice-President of the Board of Trade, held the free trade flag aloft. They argued that the protecting duty to the West Indians forced the British working class to pay higher prices for sugar and so took away from them the money earned in the factories.[13] They called the duty an "obnoxious tax,"[14] a "species of parliamentary charity,"[15] which was more than the cost of production. If the Brazilians could grow sugar for nothing, if their sugar rained down from the skies, if the West Indian planters had stolen their sugar, it would have made no difference.[16] Protection, said John Bright, was an opiate which made the planters everlasting grumblers—like Oliver Twist always asking for more.[17] The cotton manufacturers, he boasted, asked for no protection and needed none,[18] conveniently forgetting the protection they had asked for a century and a half earlier against Indian goods and ignorant of the protection they would ask for three-quarters of a century later against Japanese textiles. The free traders, Bright warned, might be defeated, but they would return to the charge with renewed energy.[19] The planters' demands were impudent;[20] it was not the duty of Parliament to make sugar cultivation profitable,[21] and Bright advised them to grow cloves and nutmegs.[22]

B.   THE IRONMASTERS

As early as 1788 an abolition society was started in Birmingham and a liberal subscription collected for the cause.[23] In this society the ironmasters were prominent. Three of the Lloyd family, with their banking interests as well, were on the committee. The dominant figure, however, was Samuel Garbett.[24] Garbett was an outstanding figure of the Industrial Revolution, more reminiscent of the twentieth than the eighteenth century. In his breadth of vision, the scope of his activities, the multiplicity of his interests, he reminds us of Samuel Touchet. Like Touchet a partner in the spinning enterprise of Wyatt and Paul, Garbett was an associate of Roebuck's in the Carron Works, a shareholder with Boulton and Watt in the Albion Mills and in the copper mines of Cornwall. "There were indeed," writes Ashton, "few sides of the industrial and commercial life of his day that he did not touch." In addition his energy was thrown into the politics of industry rather than into the details of administration. He became the ironmaster's spokesman to the government.[25] This was a dangerous man indeed to have as an opponent, for Garbett, in the larger sense, was Birmingham.

At a meeting of many respectable inhabitants of Birmingham on January 28, 1788, Samuel Garbett presiding, it was decided to send a petition to Parliament. The petition stated, *inter alia*, that, "as inhabitants of a manufacturing town and neighbourhood your petitioners have the commercial interests of this kingdom very deeply at heart; but cannot conceal their detestation of any commerce which always originates in violence, and too often terminates in cruelty." Gustavus Vasa, an African, visited Birmingham, and received a sympathetic welcome.[26]

This was not to say that Birmingham was unanimous or single-minded on the issue of abolition. The manufacturers still interested in the slave trade held counter-meetings and sent counter-petitions to Parliament.[27] But Samuel Garbett, the Lloyds and others of that caliber were, from the West Indian standpoint, on the wrong side of the fence.

In 1832 Birmingham was the center of that agitation which, led by the ironmaster Attwood, brought England to the verge of revolution and culminated in the Reform Bill of 1832. Again the town was divided on the emancipation issue. A public meeting held in the Assembly Room of the Royal Hotel on April 16, 1833, was of a noisy and turbulent character and ended in disorder, the proprietor claiming damages for broken chairs and glass.[28] Birmingham was one of the many industrial centers which voted in 1833 for a shorter period of "apprenticeship" under which, by the Emancipation Act, Negro slavery was perpetuated in a modified form. Joseph Sturge was a prominent figure in the emancipation struggle. After 1833 Sturge took the lead in England in protest against the apprenticeship system. With the abolitionist Gurney he sailed to the West Indies in 1836 "with the benevolent idea of making personal inquiries as to the state of the Negro population, in the hope of obtaining further amelioration of their condition." His safe return the following year was celebrated by a public breakfast in his honor at the Town Hall, in appreciation of "his unwearied philanthropic exertions in the cause of negro emancipation."[29] This was nineteenth century and no longer eighteenth century Birmingham, and yet another vested interest had turned against the colonial system.

With Birmingham may profitably be considered Sheffield, the center of the steel industry. Sheffield's interest in the colonial system had at most been slight; "with no vested interest in the maintenance of colonial slavery, (it) offered a favourable field for the abolitionist." Sheffield, like Manchester, Birmingham and other centers of industry, was unrepresented in Parliament before 1832. It formed a part of the county of York whose representative was first Wilberforce and then Brougham—both outstanding abolitionists. "I am an advocate for the abolition of West Indian slavery," campaigned Brougham in the town in 1830, "and both root and branch I will tear it up. I have loosened it already, and if you will assist me, I will brandish it over your heads."[30]

Some part of Sheffield's assistance can be attributed to its interest in the East. In 1825 the abolitionists began a boycott of West Indian produce and urged the consumption, instead, of the sugar and rum of India. Sheffield was the center of this movement. An auxiliary society was formed in the same year for the relief of the Negro slaves. The committee organized a thorough campaign in the town. Each member took two streets in order to make a canvass as to the practicability of inducing housekeepers to adopt the use of East India produce. The committee estimated that for every six families who used East India sugar one slave less was required in the West Indies—obviously a far-fetched argument, but any stick was good enough for beating the West Indians, so long as the West Indians were beaten. "Surely," the committee urged their fellow townsmen, "to release a fellow-creature from the state of cruel bondage and misery, by so small a sacrifice, is worthy the attention of all." Sheffield rose to the occasion: the sale of East India sugar doubled in six months.[31]

In May, 1833, the Anti-Slavery Society of the town forwarded a memorial to the Prime Minister urging immediate rather than gradual emancipation.[32] To the end it protested against compensation to the slave owners and the apprenticeship scheme, and Sheffield, like Birmingham, voted ultimately for terminating the apprenticeship in the shortest possible time.[33]

C. THE WOOLEN INDUSTRY

The woolen industry, too, joined the chorus of opposition. Wilberforce and Brougham spoke, not only for the humanitarians, but also for the woolen centers. Was the House, asked Mr. Strickland for Yorkshire in 1833, to take freedom of commerce and the extension of the employment of capital as the rule in legislating, or was it to increase monopolies by restrictions? He gave the answer himself: all monopolies ought to be removed, as destructive to the progress of commerce.[34]

John Bright in cotton, Samuel Garbett in iron. These were mighty names, to be joined by one mightier still, speaking for the woolen industry—Richard Cobden. On the question of the West Indian monopoly the evangelist of free trade and the leader of the Anti-Corn Law League spoke with a vigor, a logic and a popular support that were irresistible.

The West Indians' claim to the monopoly was, in principle, an audacity. There was a time, thundered Cobden, resurrecting the shades of the Long Parliament and Charles I, when no member would have dared to rise in Parliament to make a claim on the ground of a monopoly.[35] Men of business would calculate the cost, and could not be expected to be satisfied if they found themselves paying half as much in expenses as the whole value of the colonial trade.[36] If Britain had made a present to the planters of her exports, in return for free trade with Brazil and Cuba, she would actually have gained.[37] Then what sort of trade was this? "It was precisely as if a shopkeeper should give, with every pound's worth of goods, half a sovereign to his customer." The House of Commons conducted business with less wisdom than was required for the successful management of a chandler's shop.[38]

On the argument that the differential duty in favor of West Indian sugar was intended to prohibit the consumption of slave-grown sugar Cobden poured withering scorn. What right had a people who were the largest distributors of textiles to go to Brazil with their ships full of cotton goods manufactured from slave-grown material, and then turn up the whites of their eyes, shed crocodile tears over the slaves and refuse to take slave-grown sugar in return?[39] The situation was farcical, and Cobden wrote a skit on it in the form of an imaginary interview at the Board of Trade between Lord Ripon and the Brazilian Ambassador. The Ambassador taunts the embarrassed Lord Ripon: "No religious scruples against sending slave-grown cottons into every country in the world? No religious scruples against eating slave-grown rice? No religious scruples against smoking slave-grown tobacco? No religious scruples against taking slave-grown snuff?. ... Am I to understand that the religious scruples of the English people are confined to the article of sugar?" Ripon, obviously uncomfortable, reiterates his inability to take Brazilian sugar, and pleads, in defence, the promptings of the Anti-Slavery Party led by Joseph Sturge. At this moment in walks Sturge, with a cotton cravat, a hat lined with calico, a coat sewn with cotton thread, pockets well lined with slave wrought gold and sliver. The two diplomats burst into laughter.[40]

Logic, if not humanity, was on Cobden's side. So was the Anti-Slavery Party. That party, he boasted with justice, had had its strength and headquarters in the industrial towns, and was now in the ranks of the Corn Law repealers.[41] He and they spoke with one voice. "I am the representative of the woollen industry," he asserted in 1848, "an indigenous industry, of which there is no jealousy in this House. ... I am the representative of a county which was eminent in the slavery movement. ... Now, I unhesitatingly assert that nearly all the men who led the agitation for the emancipation of the slaves, and who by their influence on public opinion aided in producing that result, are against those hon. Gentlemen in this House who advocate a differential duty on foreign sugar with a view to put down slavery abroad."[42]

D. LIVERPOOL AND GLASGOW

Perhaps the most bitter fact for the West Indians was that Liverpool, too, turned and bit the hand that had fed it. In 1807 there were still seventy-two slave traders in the town, and it was from Liverpool that the last of the English slave traders,

Captain Hugh Crow, sailed just before the abolition bill became effective.[43] But if Tarleton continued his opposition in Parliament to so necessary a measure as the abolition of the British slave trade to the foreign sugar colonies,[44] in 1807 Liverpool was also represented by William Roscoe, whose anti-slavery sentiments have already been noticed.

Whilst Liverpool still carried on the slave trade in 1807, the slave trade had become less vital to the port's existence. In 1792 one out of every twelve ships belonging to the port was engaged in the slave trade; in 1807 one out of every twenty-four.[45] In 1772, when 101 Liverpool ships were engaged in the slave trade, the dock duties were £4,552; in 1779, when, as a result of the American Revolution, only eleven ships sailed from Liverpool to Africa, the dock duties were £4,957.[46] In 1824 they were £130,000.[47] Clearly abolition could not ruin Liverpool. As Roscoe stated, the inhabitants of the town were not unanimous in opposing abolition, and to those who would be affected by the measure, he held out the enticing prospect of a trade with India by pleading that the abrogation of the East India Company's monopoly would be compensation for any loss which the abolition of the slave trade might inflict on British merchants.[48]

But if Liverpool turned against the slave trade, it still retained its interest in slavery. It was no longer, however, West Indian slavery but American, no longer sugar but cotton. The American cotton trade became the most important single trade of Liverpool. In 1802 half of Britain's cotton imports came through Liverpool, in 1812 two-thirds, in 1833 nine-tenths.[49] Liverpool had built up Manchester in the eighteenth century; Manchester blazed the trail in the nineteenth and Liverpool trudged obediently behind. In the age of mercantilism Manchester was Liverpool's hinterland, in the age of laissez faire Liverpool was Manchester's suburb.

Liverpool followed the free-trade lead given by the cotton capital. Among its representatives after 1807 it selected Canning and Huskisson, men who spoke the language of free trade, if in somewhat subdued tones. Exclusive privileges, said Huskisson in 1830, were out of fashion,[50] thereby earning the magnificent service of plate the town had bestowed on him as a "testimony of (her) sense of the benefits derived to the nation at large from the enlightened system of commercial policy brought forward by him as President of the Board of Trade."[51] Any minister, said its new representative Ewart in 1833, thinking of Manchester's goods, who should continue to impose fetters on British commerce deserved to be impeached.[52] The merchants and shipowners of the town petitioned Parliament in the same year, praying that the exclusive colonial monopoly of the home market be considered.[53] There was a powerful Brazilian Association in the town, emphasizing that, as a result of the West Indian monopoly, more than two millions of British capital were forced into other channels, giving employment to foreign shipping and paying to foreigners freights, commissions and charges, to the great loss of British shipowners.[54] The merchants and shipowners of Liverpool expressed the hope that while Parliament was legislating for the benefit of slaves in distant colonies, it would also consider the present condition and future welfare of the laboring population at home.[55]

In Glasgow, too, the West Indians lost another friend. The days of Macdowall and the sugar heiresses were over. The change can be symbolized in the vicissitudes of one Glasgow family. In the eighteenth century a humble citizen of the town, Richard Oswald, migrated to London. There, through a fortunate marriage with an heiress of great sugar plantations, he made his fortune.[56] He was for years a large dealer in slaves, owning his own factory on Bence Island in the mouth of the Sierra Leone River.[57] The wealth eventually passed to James Oswald, Glasgow's first representative in the Reformed Parliament. In 1833 Oswald presented a petition, bearing the signatures of many respectable men, praying for a reduction of the excessive duties levied on Brazilian sugar imported for refining.[58]

E. THE SUGAR REFINERS

In the nineteenth century no less than in the eighteenth Britain's ambitious plan was to become the sugar emporium of the world, to sweeten the world's tea and coffee as the Industrial Revolution had permitted her to clothe the world. This world view was in conflict not only with the declining importance of West Indian production relative to world production, but also with the persistent determination of the West Indian planters to restrict their cultivation in order to maintain monopoly prices.

The slave insurrection in Saint Domingue sent the prices of sugar in the European market spiralling. Prices rose by fifty per cent between September, 1788, and April, 1793.[59] The sugar refiners of England sent a petition to Parliament in 1792. They were no longer as modest as they had been forty years before. They blamed the evils of the West Indian monopoly, pointed to "the decay of their once flourishing manufactory," prayed for the admission of foreign sugar in British ships at higher duties, and demanded the equalization of the duties on East and British West Indian sugar.[60] Sabotage had begun, right in the West Indian planter's backyard. Public opinion unjustly blamed the refiners for the high prices.[61] But a committee set up at a public meeting to consider means of reducing the price of sugar exonerated the refiners and advocated the admission of East India sugar on equal terms as "an act of justice."[62]

The Indian question, as we have seen, was sidetracked when the rich Saint Domingan plum was dangled before the eyes of the British Government. But the issue was revived in the 1820's, when India needed to export some raw material with which to pay for British manufactures. Competition with American cotton was impossible,[63] so Indian traders, it was urged, had to choose between sugar and the sands of the Ganges.[64] The East Indians spoke free trade but their real aim was to share the West Indian monopoly of the home market. Here they and the refiners parted company. As Ricardo put it: "No exclusive protection should be granted to either the East or the West Indies, and we should be free to import our sugar from any quarter whatever. No possible injury could arise from this."[65]

The situation of the sugar refiners in 1831 was desperate. The West Indians had a monopoly of the home market. Indian sugar could be imported only at excessive duties, except for re-export. Annual acts were passed by Parliament permitting the importation of Brazilian and Cuban sugar solely for refining and re-exportation. This was clearly unsatisfactory. There was a large capital invested in the sugar refining industry, estimated at between three and four millions in 1831.[66] As a result of the prohibition of all but British West Indian sugar the industry was on the verge of ruin. The higher costs of British West Indian sugar meant that continental refiners were displacing the British in all the European markets. In 1830 there were 224 pans at work in London; in 1833 less than one-third that number. Two-thirds of the sugar refining trade in the entire country was at a complete standstill.[67]

Were the West Indian interests, asked John Wood for the sugar refiners of Preston, alone to be regarded?[68] Would Parliament, "to gratify monopolists, consent to ruin our future resources"?[69] Britain, said Huskisson of the Board of Trade, might be made the entrepôt of the sugar of the world, and might thereby give employment to her idle men and idle capital in refining that sugar for the markets of Europe. Indeed, he knew of no channel in which capital might be more beneficially employed than in sugar refining.[70] Relief from the West Indian monopoly, said William Clay for the sugar refining district of the Tower Hamlets, "would be cheaply purchased by granting the West India proprietors the full amount of the compensation proposed."[71]

This was going too fast for a government still dominated, in 1832, by the landed aristocracy and therefore sympathetic to its colonial brethren. The government adopted a temporary compromise. In return for emancipation, the right of the West Indians to the monopoly of the home market was confirmed, whilst the unrestricted importation of foreign sugar was permitted but only for refining and export to Europe.

The situation was fantastic. The explanation offered was that Brazilian and Cuban sugar was slave-grown. But so were American cotton and Brazilian coffee. If the same restrictions had been applied to foreign cotton as were applied to foreign sugar, what would have become of Britain's industrial pre-eminence in the world? The distinction between free-grown and slave-grown products was a principle for individual agency, not a

rule which could direct international commerce.[72] The capitalists wanted only cheap sugar. They could see only one thing, that
it was "monstrous" to have to depend for their supply on sugar
produced at a monopoly price.[73] They could not, as Lord Lansdowne put it, try things by a special thermometer, which rose
to boiling point on Cuban sugar, and sank to a most agreeable
temperature on Carolina cotton.[74]

F. SHIPPING AND SEAMEN

The West Indians had always pointed, in justification of their
system, to their contribution to the naval supremacy of England.
Thanks to the researches of Clarkson, England learned the price
she had to pay for this contribution. Bearding the lion in his den,
Clarkson, at much personal risk, roamed the docks of Liverpool,
Bristol and London, questioned seamen, examined muster rolls
and collected evidence which was a terrific indictment of the
effects of the slave trade, not now upon the blacks, but upon the
whites.

According to Clarkson, the proportion of deaths in the slave
trade compared to those in the Newfoundland trade was as
twenty to one.[75] Wilberforce estimated the annual losses at
one-fourth of the sailors.[76] From the muster rolls of Liverpool
and Bristol he showed Parliament that on 350 slave vessels, with
12,263 seamen, there were 2,643 deaths—twenty-one and a half
per cent—in twelve months, whereas of 462 ships engaged in
the West Indian trade, with 7,640 seamen there were only 118
deaths in seven months—or less than three per cent annually.[77]
William Smith exploded the fallacy that the slave trade was
responsible for introducing many "landsmen" to the marine.
The proportion of the landsmen, from the Bristol muster rolls,
was one-twelfth; in Liverpool it was one-sixteenth.[78] According to Lord Howick, the losses among seamen in the slave trade
were eight times the losses in the West Indian trade, and the
former was unique in the readiness with which men deserted it
on their arrival in the West Indies for the King's ships.[79] The
Abolition Committee declared that the mortality in the slave
trade was more than double that of all the other branches of
commerce in the kingdom.[80] John Newton, an authority on

the subject, spoke of the "truly alarming" loss in the slave trade.[81] Ramsay summed up the general feeling: "It forms not but destroys seamen. And this destruction of seamen is a strong argument for the abolition of it. If we have any regard to the lives of seamen, we ought to abandon a branch of trade which dissipates the men in so unprofitable a manner."[82]

By 1807 the shipowners' interest in the slave trade had declined considerably. On the average of ten years preceding 1800 the capital invested in the slave trade was less than five per cent of the total export trade of the country; in 1807 it was one and a quarter per cent. In 1805 two per cent of British export tonnage, excluding Ireland and the coastal trade, was employed in the slave trade, only four per cent of the seamen engaged in general trade.[83]

The shipowners, too, began to find the West Indian monopoly irksome. They were promised that equalization of the duties on East India sugar would give employment to forty per cent more shipping.[84] British shipping engaged in the trade to India increased four times between 1812 and 1828, and Huskisson admitted that the difficulty was to find returns from India.[85]

The shipowners were equally alive to the value of Brazilian sugar. Poulett Thomson of the Board of Trade emphasized that the importation of foreign sugar for refining was most beneficial to the interests of the British shipowners.[86] According to Ewart, such an importation would furnish freight for 120,000 tons of shipping annually from Brazil alone, while Santo Domingo (Spanish), Cuba, Manila and Singapore would provide cargoes for a further 200,000 tons.[87] Mark Philips told the House a piteous tale of vessels returning from Brazil empty—in 1832 fifty-one vessels sailed from Liverpool to Rio de Janeiro, not one of which could get a return cargo home.[88] According to William Clay, of four British vessels which had sailed monthly from Liverpool to Brazil in 1832, not one had returned with the produce with which their cargoes had been purchased.[89]

The shipowners were all for free trade, but only when someone else's monopoly was involved. In 1825 the Navigation Laws were modified. The British West Indies were given permission to trade with every part of the world. This was the thin edge of the wedge. In 1848 the Navigation Laws, the very heart and core of the colonial system, were swept away by the full tide of laissez faire as the lumber of former times. Ricardo ridiculed the roundabout and expensive way whereby exchanges of produce were carried on. He quoted one instance where American hides were taken from Marseilles to Rotterdam. Not finding a market, they were taken back to Marseilles, whence they were sent to Liverpool. At Liverpool they were seized on the ground that they were imported in a French vessel, and released only on the condition that they should be sent back to New York. The Spaniard, Ricardo continued, was not permitted by the English Navigation Laws to take in a cargo of sugar at Cuba for delivery to a French port, where he would take in wine for England. In England he would be met by a custom house officer, who would tell him that he could not land his cargo. "Why?" the Spaniard would inquire. "I understood you wanted wine." "So we do," the officer would reply. Then the Spaniard would say, "I will exchange my wine for your earthenware." "That will not do," replies the officer. "It must be brought by Frenchmen on a French ship." "But the French do not want your earthenware." "We cannot help that," the officer replies. "We must not let you violate our Navigation Laws." If the Spaniards wanted earthenware, concluded Ricardo, the French sugar, and the English wine, "why on earth should we forbid the natural course of the transaction?"[90]

The shipowners would have none of it. They had voted against the monopoly of corn and the monopoly of sugar but would not relinquish the monopoly of shipping. Where corn and sugar were on the run, shipping could enjoy no immunity. In 1848 the Navigation Laws were repealed. The final nail was driven into the coffin of mercantilism when Ricardo advised the advocates of the "long voyage" to sail their cargo three times round the British Isles.[91]

· 10 ·

"THE COMMERCIAL PART

OF THE NATION"

AND SLAVERY

THE CAPITALISTS had first encouraged West Indian slavery and then helped to destroy it. When British capitalism depended on the West Indies, they ignored slavery or defended it. When British capitalism found the West Indian monopoly a nuisance, they destroyed West Indian slavery as the first step in the destruction of West Indian monopoly. That slavery to them was relative not absolute, and depended on latitude and longitude, is proved after 1833 by their attitude to slavery in Cuba, Brazil and the United States. They taunted their opponents with seeing slavery only where they saw sugar and limiting their observation to the circumference of a hogshead.[1] They refused to frame their tariff on grounds of morality, erect a pulpit in every custom house, and make their landing-waiters enforce anti-slavery doctrines.[2]

Before and after 1815 the British government tried to bribe the Spanish and Portuguese governments into abolition of the slave trade—in 1818 Spain was given £400,000 in return for a promise to do so. All to no avail. The treaties were treated as scraps of paper, as abolition would have ruined Cuba and Brazil. The British government, therefore, urged on by the West Indians, decided to adopt more drastic measures. Wellington was sent to the international conference at Verona to

169

propose that the Continental Powers boycott the produce of countries still engaged in the slave trade. If he were met with the inquiry, whether Britain was similarly prepared to exclude the produce of slave-trading countries imported not for consumption but in transit, he was to express his readiness to refer that proposition for immediate consideration to his government.[3] These instructions did little justice to the perspicacity of the Continental statesmen. Wellington's proposal was received in silence, and he observed "those symptoms of disapprobation and dissent which convince me not only that it will not be adopted, but that the suggestion of it is attributed to interested motives not connected with the humane desire of abolishing the slave trade!"[4] As Canning reported to his cabinet: "The proposed refusal to admit Brazilian sugar into the dominions of the Emperors* and the King of Prussia was met (as might be expected) with a smile; which indicated on the part of the continental statesmen a suspicion that there might be something of self-interest in our suggestion for excluding the produce of rival colonies from competition with our own, and their surprise that we should consent to be the carriers of the produce which we would fain dissuade them from consuming."[5]

It was clearly what a member of Parliament was later to call "lucrative humanity."[6] The independence of Brazil gave Canning a better opportunity. Recognition in return for abolition.[7] But there was a danger that France would recognize Brazil on condition that the slave trade be continued.[8] What then of the British carrying trade and British exports? "There are immense British interests engaged in the trade with Brazil," Canning reminded Wilberforce, "and we must proceed with caution and good heed; and take the commercial as well as moral feelings of the country with us."[9] Morality or profit? Britain had to choose. "You argue," wrote Canning candidly to Wilberforce, "against the acknowledgment of Brazil unpurged of Slave Trade ... you are surprised that the Duke of Wellington has not been instructed to say that he will give up the trade with

---

*Of Russia and Austria-Hungary.

Brazil, (for that is, I am afraid, the amount of giving up the import and re-export of the sugar and cotton), if Austria, Russia and Prussia will prohibit her produce. In fair reasoning, you have a right to be surprised, for we ought to be ready to make sacrifices when we ask them, and I am for making them; but who would dare to promise such a one as this without a full knowledge of the opinions of the commercial part of the nation?"[10]

The commercial part of the nation did not leave Canning long in doubt. A bill had already been presented in Parliament in 1815 to proscribe the slave trade as an investment for British capital. Baring, of the great banking house which was to have such intimate relations with independent Spanish America, issued a solemn warning that every commercial organization in Britain would petition against it,[11] and the House of Lords threw it out.[12] In 1824 one hundred and seventeen merchants of London petitioned for the recognition of the independence of South America—the petitioners were, in a word, the city of London.[13] The President, Vice-President and members of the Chamber of Commerce of Manchester declared that the opening of the South American market to British industry would be an event which must produce the most beneficial results to British commerce.[14] British capitalism could no longer be content with smuggling.

This South American market, Brazil in particular, was based on slave labor and required the slave trade. The British capitalists, therefore, began a vigorous campaign against their government's policy of forcible suppression of the slave trade by stationing warships on the African coast. The policy was expensive, exceeding the annual value of the total trade with Africa. African exports were £154,000 in 1824; imports £118,000 in British goods and £119,000 in foreign. This was the great extent of commerce, said Hume, for which the country was to make such a vast sacrifice of human life on the deadly slave coast.[15] Humanity for English sailors demanded its abandonment. If some abolitionists were suffering from a humane delusion, why should they be allowed to delude the English Parliament?[16] The British people could not afford to become purchasers on such extravagant terms of indulgences for Africa.[17]

All this was before 1833, contemporaneous with the capitalist attacks on West Indian slavery. After 1833 the capitalists were still involved in the slave trade itself. British goods, from Manchester and Liverpool, cottons, fetters and shackles, were sent direct to the coast of Africa or indirectly to Rio de Janeiro and Havana, where they were used by their Cuban and Brazilian consignees for the purpose of purchasing slaves.[18] It was said that seven-tenths of the goods used by Brazil for slave purchases were British manufactures,[19] and it was whispered that the British were reluctant to destroy the barracoons on the coast because they would thereby destroy British calicoes.[20] In 1845 Peel refused to deny the fact that British subjects were engaged in the slave trade.[21] The Liverpool representative in Parliament, questioned point blank, was not prepared to contradict that Liverpool exports to Africa or elsewhere were appropriated to "some improper purpose."[22] British banking firms in Brazil financed the slave traders and insured their cargoes, thereby earning the goodwill of their hosts. British mining companies owned and purchased slaves whose labor they employed in their enterprises. "We must needs adopt the painful conclusion," said Brougham with reference to Cuban and Brazilian development, "that in great part at least such an ample amount of capital as was required, must have belonged to the rich men of this country."[23] John Bright was well aware of the interests of his Lancashire constituents when he argued eloquently in 1843 against a bill prohibiting the employment of British capital, however indirectly, in the slave trade on the ground that it would be a dead letter, and that the matter should be left to the honorable and moral feelings of individuals.[24] In that very year, British firms handled three-eighths of the sugar, one-half of the coffee, five-eighths of the cotton exported from Pernambuco, Rio de Janeiro and Bahia.[25]

The capitalists had had enough of Britain's "noble experiment." Commerce was the great emancipator.[26] The only way to put down slavery was to trust to the eternal and just principles of free trade.[27] Leave the slave trade alone, it would commit suicide. If the miscreants of any nation chose to engage in it, their guilt be upon their own heads; leave to a higher tribunal the moral government of the world.[28] The money expended in fruitless efforts to suppress the slave trade could be more beneficially and philosophically employed at home.[29] Bright criticized as audacity the idea that justice to Africa should be done at the expense of injustice to England.[30] They had a great deal to do at home, argued Cobden, within a stone's throw of the Houses of Parliament, before they embarked on a scheme of redeeming from barbarism the whole of Africa.[31] The activities of the British squadron on the African coast were described as buccaneering expeditions,[32] which weeded England annually of her best and bravest and desolated countless English firesides.[33] There were other occasions on which to devote attention to the social happiness of the world, other means of endeavoring to advance that happiness, and they should not interfere violently by fiscal regulations with the feelings of others.[34] Public opinion in the slave trading countries must be won over to the cause of humanity, not alienated by a policy of coercion, and the Brazilians could not be expected to travel the humanitarian road faster than the English had done.[35] Britain's "blundering and ignorant humanity" had only aggravated the sufferings of the slaves.[36] They had used, said Hutt, "the utmost latitude, one might say licentiousness, of means—public money to any extent—naval armaments watching every shore and every sea where a slave ship could be seen or suspected—courts of special judicature in half of the intertropical regions of the globe—diplomatic influence and agency such perhaps as this country never before concentrated on any public object."[37] Despite all this, the slave trade had increased. It was a wild crusade, and not all the forces of the British Navy, not all the resources of the British Treasury could suppress it.[38] They had been laboring for thirty years, and not even a lunatic would entertain any optimistic illusion about their future success.[39] Had the British government surrendered its reason to philanthropy?[40] Had it prostituted its diplomacy to the purposes of an unreasonable fanaticism?[41] It was curious to see administrations, not distinguished by devotion to constitutional liberties at home, assuming that a distant and barbarous people had more claims on their conscience than their own countrymen.[42] The nations were disgusted with "this philanthropic cant."[43] These vagaries, this rash and idle system[44] must be abandoned, as sinster and spurious philanthropy,[45] costly and abortive experiments,[46] which hazarded the peace of the world.[47] The laws of Heaven did not authorize the British people to keep the whole world in a pother about the slave trade.[48]

Where was Palmerston? The slave trade has been called Palmerston's "benevolent crotchet" and he emerges in our textbooks as the persistent opponent of the slave trade. In office Palmerston accomplished little. Out of office he goaded the government to greater efforts to accomplish what he had failed to do. A simple motion for returns of the slave trade between 1815 and 1843 was accompanied by a speech which fills over twenty-five columns in Hansard; a rhetorical display crowned by a magnificent peroration, which might have been culled from anti-slavery speeches of the last half-century, accompanied a simple innocuous motion.[49] As if he were appealing to Parliament and the country for full appreciation of his labors in the cause, once every month he drew attention to those labors.[50] But when Manchester's representative emphasized the difficulties which Britain's suppression policy was causing with the Brazilian government and deprecated armed interference, Palmerston spoke about France, Cuba, the Imaum of Muscat, everything but the Brazilian slave trade.[51] And with the parliamentary campaign against the suppression policy at its height, Palmerston contented himself with the hope that "no Committee will recommend a course the reverse of that which we have been pursuing . . . . no one will be found to say that we ought to retrace our steps."[52] They had given proof, he thought, of their zeal for the suppression of the slave trade, and if they prohibited the importation of Brazilian sugar, Brazil would think that they did not really believe that free labor was cheaper than slave.[53] In urging the Spanish claim to reciprocity, he warned that they would lose their trade with Spain (Cuba) as they were losing it with Brazil, all because of the "absurd tariff and mischievous policy" of the government. "They have sacrificed the commercial interests of the country in the Brazilian trade, in the Spanish trade, and I fear, also in other quarters about to follow, and all for the purpose of maintaining a favourite crotchet, based upon hypocritical pretences."[54] The "last candle of the nineteenth century" had been snuffed out.

Disraeli, too, condemned the suppression of the slave trade on grounds of economy and as questionable policy which involved Britain in difficulties in every court and in every colony.[55] Wellington called it criminal—"a breach of the law of nations—a breach of treaties."[56] Even Gladstone was forced to choose between the needs of the British capitalists and the needs of the West Indian planters. In 1841 he was all for suppression, and asked the capitalists whether, for small and paltry pecuniary advantages, they were prepared to forgo the high title and noble character they had earned before the whole world. Were they dragging every inconsistency into the light for the purpose of using it as a plea for further and more monstrous inconsistency, or in order to substitute a uniformity in wrong for an inconsistent acknowledgment of what was right?[57] In 1850, however, he condemned the policy of suppression as anomalous and preposterous. "It is not an ordinance of Providence that the government of one nation shall correct the morals of another."[58]

Ironically enough, it was the former slave owners of the West Indies who now held the humanitarian torch. Those who, in 1807, were lugubriously prophesying that abolition of the British slave trade would "occasion diminished commerce, diminished revenue and diminished navigation; and in the end sap and totally remove the great cornerstone of British prosperity,"[59] were, after 1807, the very men who protested against "a system of man-stealing against a poor and inoffensive people."[60] Barham, a West Indian, introduced the bill of 1815 to make penal the employment of British capital in the foreign slave trade, and even to make the insurance of ships in the slave trade criminal.[61] Among the remedies suggested by the West India interest in 1830 to meet the increasing distress of the colonies was a resolution "to adopt more decisive measures than any that have hitherto been employed to stop the foreign slave trade; on the effectual suppression of which the prosperity of the British West Indian colonies ... ultimately depend(s)."[62] Jamaican envoys, sent to Britain in 1832, declared that "the colonies were easily reconciled to the abolition of a barbarous commerce, which the advanced civilization of the age no longer permitted to exist; but they have thought, and apparently with reason, that the philanthropists should not have been satisfied with the extinction of the British trade."[63] A great mass movement for abolition of the slave trade developed in Jamaica in 1849. All classes, colors, parties and sects were united on the question of justice to Africa. They denounced the slave trade and slavery as "opposed to humanity—productive of the worst evils to Africa—degrading to all engaged in the traffic, and inimical to the moral and spiritual interests of the enslaved," and pleaded that "the odious term 'slave' (be) expunged from the vocabulary of the universe." "SLAVERY MUST FALL, and, when it falls, JAMAICA WILL FLOURISH." England, they declared pointedly, had gone to war for less justifiable causes.[64]

The British capitalists, however, remained unimpressed. In 1857 an editorial in the London *Times* declared: "We know that for all mercantile purposes England is one of the States, and that, in effect, we are partners with the Southern planter; we hold a bill of sale over his goods and chattels, his live and dead stock, and take a lion's share in the profits of slavery. ... We fête Mrs. Stowe, cry over her book, and pray for an anti-slavery president..., but all this time we are clothing not only ourselves, but all the world besides, with the very cotton picked and cleaned by 'Uncle Tom' and his fellow-sufferers. It is our trade. It is the great staple of British industry. We are Mr. 'Legree's' agents for the manufacture and sale of his cotton crops."[65] British capitalism had destroyed West Indian slavery, but it continued to thrive on Brazilian, Cuban and American slavery. But West Indian monopoly had gone for ever. In the Civil War the British government nearly recognized the Confederacy. By a supreme irony it was left for the West Indian, Gladstone, to remind an audience in Newcastle that the American Civil War had "perhaps become the most purposeless of all great civil wars that have ever been waged," and that "there is no doubt that Jefferson Davis and other leaders of the South have made an army; they are making, it appears, a navy; and they have made what is more than either, they have made a nation."[66]

· 11 ·

THE "SAINTS" AND SLAVERY

THIS STUDY has deliberately subordinated the inhumanity of the slave system and the humanitarianism which destroyed that system. To disregard it completely, however, would be to commit a grave historical error and to ignore one of the greatest propaganda movements of all time. The humanitarians were the spearhead of the onslaught which destroyed the West Indian system and freed the Negro. But their importance has been seriously misunderstood and grossly exaggerated by men who have sacrificed scholarship to sentimentality and, like the scholastics of old, placed faith before reason and evidence. Professor Coupland, in an imaginary interview with Wilberforce, asks him: "What do you think, sir, is the primary significance of your work, the lesson of the abolition of the slave system?" The instant answer is: "It was God's work. It signifies the triumph of His will over human selfishness. It teaches that no obstacle of interest or prejudice is irremovable by faith and prayer."[1]

This misunderstanding springs, in part, from a deliberate attempt by contemporaries to present a distorted view of the abolitionist movement. When the slave trade was abolished in 1807, the bill included a phrase to the effect that the trade was "contrary to the principles of justice, humanity and sound policy." Lord Hawkesbury objected; in his opinion the words "justice and humanity" reflected on the slave traders. He therefore moved an amendment excluding those words. In so doing he confined the necessity of abolition solely to expediency.

The Lord Chancellor protested. The amendment would take away the only ground on which the other powers could be asked to co-operate in abolition. The Earl of Lauderdale declared that the words omitted were the most essential in the bill. The omission would lend color to the suspicion in France that British abolition was dictated by the selfish motive that her colonies were well-stocked with Negroes. "How, in thus being supposed to make no sacrifice ourselves, could we call with any effect upon foreign powers to co-operate in the abolition?" The Lords voted for the original version.[2]

The British humanitarians were a brilliant band. Clarkson personifies all the best in the humanitarianism of the age. One can appreciate even today his feelings when, in ruminating upon the subject of his prize-winning essay, he first awoke to the realization of the enormous injustice of slavery. Clarkson was an indefatigable worker, who conducted endless and dangerous researches into the conditions and consequences of the slave trade, a prolific pamphleteer whose history of the abolition movement is still a classic. His labors in the cause of justice to Africa were accomplished only at the cost of much personal discomfort, and imposed a severe strain on his scanty resources. In 1793 he wrote a letter to Josiah Wedgwood which contains some of the finest sentiments that motivated the humanitarians. He needed money and wished to sell two of his shares in the Sierra Leone Company, founded in 1791 to promote legitimate commerce with Africa. "But," he pointed out, "I should not chuse to permit anyone to become a purchaser, who would not be better pleased with the good resulting to Africa than from great commercial profits to himself; not that the latter may not be expected, but in case of a disappointment, I should wish his mind to be made easy by the assurance that he has been instrumental in introducing light and happiness into a country, where the mind was kept in darkness and the body nourished only for European chains."[3] Too impetuous and enthusiastic for some of his colleagues,[4] Clarkson was one of those friends of whom the Negro race has had unfortunately only too few.

Then there were James Stephen, the father, and James Stephen, the son. The father had been a lawyer in the West Indies and knew conditions at first hand. The son became the first outstanding permanent under-secretary of the Colonial Office, the "Oversecretary Stephen" and "Mr. Mother Country" of unfriendly jibes. In this capacity he held a watching brief for his helpless constituents, the Negro slaves. He was constantly spurring on Wilberforce to greater and more public efforts instead of the policy of memorials and interviews with ministers. The only thing to check colonial crimes was to "blazon them to the English public, and arm ourselves with public indignation."[5] Stephen was not impressed with the planter's arguments. "The deprivation of a mansion or an epuipage painful though it may be is hardly to be set against the protracted exclusion from those common advantages of human life under which from the admitted facts of the case the slaves are proved to be labouring. . . .[6] The ultimate end of human society—the security of life, property and reputation—must be preferred to its subordinate ends—the enjoyment of particular franchises."[7] It was trusteeship in its noblest form and finest language. Stephen drafted the Emancipation Bill, which included concessions he was loth to make to the planters. Where the others sat back and congratulated themselves, the permanent under-secretary continued to watch colonial legislation with jealousy and distrust. "Popular franchises in the hands of the masters of a great body of slaves," he wrote in 1841, "were the worst instruments of tyranny which were ever yet forged for the oppression of mankind."[8] In those days and under such an administrator Crown Colony government was a notable step in the protection of weaker peoples.

One of the earliest, ablest and most diligent of the abolitionists was James Ramsay, who, as a rector in the West Indies, had had some twenty years' experience of slavery. "The only use," he wrote to Wilberforce in 1787, "I can be of in the business is as a pioneer to remove obstacles; use me in this way and I shall be happy."[9] He knew from experience the heavy mortality occasioned by the slave trade among the white sailors; he could speak at first hand of the heavy mortality occasioned among

the slaves by excessive toil on the plantations.[10] The planters pursued him with a relentlessness reserved for him alone.
"Ramsay is dead," boasted one of them, "I have killed him."

Besides these men Wilberforce with his effeminate face
appears small in stature. There is a certain smugness about
the man, his life, his religion. As a leader, he was inept,
addicted to moderation, compromise and delay. He deprecated
extreme measures and feared popular agitation. He relied for
success upon aristocratic patronage, parliamentary diplomacy
and private influence with men in office.[11] He was a lobby-
ist, and it was a common saying that his vote could safely be
predicted, for it was certain to be opposed to his speech.[12] "Generally," said Tierney, "his phraseology is adapted to suit either
party; and if, now and then, he loses the balance of his argument and bends a little to one side, he quickly recovers himself
and deviates as much in an opposite direction as will make a
fair division of his speech on both sides of the question."[13] But
he was a persuasive and eloquent speaker, with a melodious
voice which earned him the sobriquet of "the nightingale of the
House." Above all he had the reputation of being otherworld-
minded, and it is certain that this reputation for saintliness and
his disinterestedness in the cause were powerful factors in Pitt's
prodding that he should lead the parliamentary crusade.

These were the men whom the planters called visionaries and
fanatics, and likened to hyenas and tigers.[14] With the aid of
the others, Macaulay, Wesley, Thornton and Brougham, they
were successful in raising anti-slavery sentiments almost to the
status of a religion in England, and these religious reformers
who made Clapham into more than a railway junction were not
inappropriately nicknamed "the Saints." The very emotionalism
which such a phenomenon arouses calls for greater caution on
the part of the student of the social sciences. For if, as so many
have held, slavery falls into the realm of theology, monopoly
most emphatically does not.

The abolitionists were not radicals. In their attitude to
domestic problems they were reactionary. The Methodists
offered the English worker Bibles instead of bread and Wesleyan
capitalists exhibited open contempt for the working class.

Wilberforce was familiar with all that went on in the hold
of a slave ship but ignored what went on at the bottom of
a mineshaft. He supported the Corn Laws, was a member of
the secret committee which investigated and repressed working class discontent in 1817, opposed feminine anti-slavery
associations, and thought the First Reform Bill too radical.[15]

The initial error into which many have fallen is the assumption that the abolitionists, from the very outset, never concealed
their intention of working for complete emancipation. The abolitionists for a long time eschewed and repeatedly disowned any
idea of emancipation. Their interest was solely in the slave
trade, whose abolition, they thought, would eventually lead,
without legislative interference, into freedom. On three occasions the Abolition Committee explicity denied any intention
of emancipating the slaves.[16] Wilberforce in 1807 publicly disowned such intentions.[17] The Bishop of Rochester asserted that
the abolitionists proceeded upon no visionary notions of equality and imprescriptible rights of men; they strenuously upheld
the gradations of civil society.[18] In 1815 the African Institution stated clearly that it looked for emancipation from the
slaveowners.[19]

It was not until 1823 that emancipation became the avowed
aim of the abolitionists. The chief reason was the persecu-
tion of the missionaries in the colonies—the death of Smith
in Guiana, the expulsion of Shrewsbury in Barbados, the perse-
cution of Knibb in Jamaica. Even then emancipation was to be
gradual. "Nothing rash," warned Buxton, "nothing rapid, nothing abrupt, nothing bearing any feature of violence." Above all,
pas de zèle. Slavery would never be abolished. "It will subside; it
will decline; it will expire; it will, as it were, burn itself down
into its socket and go out. . . . We shall leave it gently to decay
—slowly, silently, almost imperceptibly, to die away and to
be forgotten."[20] As in the United States, slavery was to wither
away. The hope was not realized in England either, though the
West Indians were too weak and few to fight a civil war.

This was the situation in 1830, when the July Revolution
broke out in France and fanned the flames of parliamentary
reform in England. The abolitionists were still lobbying and

temporizing, sending memorials and deputations to ministers, while colonial slavery and colonial monopoly continued
unabated. "It was therefore necessary that another order of men,
of bolder and more robust, if somewhat less refined, natures
should now appear to take the work in hand, not so much to
supersede as to supplement the exertions of their more wary
and hesitating colleagues."[21] Conservatives and radicals clashed
in a great anti-slavery meeting in May, 1830. Buxton had
proposed the usual resolutions, "admirably worded; admirably
indignant, but—admirably prudent." Pownall rose to put his
amendment—immediate abolition. The effect on the delegates
was electric. Buxton deprecated, Brougham interposed, Wilberforce waved his hand for silence, but the amendment was
eventually put and "carried with a burst of exulting triumph."[22]
The new policy was admirably stated by one of Sturge's friends:
"Sin will lie at our door if we do not agitate, agitate, agitate.
. . . The people must emancipate the slaves, for the government
never will."[23]

As far as the abolitionist leadership was concerned, however,
their attitude to West Indian slavery must be seen in its relation
to slavery in other parts of the world. Their condemnation of
slavery applied only to the Negro and only to the Negro in the
British West Indies. First, India.

In their campaign against the West Indian planters the
abolitionists inaugurated what Cochin has called "a sort of
pious and silly crusade."[24] They urged their sympathisers
to boycott slave-grown produce in favor of the free-grown
produce of India. This crusade was recommended by the
Abolition Committee in 1795[25] and by many pamphleteers.
William Fox in 1792 informed the British people that in
every pound of sugar they consumed two ounces of human
flesh.[26] By an elaborate mathematical computation it was estimated that if one family using five pounds of sugar a week
would abstain for twenty-one months, one Negro would be
spared enslavement and murder.[27] The consumer of sugar
was really "the prime mover, *the grand cause of all the horrible
injustice.*"[28] By substituting East for West Indian sugar, the

Peckham Ladies' African Anti-Slavery Association was informed, they were undermining the system of slavery in the safest, easiest and most effective manner.[29] An abolitionist leaflet was circulated, entitled "The Negro Slave's Complaint to the Friends of Humanity." The Negro pleaded: "And now, massa, you be de *friend of freedom*, good man, pity poor Negro, me beg buy de East Sugar, no slave sugar, de free, and den my massa vill tink and say, ve no much sell de slave sugar, slaves must be no slaves, must be free, and ve pay de vages, and den vill vork villing and do more work, and ve den sell more *sugar*, and get more of de money. — De men at de East be vise men, and de vise men at de East no slave—make sugar free, free, free."[30] Not only sugar but cotton. A movement was started among the ladies to encourage the consumption of free-grown cotton,[31] which, according to Gurney, would do more to abolish slavery in America than all the abolitionist pamphlets.[32] As the Irish abolitionists put it, their aim was to "universalize the use of free labour tropical produce."[33]

But the wise men of the East were no more impeccable than the sinful planters of the West. The act emancipating the slaves in the British West Indies passed its third reading on August 7, 1833. Forty-eight hours before, the East India Company's Charter had come up for renewal in the House of Lords. The bill included a clause which declared that slavery "should be abolished" in India. Lord Ellenborough expressed his astonishment that such a proposition should ever have entered the head of any statesman. Lord Auckland defended the bill: "It had been framed with the utmost caution consistent with the destruction of an odious system; as well as the utmost care not to interfere with the domestic manners of the natives." The Duke of Wellington called upon their Lordships to deal lightly with the question, as they valued the maintenance of British India. It was a violent innovation, altogether uncalled for, which would produce the greatest dissatisfaction, if not absolute insurrection.[34]

Repeated declarations were later made in Parliament on behalf of the government that the East India Company was preparing legislation with a view to the "amelioration" of slavery and that such legislation would be produced in Parliament. But the promised legislation never was forthcoming. "The government of India were taking such steps to ameliorate the condition of slavery as, at no distant period, should lead to its total extinction."[35] This was in 1837. By 1841 none of the rules and regulations for the mitigation of slavery had been produced.[36] And when the question of equalizing the duties on East Indian rum came up and it was argued that East Indian rum was slave produce, Prime Minister Peel replied that "to postpone the equalization . . . until he had actually settled that abolition, would be deferring its operation to a much more distant period than even the most ardent advocates of the West Indians could wish."[37] In defence of the East Indians it was pleaded, in 1842, that they had prohibited the selling of children into slavery in periods of scarcity.[38] Ten years after Britain's "great atonement," the Earl of Auckland would not deny that "some condition of servitude, more or less painful, might not still exist";[39] and Peel considered that such measures as had been adopted "appeared well calculated to arrest the progress of slavery, and check abuses, and when carried out in all parts of India under our control or which we could influence, would go a long way to suppress slavery."[40]

Yet this was the tropical produce that the abolitionists were recommending to the people of England. Clarkson called on them to "shew their abhorrence of the planters' system by leaving off the use of their produce,"[41] and as late as 1840 was still looking to the East India Company to extirpate slavery "by means that are perfectly *moral and pacific* . . . namely, by the *cultivation of the earth* and by the employment of *free labour*."[42]

The abolitionists did this not out of ignorance. As an apology for the East India Company, Zachary Macaulay urged that "they had obtained dominion over countries which had been previously under the Hindu and Mogul Government. They therefore could not be blamed if, when they came into possession of those countries, they found principles acted upon with which, however adverse to their feelings, it would be unsafe to interfere, without due caution."[43] In 1837 Buxton expressed the fear that sugar would produce a system of slavery in the East as disgraceful as it had produced in the West. The government spokesman assured him it would not. Buxton "was much obliged ... for that assurance."[44] In 1843 Brougham was still looking forward with sanguine hope to the abolition of slavery in India, "a consummation not to be accomplished so much by legislation, or by doing violence to property," as by encouraging the native slave owners to declare their children free after a certain date.[45]

Some of the Clapham Sect had East Indian interests and "perhaps their detestation of West Indian slavery was sharpened by a sense of the unfair discrimination of the sugar duties in favour of the West Indies and against the growing sugar plantations of India."[46] The Thorntons owned East India stock;[47] one of the family participated in the debate at East India House in 1793 on the sugar trade, and denied the existence of any compact in favor of the West Indian monopoly.[48] Zachary Macaulay had shares in the East India Company, and was one of the nine signatories who summoned the meeting of the Court of Proprietors in 1823 to discuss the sugar question.[49] In a powerful pamphlet in 1823 he declared that the West Indians "have no more right to claim the continuance of a protecting duty on sugar, to the manifest wrong of India and of Great Britain, than they had before a right to claim the continuance of the Slave Trade, to the manifest wrong of Africa."[50] Macaulay's speech in the debate at East India House on the sugar trade in 1823 was such a diatribe against slavery that a subsequent speaker had to remind him that "if the slave trade were ten times worse than it had been stated to be, they were not met to consider that question."[51]

More important than Thornton or Macaulay was James Cropper. A prominent abolitionist, Cropper was the greatest importer of East India sugar into Liverpool, and was the founder and head of the independent East India house, Cropper, Benson and Company of Liverpool, with a trade of a thousand pounds a day.[52] Cropper was aware that his private interests rendered his motives liable to suspicion.[53] West Indians recalled that he had once imported slave-grown cotton from the United

States.[54] Cropper's own explanation is as follows: "I saw that hideous monster, slavery, gasping, as it were, in the agonies of death, seeking for the support which could alone continue its existence. . . . I could not suffer the fear of reproaches, on account of being interested, to get the better of the paramount feeling of humanity and duty. I durst not encounter the reproaches of my own conscience."[55] In his anti-slavery arguments he refused to steer clear of commercial considerations. Slavery, he wrote, "can be lucrative only on *fertile soils*, and amongst a *scanty population* as in the new states in America, where two days' labour will purchase an acre of land."[56] Discussing the abolition of slavery in Europe, the Northern states of the Union and certain parts of South America, he reached the conclusion that the fact that emancipation had not been extensive where slave labor was profitable showed that "the efforts of benevolent men have been most successful when cooperating with natural causes."[57] When he wrote lyrically of Britain's manufacturing skill and industry, "unshackled by bounties, unaided by useless monopolies, thriving with unrestrained freedom,"[58] he was thinking less of West Indian slavery than of West Indian monopoly. Why should Britain not supply the Continent with refined sugar as well as with manufactured cotton?[59] But when the West Indians asked him pointedly whether he meant to introduce Brazilian as well as Indian sugar, he replied that all sugar should be admitted at a uniform duty, on the condition that Brazil and Cuba agreed to abolish the slave trade.[60] What then had become of his "natural causes"? His dual position of humanitarian and economist forced him into inconsistencies. In his home a special dinner service portrayed a Negro in chains, and in 1837 he purchased 12,000 small bottles which he filled with samples of free-grown sugar and coffee and distributed among sympathisers and members of Parliament.[61] But the support of Liverpool's "benevolent townsman"[62] did untold harm to the cause of humanitarianism.

Thomas Whitmore, East Indian leader in Parliament, was a vice-president of the Anti-Slavery Society and was at one time candidate for succession to the leadership of the Anti-Slavery party.[63] Wilberforce's diary for May 22, 1823, the date of

Whitmore's motion on the sugar duties, reads: "None interested for the question but the East Indians and a few of us Anti-Slavers, and the West Indians and government against us."[64] The two tellers for the East Indian side were Whitmore and Buxton.[65] Of all the abolitionists, only one, Brougham, was opposed to equalization of the duties, on the ground that it would very speedily lay waste the whole of the West Indian archipelago.[66]

This connection between East Indians and certain abolitionists has not been fully appreciated. Coupland is clearly unhappy about the whole thing, as is seen in his concern with the "sincerity" of both groups.[67] Klingberg speaks of "co-operation."[68] Burn is convinced that the attacks on Cropper's disinterestedness were unfounded.[69] Ragatz' explanation is the most satisfactory of all: Cropper's was "one of those occasional cases in which conduct is not primarily influenced by self-interest though they may accidentally coincide."[70] The real significance, however, of the abolitionists' support of East India, and later of Brazilian sugar, is that the issues involved were not only the inhumanity of West Indian slavery but the unprofitableness of West Indian monopoly.

After India, Brazil and Cuba. By no stretch of imagination could any humanitarian justify any proposal calculated to rivet the chains of slavery still more firmly on the Negroes of Brazil and Cuba. That was precisely what free trade in sugar meant. For after 1807 the British West Indians were denied the slave trade, and after 1833 slave labor. If the abolitionists had recommended Indian sugar, incorrectly, on the humanitarian principle that it was free-grown, it was their duty to their principles and their religion to boycott the slave-grown sugar of Brazil and Cuba. In failing to do this it is not to be inferred that they were wrong, but it is undeniable that their failure to adopt such a course completely destroys the humanitarian argument. The abolitionists, after 1833, continued to oppose the West Indian planters who now employed free labor. Where, before 1833, they had boycotted the British slave owner, after 1833 they espoused the cause of the Brazilian slave owner.

The abolitionists at first had not confined their attention to the British slave trade. They had dreamed of nothing short of the total and universal abolition of the slave trade. They took advantage of the return of peace in 1815 and the international conferences then in vogue to disseminate their views. They sent whole "loads of humbug" to Parliament;[71] in thirty-four days in 1814, they sent 772 petitions with a million signatures.[72] They denounced the paper declaration of the Congress of Vienna against the slave trade, where they had won over Britain's plenipotentiary, Wellington, and were even prepared to go to war for abolition.[73] They gained the support of the Tsar of Russia.[74] They sent a special observer, Clarkson, to the Congress of Aix-la-Chapelle. They were ready to fight France all over again to prevent French reconquest of Saint Domingue,[75] and were unwilling to recognize the independence of Brazil from Portugal without an explicit promise to renounce the slave trade. They forced the British government, by their "friendly violence,"[76] to station a squadron on the African coast to suppress the slave trade by force.

The pressure on the government was terrific. The government pleaded for time, for caution. "Morals," said Castlereagh, "were never well taught by the sword."[77] He begged the humanitarians to "moderate their virtuous feelings, and put their solicitude for Africa under the dominion of reason."[78] But the abolitionists gave the government no peace. As Liverpool confessed on one occasion to Wilberforce: "If I were not anxious for the abolition of the slave trade on principle, I must be aware of the embarrassment to which any government must be exposed from the present state of that question in this country."[79] The government was considerably hampered in its foreign relations for they knew that all negotiations were futile. But they never dared to say so openly. "We shall never succeed," wrote Wellington to Aberdeen, "in abolishing the foreign slave trade. But we must take care to avoid to take any steps which may induce the people of England to believe that we do not do everything in our power to discourage and put it down as soon as possible."[80]

In an unforgettable general election in 1831, in which candidates were quizzed on their views on slavery, the abolitionists dragged Negroes to election with golden chains, and, where they could find no Negroes, chimney sweeps. They placarded the hustings all over the kingdom with full-length pictures of white planters flogging Negro women.[81] In their campaigns they appealed to the hearts and consciences of British women, and even approached children. Leeds published an anti-slavery series for juvenile readers. An anti-slavery dial was manufactured, so that benevolent people, enjoying the domestic comforts of an evening fireside in England, would know that the Negroes were toiling on the plantations under the oppressive heat of a tropical sun.[82] This was in the years before 1833. Bliss was in that dawn.

But even in that dawn the storm clouds had begun to gather. The abolitionists were boycotting the slave-grown produce of the British West Indies, dyed with the Negro's blood. But the very existence of British capitalism depended upon the slave-grown cotton of the United States, equally connected with slavery and polluted with blood. The West Indian could legitimately ask whether "slavery was only reprehensible in countries to which those members do not trade, and where their connections do not reside."[83] The answers given were curious. The person who received slave-grown produce from America dealt in the produce of labor performed by slaves who were not his fellow subjects, and there was not, in the slavery of the United States, any evidence of that destruction of human life which was one of the most appalling features of the system in the British West Indies.[84] The boycotters of West Indian sugar sat upon chairs of Cuban mahogany, before desks of Brazilian rosewood, and used inkstands of slave-cut ebony; but "it would do no good to go round and inquire into the pedigree of every chair and table." In a country like England total abstinence from slave produce was impossible, unless they wished to betake themselves to the woods and live on roots and berries.[85] As the Newcastle abolitionists argued, only "the unnecessary purchase of one iota of slave produce involves the purchaser in the guilt of the slaveholder."[86]

Was Brazilian sugar necessary? The capitalists said yes; it

was necessary to keep British capitalism going. The abolitionists took the side of the capitalists. In 1833, Lushington, one
of the oldest of the abolitionists, representing a sugar refining
district, begged the government not to lose an hour in granting
relief to his constitutents, who asked for no bounty, no unfair
advantages, no unjust monopoly.[87] He had in mind the sugar
refiners of the Tower Hamlets, not the Negroes of the British West Indies. Buxton took a curious position. If it could
be shown that the foreign sugar to be imported would be consumed at home, instead of being exported, he would vote no.
But it required one-third more labor to refine sugar in Brazil
and then import it into Britain in a refined state. In permitting, therefore, foreign sugar to be refined in Britain, they were
substituting British machinery at home for slave labor abroad,
and consequently to that extent diminishing slave labor and dis-
couraging the slave trade.[88] Parliament was astonished.[89] Well
might it be.

This was in September, 1831. Two years later Buxton was
rejoicing in the success of his labors. "A mighty work is accomplished as far as this country is concerned."[90] The Emancipation
Act marked the end of the abolitionist efforts. They were satisfied. It never dawned upon them that the Negro's freedom could
be only nominal if the sugar plantation was allowed to endure.
When Gladstone, in 1848, still claimed the protecting duty
for the planters, he most emphatically stated it had nothing to
do with the Negro. He could see "no reason why we should
throw away the funds of the country in giving a further stimulus to that condition, which is one of comfort fully adequate
to their scale in society and their desires."[91] The abolitionists
were silent. It never occurred to them that the Negro might
want the land. In Antigua, where all the land was appropriated,
planters and slaves flocked to the churches when the news of
emancipation reached the island, thanked God for the blessings
of freedom, and returned to their labors, the slaves now raised
to the dignity of landless wage earners paid twenty-five cents a
day. The same was true of Barbados, where similar conditions
prevailed, except that the Barbadians omitted the thanksgiv-
ing. Where were the abolitionists? "The Negro race," wrote

Buxton, "are blessed with a peculiar aptitude for the reception of moral and religious instruction, and it does seem to me that there never was a stronger call on any nation than there is now on us to meet this inclination in them, to supply them amply with the means of instruction, to dispatch missionaries, to institute schools, and to send out Bibles. It is the only compensation in our power. It is an abundant one! We may in this manner recompense all the sorrows and sufferings we have inflicted and be the means of making in the end their barbarous removal from their own land the greatest of blessings to them."[92] Similarly for Africa. In 1840 Gurney wrote that "the ultimate and only radical cure of the vices and miseries of Africa is Christianity. . . . We must never forget the paramount value of Evangelization."[93]

The barbarous removal of the Negroes from Africa continued for at least twenty-five years after 1833, to the sugar plantations of Brazil and Cuba. Brazilian and Cuban economy depended on the slave trade. Consistency alone demanded that the British abolitionists oppose this trade. But that would retard Brazilian and Cuban development and consequently hamper British trade. The desire for cheap sugar after 1833 overcame all abhorrence of slavery. Gone was the horror which once was excited at the idea of a British West Indian slave-driver armed with a whip; the Cuban slave-driver, armed with whip, cutlass, dagger and pistols, and followed by bloodhounds, aroused not even comment from the abolitionists. Exeter Hall, the center of British humanitarianism, yielded to the Manchester School, the spearhead of British free trade.

The abolitionists, once so belligerent where the slave trade was concerned, were now pacifists. Buxton wrote a book condemning the slave squadron and the policy of forcible suppression of the slave trade as causing aggravated suffering to multiplied numbers.[94] Sturge reorganized the Anti-Slavery Society on a purely pacific basis. "The utter failure," said Wilberforce, junior, Bishop of Oxford, at a great abolitionist meeting in 1840, "of every attempt by treaty, by remonstrance, and by naval armaments to arrest the progress of the slave trade, proves the necessity of resorting to a preventive policy founded on different and higher principles."[95] Young Buxton "could not but see that those high principles by which this country had been guided for many years were now supplanted by others which, though important in themselves, were far inferior to those principles on which he had acted in former years."[96] Brougham's philanthropy was excited only by sugar and not by cotton, only by the slave trade and not by slavery, only by the slave trade between Africa and Brazil and not by the slave trade between Virginia and Texas. He condemned as "a gross perversion of the doctrines of free trade" the policy of obtaining "cheap sugar at the heavier cost of piracy, and torture, and blood."[97] He knew it would be madness to exclude American cotton, so taking as his standard of measurement not slavery but the slave trade, he argued that while he had no right to interfere in the domestic institutions of independent states, he had every right to demand the enforcement of treaties signed by independent states.[98] According to his interpretation the United States did not carry on the slave trade. There was a difference, he contended, between slave-grown sugar in Louisiana, increased by the natural increase of the slaves or more efficient cultivation, and slave-grown sugar in Brazil, increased by "the unnatural, forced, and infernal traffic in Africans carried on by force and fraud."[99]

Perhaps the greatest single speech ever made on the slavery question was the speech of Thomas Babington Macaulay, later Lord Macaulay, in 1845. It was a masterpiece of clarity and lucidity, befitting a great historian. It had one defect: it was pro-slavery and not anti-slavery. "My especial obligations in respect to negro slavery," said Macaulay tartly, "ceased when slavery itself ceased in that part of the world for the welfare of which I, as a member of this House, was accountable." He refused to turn the fiscal code of the country into a penal code for the purpose of correcting vices in the institutions of independent states, or the tariff into "an instrument for rewarding the justice and humanity of some foreign governments, and for punishing the barbarity of others." He boldly faced the inconsistency of importing Brazilian sugar for refining but not for consumption. "We import the accursed thing; we bond it; we employ our skill and machinery to render it more alluring to the eye and to the palate; we export it to Leghorn and Hamburg; we send it to all the coffee houses of Italy and Germany; we pocket a profit on all this; and then we put on a Pharisaical air, and thank God that we are not like those sinful Italians and Germans who have no scruple about swallowing slave-grown sugar."[100] They dared not prohibit the importation of Brazilian sugar, unless they wished to make Germany a Warwickshire and Leipzig another Manchester.[101] "I will not have two standards of right. . . . I will not have two weights or two measures. I will not blow hot and cold, play fast and loose, strain at a gnat and swallow a camel."[102]

All the great names were here—Wilberforce, Buxton, Macaulay, Brougham. All but Clarkson, a voice in the wilderness calling for the exclusion of all articles produced by manacled and fettered hands.[103] Yet even Clarkson in 1839 opposed suppression on the curious ground that it was "but putting money into the pockets of our men of war."[104]

Slavery was now regarded in a different light. Mr. Wilson was not prepared to say that, because the relation between employer and employed was that of master and slave, it should be branded as injustice and oppression.[105] The member for Oxford University opposed the slave trade and was prepared for war, if necessary, to suppress it,[106] but he had never accepted the view that property in man was illegal.[107] The political economist, M'Culloch, recalled that without slavery the tropics could never have been cultivated and that, as an institution, it was not justly open to the opprobrium and denunciation applied to it.[108] Look at the system of slavery more calmly, lectured Professor Merivale at Oxford; it was a great social evil, but one differing in degree and quality, not in kind, from many other social evils they were compelled to tolerate, such as the great inequality of fortunes, pauperism, or the overworking of children.[109]

Disraeli, like many to follow in Britain and the United States, condemned emancipation as the greatest blunder ever committed by the English people. It was "an exciting topic . . . addressed to an insular people of strong purpose, but very deficient information."[110] This was not a hasty judgment in the course of a brilliant oratorical performance. It was a considered opinion, which he deliberately repeated in his *Life of Lord George Bentinck*. "The movement of the middle class for the abolition of slavery was virtuous, but it was not wise. It was an ignorant movement. The history of the abolition of slavery by the English and its consequences, would be a narrative of ignorance, injustice, blundering, waste, and havoc, not easily paralleled in the history of mankind."[111]

Even the intellectuals were engulfed. Coleridge had been awarded the Browne Gold Medal at Cambridge for an ode on slavery and had abstained from sugar. But in 1811 he sneered at the "philanthropy-trade," accused Wilberforce of caring only for his own soul, and criticized Clarkson as a man made vain by benevolence, "the moral steam engine or the giant with one idea";[112] while in 1833 he was strongly opposed to frequent discussions of the *"rights"* of the Negroes who should be "taught to be thankful for the providence which has placed them within the reach of the means of grace."[113] In 1792 Wordsworth was completely indifferent to the "novel heat of virtuous feeling" which was spreading through England.[114] His famous sonnets to Clarkson, Toussaint L'Ouverture, and the "white-robed Negro" are merely magnificent rhetoric and, not accidentally, lack the depth of his finest poetry. In 1833 he pleaded that slavery was in principle monstrous but was not the worst thing in human nature; it was not in itself at all times and under all circumstances to be deplored, and in 1840 he refused to be publicly associated with the abolitionists.[115] Southey favored compulsory manumission by which slavery would, with reasonable hope, be extinguished in the course of a generation.[116]

But reaction at its blackest and cheapest was personified by Carlyle. He wrote an essay on "The Nigger Question," sneering at the "Exeter-Hallery and other tragic Tomfoolery" which, proceeding on the false principle that all men were equal, had made of the West Indies a Black Ireland. Would horses be the next to be emancipated? he asked. He contrasted the "beautiful Blacks sitting there up to the ears in pumpkins, and doleful Whites sitting here without potatoes to eat." It was only the white man who had given value to the West Indies, and the "indolent two-legged cattle" should be forced to work. The abuses of slavery should be abolished, and the precious thing in it saved: the Negro "has an indisputable and perpetual *right* to be compelled ... to do competent work for his living." It was not that Carlyle hated the Negro. No, he liked him, and found that "with a pennyworth of oil, you can make a handsome glossy thing of poor Quashee." The black African, alone of wild men, could live among civilized men, but he could be useful in God's creation only as a perpetual servant, unless the British West Indies were to become, like Haiti, "a tropical dog-kennel," black Peter exterminating black Paul.[117] Public opinion, as Lord Denman moaned, had undergone a lamentable and disgraceful change.[118]

· 12 ·

THE SLAVES AND SLAVERY

WE HAVE CONSIDERED the different attitudes to slavery of the British Government, the British capitalists, the absentee British West Indian planters, and the British humanitarians. We have followed the battle of slavery in the home country. It would be a grave mistake, however, to treat the question as if it were merely a metropolitan struggle. The fate of the colonies was at stake, and the colonists themselves were in a ferment which indicated, reflected, and reacted upon the great events in Britain.

First, there were the white planters, who had to deal not only with the British Parliament but with the slaves. Secondly, there were the free people of color. And, thirdly, there were the slaves themselves. Most writers on this period have ignored them. Modern historical writers are gradually awaking to the distortion which is the result of this.[1] In correcting this deficiency they correct an error which the planters and the British officials and politicians of the time never made.

First, the planters. In 1823 the British government adopted a new policy of reform towards West Indian slavery. The policy was to be enforced, by orders in council, in the Crown Colonies of Trinidad and British Guiana; its success, it was hoped, would encourage the self-governing colonies to emulate it spontaneously. The reforms included: abolition of the whip; abolition of the Negro Sunday market, by giving the slaves another day off, to permit them time for religious instruction; prohibition of the flogging of female slaves; compulsory manumission of field and domestic slaves; freedom of female children born after 1823; admissibility of evidence of slaves in courts of law; establishment of savings banks for slaves; a nine-hour day; and the appointment of a Protector of Slaves whose duty it was, among other things, to keep an official record of the punishments inflicted on the slaves. It was not emancipation but amelioration, not revolution but evolution. Slavery would be killed by kindness.

The reply of the planters, in the Crown Colonies as well as in the self-governing islands, was an emphatic refusal to pass what they considered "a mere catalogue of indulgencies to the Blacks."[1a] They knew that all such concessions meant only further concessions.

Not one single recommendation received the unanimous approval of the West Indian planters. They were roused to fury especially by the proposals for the prohibition of the flogging of female slaves and the abolition of the Negro Sunday market.

From the planters' standpoint, it was necessary to punish women. Even in civilized societies, they argued, women were flogged, as in the houses of correction in England. "Our black ladies," said Mr. Hamden in the Barbados legislature, "have rather a tendency to the Amazonian cast of character; and I believe that their husbands would be very sorry to hear that they were placed beyond the reach of chastisement."[2]

On the question of the abolition of the Negro Sunday market, Barbados refused to surrender one-sixth of its already reduced income.[3] Jamaica replied that the "pretence of having time for religoius duties" would merely encourage idleness among the slaves.[4] So great was the opposition of the planters that the governor deemed any attempt at alteration highly imprudent and could see no alternative but leaving it "to the operation of time and that change of circumstances and opinions which is slowly but surely leading to the improvement of the habits and manners of the slaves."[5] It was a true and important fact that, with time, mere contact with civilization improved the slave, but the slave was in no mood for the inevitability of gradualism.

The whip, argued the planters, was necessary if discipline was to be maintained. Abolish it, "and then adieu to all peace and comfort on plantations."[6] A Trinidad planter called it "a most unjust and oppressive invasion of property" to insist on a nine-hour day for full-grown slaves in the West Indies, while the English factory owner could exact twelve hours' labor from children in a heated and sickly atmosphere.[7] In Jamaica the bill for admitting slave evidence aroused a great and violent clamor, and it was rejected on the second reading by a majority of thirty-six to one.[8] The Assembly of the island postponed the savings banks clause to a future session,[9] and the governor dared not even mention the question of the freedom of female children.[10] The legislature of British Guiana decided that "if the principle of manumission *invito domino* is to be adopted, it is more for their consistency and for the interests of their constituents that it should be done *for* them than *by* them."[11] In Trinidad the number of manumissions declined considerably,[12] while appraisals for manumission increased suddenly:[13] "the possibility of sworn appraisers pronouncing an unjust decision," Stephen confessed, "was not contemplated and is not provided against."[14] One manager in Trinidad talked of "the silly orders in council," and in recording punishments resorted to language unbefitting his responsibility and insulting to the framers of the legislation.[15] The office of Protector of Slaves in British Guiana was a "delusion": "There is no protection for the Slave Population," wrote the incumbent in 1832, "I am desperately unpopular. . . ."[16]

Not only did the West Indian planters question the specific proposals of the British Government, they also challenged the right of the imperial parliament to legislate on their internal affairs and issue "arbitrary mandates . . . so positive and unqualified in point of matter, and so precise and peremptory in point of time."[17] From Barbados the governor reported that any attempt at dictation gave rise to instant irritation and opposition.[18] The inconsistency of slave owners talking of rights and liberties was dismissed as "the clamour of ignorance." Look to history, expostulated Hamden, "you will there find that no nations in the world have been more jealous of their liberties than those amongst whom the institution of slavery existed."[19]

In Jamaica the excitement reached fever pitch. The Assembly vowed that it would "never make a deliberate surrender of their undoubted and acknowledged rights" by legislating in the manner prescribed[20] "upon a subject of mere municipal regulation and internal police."[21] If the British Parliament was to make laws for Jamaica, it must exercise that prerogative without a partner.[22] The doctrine of the transcendental power of the imperial parliament was declared to be subversive of their rights and dangerous to their lives and properties.[23] According to the governor, "the undoubted rights of the British Parliament have been wantonly and repeatedly denied, (and) unless the arrogance of such pretensions is effectually curbed, His Majesty's authority in this colony will exist only in name."[24] Two Jamaican deputies, sent to England in 1832 to lay their grievances before the home authorities, pointedly uncovered the *arcana imperii:* "We owe no more allegiance to the inhabitants of Great Britain than we owe to our brother colonists in Canada. . . . we do not for a moment acknowledge that Jamaica can be cited to the bar of English opinion to defend her laws and customs."[25] One member of the island assembly went further: "as for the King of England," he asked, "what right I should be glad to know has he to Jamaica except that he stole it from Spain?"[26] A West Indian in Parliament reminded the British people that "by persisting in the question of right we lost America."[27] Talk of secession was rife. The home government was warned that there was constant communication in Jamaica with individuals in the United States,[28] and that feelers had been put out by some planters to the United States Government.[29] The cabinet took the matter sufficiently seriously to question the governor about the matter.[30] Had not Saint Domingue, in similar circumstances, offered itself to Britain?

This was more than the language of desperate men or an insane flouting of the "temperate but authoritative admonition"[31] of the imperial authorities. It was a lesson not so much to the public of Great Britain as to the slaves of the West Indies.

If the governor of Jamaica found in the planters "a greater reluctance to part with power over the slave than might have been expected in the present age,"[32] it is obvious how the recalcitrance of the plantocracy appeared to the slaves. The Negroes, least of all people, were likely to forget that, in the words of the governor of Barbados, *"the love of power of* these planters over the poor Negroes, each in his little sugar dominion, has found as great an obstacle to freedom as *the love of their labor."*[33] Emancipation would come not from the planters but despite the planters.

Whilst the whites were plotting treason and talking of secession, the free people of color were steadfastly loyal. They deprecated "a dissolution of the ties which bind us to the Mother Country as the greatest calamity that could possibly befall ourselves and our posterity."[34] To their great credit, the governor of Trinidad reported, they had not participated in those meetings "whereat so much pains have been taken to sow the seeds of discontent in the colony both among the free and the slave population."[35] Whilst the whites were refusing to hold office, the mulattoes were insisting on their right to public service.[36] They were loyal not from inherent virtue but because they were too weak to gain their rights on their own behalf and could see no prospect of their own emancipation except through the British government. Furthermore, the local governments, in so far as they were trying to carry out the policy of the anti-monopolists, had to lean on them. In Barbados, wrote the governor, the balance of refinement, morals, education, and energy was on the side of the mulattoes, whilst the whites had nothing but old rights and prejudices to maintain their illiberal position. "You will see," he advised the home government, "a large policy in present circumstances in bringing these castes forward. They are a sober, active, energetic and loyal race; and I could equally depend on them if need came, against either slaves or white militia."[37]

Contrary to popular and even learned belief, however, as the political crisis deepened in Britain, the most dynamic and powerful social force in the colonies was the slave himself. This aspect of the West Indian problem has been studiously ignored, as if the slaves, when they became instruments of production, passed for men only in the catalogue. The planter looked upon slavery as eternal, ordained by God, and went to great lengths to justify it by scriptural quotations. There was no reason why the slave should think the same. He took the same scriptures and adapted them to his own purposes. To coercion and punishment he responded with indolence, sabotage and revolt. Most of the time he merely was as idle as possible. That was his usual form of resistance—passive. The docility of the Negro slave is a myth. The Maroons of Jamaica and the Bush Negroes of British Guiana were runaway slaves who had extracted treaties from the British Government and lived independently in their mountain fastnesses or jungle retreats. They were standing examples to the slaves of the British West Indies of one road to freedom. The successful slave revolt in Saint Domingue was a landmark in the history of slavery in the New World, and after 1804, when the independent republic of Haiti was established, every white slaveowner, in Jamaica, Cuba, or Texas, lived in dread of another Toussaint L'Ouverture. It is inconceivable a priori that the economic dislocation and the vast agitations which shook millions in Britain could have passed without effect on the slaves themselves and the relation of the planters to the slaves. Pressure on the sugar planter from the capitalists in Britain was aggravated by pressure from the slaves in the colonies. In communities like the West Indies, as the governor of Barbados wrote, "the public mind is ever tremblingly alive to the dangers of insurrection."[38]

Not nearly as stupid as his master thought him and later historians have pictured him, the slave was alert to his surroundings and keenly interested in discussions about his fate. "Nothing," wrote the governor of British Guiana in 1830, "can be more keenly observant than the slaves are of all that affects their interests."[39] The planters openly discussed the question of slavery in the presence of the very people whose future was under consideration. "If the turbulent meetings which are held here among the proprietors," wrote the governor of Trinidad in 1832, "are countenanced, nothing that may occur need be matter of surprise. . . ."[40] The local press added to the inflammable material. A Trinidad paper called the order in council "villainous,"[41] another spoke of "the *ridiculous* provisions of the ruinous Code Noir."[42] One judge refused to sit on any trial arising out of the order in council and walked out of court.[43] The planters have been blamed for this reckless attitude. But they could not help it. It is a feature of all deep social crises. Before the French Revolution the French court and aristocracy discussed Voltaire and Rousseau not only freely but, in certain spheres, with real intellectual appreciation. The arrogant behavior and intemperate language of the planters, however, served only to inflame the minds of the already restless slaves.

The consensus of opinion among the slaves, whenever each new discussion arose or each new policy was announced, was that emancipation had been passed in England but was withheld by their masters. The governor of Jamaica reported in 1807 that abolition of the slave trade was construed by the slaves as "nothing less than their general emancipation."[44] In 1816 the British Parliament passed an act making compulsory the registration of all slaves, to prevent smuggling in violation of the abolition law. The slaves in Jamaica were of the impression that the bill "contemplates some dispositions in their favour which the Assembly here supported by the inhabitants generally are desirous to withhold,"[45] and the planters had to recommend a parliamentary declaration that emancipation was never contemplated.[46] A similar misunderstanding prevailed among the slaves in Trinidad[47] and Barbados.[48] All over the West Indies the slaves were asking "why Bacchra no do that King bid him?"[49] So deeply was the idea imbedded in the minds of the slaves that some great benefit was intended for them by the home government in opposition to their masters that they eagerly seized upon every trifling circumstance in confirmation.[50] Every change of governor was interpreted by them as emancipation. The arrival of D'Urban in British Guiana in 1824 was construed by the slaves as involving "something interesting to their prospects."[51] The governor of Trinidad went on leave in 1831; the Negroes had it that he "was to bring out emancipation for all the slaves."[52] Mulgrave's arrival in Jamaica in 1832 created great excitement. At a review near Kingston he was followed around by a greater number of slaves than had ever assembled before in the island, all with one idea in their minds, that he had "come out with emancipation in his pocket."[53] The appointment of Smith as governor of Barbados in 1833 was understood by the slaves as meaning general emancipation. His arrival in the island gave rise to a considerable number of desertions from distant plantations to Bridgetown "to ascertain if the Governor had brought out freedom or not."[54]

The slaves, however, were not prepared to wait for freedom to come to them as a dispensation from above. The frequency and intensity of slave revolts after 1800 reflect the growing tensions which reverberated in the stately halls of Westminster.

In 1808 a slave revolt broke out in British Guiana. The revolt was betrayed and the ringleaders arrested. They consisted of "the drivers, tradesmen, and other most sensible slaves on the estates,"[55] that is, not the field hands but the slaves who were more comfortably off and better treated. In the same way a rebel in Jamaica in 1824, who committed suicide, openly admitted that his master was kind and indulgent, but defended his action on the ground that freedom during his lifetime had been withheld only by his master.[56] It was a danger signal. Toussaint L'Ouverture in Saint Domingue had been a trusted slave coachman.

In 1816 came the turn of Barbados. It was a rude shock for the Barbadian planters who flattered themselves that the good treatment of the slaves would "have prevented their resorting to violence to establish a claim of natural right which by long custom sanctioned by law has been hitherto refused to be acknowledged."[57] The rebels, when questioned, explicitly denied that ill treatment was the cause. "They stoutly maintained however," so the commander of the troops wrote to the governor, "that the island belonged to them, and not to white men, whom they proposed to destroy, reserving the females."[58] The revolt caught the planters off their guard, and only its premature breaking out, as a result of the intoxication of one of the rebels, prevented it from engulfing the entire island.[59] The Jamaican planters could see in the revolt nothing but "the first fruits of the visionary schemes of a few hotheaded philanthropic theorists, ignorant declaimers, and bigotted fanatics."[60] All they could think of was urgent representations to the governor to recall a detachment that had sailed a few days before to England and to detain the remainder of the regiment in Jamaica.[61]

But the tension was rapidly mounting. British Guiana in 1808, Barbados in 1816. In 1823 British Guiana went up in flames, for the second time. Fifty plantations revolted, embracing a population of 12,000. Here again the revolt was so carefully and secretly planned that it took the planters unawares. The slaves demanded unconditional emancipation. The governor expostulated with them—they must go gradually and not be precipitate. The slaves listened coldly. "These things they said were no comfort to them, God had made them of the same flesh and blood as the whites, that they were tired of being slaves to them, that they should be free and they would not work any more." The governor assured them that "if by peaceful conduct they deserved His Majesty's favor they would find their lot substantially though gradually improved, but they declared they would be free."[62] The usual severities followed, the revolt was quelled, the planters celebrated and went their way, unheeding. Their sole solicitude was the continuation of the martial law that had been declared.[63]

"Now the ball has begun to roll," wrote the governor of Barbados confidentially to the Secretary of State for the Colonies when he heard the news of the Guiana revolt, "nobody can say when or where it is to stop."[64] The next year the slaves on two plantations in the parish of Hanover in Jamaica revolted. The revolt was localized and suppressed by a large military force and the ringleaders executed. The slaves as a group, however, could only with difficulty be restrained from interfering with the execution. In addition, the executed men, wrote the governor, "were fully impressed with the belief that they were entitled to their freedom and that the cause they had embraced was just and in vindication of their own rights." According to one of the leaders, the revolt had not been subdued, "the war had only begun."[65]

Outward calm was restored in British Guiana and in Jamaica, but the Negroes continued restless. "The spirit of discontent is anything but extinct," wrote the governor of British Guiana, "it is alive as it were under its ashes, and the negro mind although giving forth no marked indication of mischief to those not accustomed to observe it, is still agitated, jealous and suspicious."[66] The governor cautioned against further delay, not only for the sake of the intrinsic humanity and policy of the measure, but that expectation and conjecture might cease and the Negroes be released from that feverish anxiety which would continue to agitate them, until the question was set definitely at rest.[67] No state of the Negro mind was so dangerous as one of undefined and vague expectation.[68]

This was in 1824. Seven years later the same discussions about property and compensation and vested rights were still going on. In 1831 the slaves took the matter into their own hands. An insurrectionary movement developed in Antigua. The governor of Barbados had to send reinforcements.[69] In Barbados itself the idea prevailed that the King had granted emancipation but the governor was withholding the boon, while a rumor spread that, in the event of insurrection, the King's troops had received positive orders not to fire upon the slaves.[70]

The climax came with a revolt in Jamaica during the Christmas holidays. Jamaica was the largest and most important British West Indian colony, and had more than half the slaves in the entire British West Indies. With Jamaica on fire, nothing could stop the flames from spreading. An "extensive and destructive insurrection" broke out among the slaves in the western district.[71] The insurrection, reported the governor, "was not occasioned by any sudden grievance or immediate cause of discontent, it had been long concerted and at different periods deferred." The leaders were slaves employed in situations of the greatest confidence, who were consequently exempted from all hard labor. "In their position motives no less strong than those which appear to have actuated them—a desire of effecting their freedom, and in some cases of possessing themselves of the property belonging to their masters—could have influenced their conduct."[72]

The West Indian planters, however, saw in these slave revolts nothing but an opportunity of embarrassing the mother country and the humanitarians. From Trinidad the governor wrote as follows in 1832: ". . . the island, as far as the slaves are concerned, is quite tranquil and very easily could be kept so if such was the desire of those who ought to guide their endeavours in this way. . . . It would almost appear to be the actuating motives of some leading people here to drive the Government to abandon its principles, even at the risk of exciting the slaves to insurrection."[73] The governor of Jamaica encountered the same situation: "There is no doubt that there would be those short sighted enough to enjoy at the moment any disturbance on the part of the Negroes arising from disappointment which these persons despairing of their own prospects would consider as some consolation from its entailing embarrassment on the British Government."[74] The West Indian planter, in the words of Daniel O'Connell, continued to sit, "dirty and begrimed over a powder magazine, from which he would not go away, and he was hourly afraid that the slave would apply a torch to it."[75]

But the conflict had left the stage of abstract political discussion about slaves as property and political measures. It had become translated into the passionate desires of people. "The question," wrote a Jamaican to the governor, "will not be left to the arbitrament of a long angry discussion between the Government and the planter. The slave himself has been taught that there is a third party, and that party himself. He knows his strength, and will assert his claim to freedom. Even at this moment, unawed by the late failure, he discusses the question with a fixed determination."[76] From Barbados the governor emphasized the "double cruelty" of suspense—it paralyzed the efforts of the planters, and drove the slaves, who had been kept in years of hope and expectation, to sullen despair.[77] Nothing could be more mischievous, he warned, than holding out to the slaves from session to session that their freedom was coming.[78] It was most desirable, he wrote a fortnight later, that "the state of this unhappy people should be early considered and decided on by the Home Authorities, for the state of delusion they are labouring under renders them obnoxious to their owners and in some instances encreases the unavoidable misery of their condition."[79]

In 1833, therefore, the alternatives were clear: emancipation from above, or emancipation from below. But EMANCIPATION. Economic change, the decline of the monopolists, the development of capitalism, the humanitarian agitation in British churches, contending perorations in the halls of Parliament, had now reached their completion in the determination of the slaves themselves to be free. The Negroes had been stimulated to freedom by the development of the very wealth which their labor had created.

CONCLUSION

THIS STUDY, though treating specifically of Britain, has been given the general title of "Capitalism and Slavery." The title "British Capitalism and Slavery," though pedantically more accurate, would nevertheless have been generically false. What was characteristic of British capitalism was typical also of capitalism in France. Gaston-Martin writes: "There was not a single great shipowner at Nantes who, between 1714 and 1789, did not buy and sell slaves; there was not one who sold only slaves; it is almost as certain that none would have become what he was if he had not sold slaves. In this lies the essential importance of the slave trade: on its success or failure depended the progress or ruin of all the others."[1]

Britain, far ahead of the rest of the world, and France were the countries which ushered in the modern world of industrial development and parliamentary democracy with its attendant liberties. The other foreign stream which fed the accumulation of capital in Britain, the trade with India, was secondary in the period we have presented. It was only with the loss of the American colonies in 1783 that Britain turned to the serious exploitation of her Indian possessions.

The crisis which began in 1776 and continued through the French Revolution and the Napoleonic wars until the Reform Bill of 1832, was in many respects a world crisis similar to the crisis of today, differing only in the more comprehensive range, depth and intensity of the present. It would be strange if the study of the previous upheaval did not at least leave us with certain ideas and principles for the examination of what is going on around us today.

1. *The decisive forces in the period of history we have discussed are the developing economic forces.*

These economic changes are gradual, imperceptible, but they have an irresistible cumulative effect. Men, pursuing their interests, are rarely aware of the ultimate results of their activity. The commercial capitalism of the eighteenth century developed the wealth of Europe by means of slavery and monopoly. But in so doing it helped to create the industrial capitalism of the nineteenth century, which turned round and destroyed the power of commercial capitalism, slavery, and all its works. Without a grasp of these economic changes the history of the period is meaningless.

2. *The various contending groups of dominant merchants, industrialists and politicians, while keenly aware of immediate interests, are for that very reason generally blind to the long-range consequences of their various actions, proposals, policies.*

To the large majority of those responsible for British policy the loss of the American colonies seemed a catastrophe. In reality, as was rapidly seen, it proved the beginning of a period of creative wealth and political power for Britain which far exceeded all the undoubted achievements of the previous age. From this point of view, the problem of the freedom of Africa and the Far East from imperialism will be finally decided by the necessities of production. As the new productive power of 1833 destroyed the relations of mother country and colonies which had existed sixty years before, so the incomparably greater productive power of today will ultimately destroy any relations which stand in its way. This does not invalidate the urgency and validity of arguments for democracy, for freedom now or for freedom after the war. But *mutatis mutandis*, the arguments have a familiar ring. It is helpful to approach them with some experience of similar arguments and the privilege (apparently denied to active contemporaries) of dispassionate investigation into what they represented.

3. *The political and moral ideas of the age are to be examined in the very closest relation to the economic development.*

Politics and morals in the abstract make no sense. We find the British statesmen and publicists defending slavery today, abusing slavery tomorrow, defending slavery the day after. Today they are imperialist, the next day anti-imperialist, and equally pro-imperialist a generation after. And always with the same vehemence. The defence or attack is always on the high moral or political plane. The thing defended or attacked is always something that you can touch and see, to be measured in pounds sterling or pounds avoirdupois, in dollars and cents, yards, feet and inches. This is not a crime. It is a fact. It is understandable at the time. But historians, writing a hundred years after, have no excuse for continuing to wrap the real interests in confusion.* Even the great mass movements, and the anti-slavery mass movement was one of the greatest of these, show a curious affinity with the rise and development of new interests and the necessity of the destruction of the old.

4. *An outworn interest, whose bankruptcy smells to heaven in historical perspective, can exercise an obstructionist and disruptive effect which can only be explained by the powerful services it had previously rendered and the entrenchment previously gained.*

How else explain the powerful defence put up by the West Indians when any impartial observer, if such existed, could have seen that their time was up? However, in a simplified account such as history always must be, the carefully chosen representative, contemporary utterances give a misleading effect of clarity of aim and purpose.

5. *The ideas built on these interests continue long after the interests have been destroyed and work their old mischief, which is all the more mischievous because the interests to which they corresponded no longer exist.*

---

*Of this deplorable tendency Professor Coupland of Oxford University is a notable example.

Such are the ideas of the unfitness of the white man for labor in the tropics and the inferiority of the Negro which condemned him to slavery. We have to guard not only against these old prejudices but also against the new which are being constantly created. No age is exempt.

The points made above are not offered as solutions of present-day problems. They are noted as guide-posts that emerge from the charting of another sea which was in its time as stormy as our own. The historians neither make nor guide history. Their share in such is usually so small as to be almost negligible. But if they do not learn something from history, their activities would then be cultural decoration, or a pleasant pastime, equally useless in these troubled times.

NOTES

CHAPTER I

1. C. M. Andrews, *The Colonial Period of American History* (New Haven, 1934-1938), I, 12-14, 19-20.

2. N. M. Crouse, *The French Struggle for the West Indies, 1665-1713* (New York, 1943), 7.

3. Adam Smith, *The Wealth of Nations* (Cannan edition, New York, 1937), 538. To this Smith added a political factor, "liberty to manage their own affairs in their own way".

4. H. Merivale, *Lectures on Colonization and Colonies* (Oxford, 1928 edition), 262.

5. *Ibid.*, 385. The description is Lord Sydenham's, Governor-General of Canada.

6. Merivale, *op. cit.*, 256.

7. *Ibid.*

8. R. B. Flanders, *Plantation Slavery in Georgia* (Chapel Hill, 1933), 15-16, 20.

9. Merivale, *op. cit.*, 269.

10. M. James, *Social Problems and Policy during the Puritan Revolution, 1640-1660* (London, 1930), 111.

11. Adam Smith, *op. cit.*, 365.

12. J. Cairnes, *The Slave Power* (New York, 1862), 39.

13. G. Wakefield, *A View of the Art of Colonization* (London, 1849), 323.

14. Adam Smith, *op. cit.*, 365-366.

15. Merivale, *op. cit.*, 303. Italics Merivale's.

16. M. B. Hammond, *The Cotton Industry: An Essay in American Economic History* (New York, 1897), 39.

17. Cairnes, *op. cit.*, 44; Merivale, *op. cit.*, 305-306. On soil exhaustion and the expansion of slavery in the United States see W. C. Bagley, *Soil Exhaustion and the Civil War* (Washington, D. C., 1942).

18. Merivale, *op. cit.*, 307-308.

19. J. A. Saco, *Historia de la Esclavitud de los Indios en el Nuevo Mundo* (La Habana, 1932 edition), I, Introduction, p. xxxviii. The Introduction is written by Fernando Ortíz.

20. A. W. Lauber, *Indian Slavery in Colonial Times within the Present Limits of the United States* (New York, 1913), 214-215.

21. J. C. Ballagh, *A History of Slavery in Virginia* (Baltimore, 1902), 51.

22. F. Ortíz, *Contrapunteo Cubano del Tabaco y el Azúcar* (La Habana, 1940), 353.

23. *Ibid.*, 359.

24. Lauber, *op. cit.*, 302.

25. C. M. Haar, "White Indentured Servants in Colonial New York," *Americana* (July, 1940), 371.

26. *Cambridge History of the British Empire* (Cambridge, 1929), I, 69.

27. See Andrews, *op. cit.*, I, 59; K. F. Geiser, *Redemptioners and Indentured Servants in the Colony and Commonwealth of Pennsylvania* (New Haven, 1901), 18.

28. *Cambridge History of the British Empire*, I, 236.

29. C. M. MacInnes, *Bristol, a Gateway of Empire* (Bristol, 1939), 158-159.

30. M. W. Jernegan, *Laboring and Dependent Classes in Colonial America, 1607-1783* (Chicago, 1931), 45.

31. H. E. Bolton and T. M. Marshall, *The Colonization of North America, 1492-1783* (New York, 1936), 336.

32. J. W. Bready, *England Before and After Wesley—The Evangelical Revival and Social Reform* (London, 1938), 106.

33. *Calendar of State Papers, Colonial Series*, V, 98. July 16, 1662.

34. Geiser, *op. cit.*, 18.

35. See G. Mittelberger, *Journey to Pennsylvania in the year 1750* (Philadelphia, 1898), 16; E. I. McCormac, *White Servitude in Maryland* (Baltimore, 1904), 44, 49; "Diary of John Harrower, 1773-1776," *American Historical Review* (Oct., 1900), 77.

36. E. Abbott, *Historical Aspects of the Immigration Problem, Select Documents* (Chicago, 1926), 12n.

37. Bready, *op. cit.*, 127.

38. L. F. Stock (ed.), *Proceedings and Debates in the British Parliament respecting North America* (Washington, D. C., 1924-1941), I, 353 n, 355; III, 437 n, 494.

39. *Calendar of State Papers, Colonial Series*, V, 221.

40. *Ibid.*, V, 463. April, 1667(?)

41. Stock, *op. cit.*, V, 229 n.

42. Jernegan, *op. cit.*, 49.

43. J. D. Lang, *Transportation and Colonization* (London, 1837), 10.

44. Merivale, *op. cit.*, 125.

45. J. D. Butler, "British Convicts Shipped to American Colonies," *American Historical Review* (Oct., 1896), 25.

46. J. C. Jeaffreson (ed.), *A Young Squire of the Seventeenth Century. From the Papers (A.D. 1676-1686) of Christopher Jeaffreson* (London, 1878), I, 258. Jeaffreson to Poyntz, May 6, 1681.

47. For Cromwell's own assurance for this, see Stock, *op. cit.*, I, 211. Cromwell to Speaker Lenthall, Sept. 17, 1649.

48. V. T. Harlow, *A History of Barbados, 1625-1685* (Oxford, 1926), 295.

49. J. A. Williamson, *The Caribbee Islands Under the Proprietary Patents* (Oxford, 1926), 95.

50. *Calendar of State Papers, Colonial Series*, XIII, 65. Joseph Crispe to Col. Bayer, June 10, 1689, from St. Christopher: "Besides the French we have a still worse enemy in the Irish Catholics." In Montserrat the Irish, three to every one of the English, threatened to turn over the island to the French (*Ibid.*, 73. June 27, 1689). Governor Codrington from Antigua preferred to trust the defence of Montserrat to the few English and their slaves rather than rely on the "doubtful fidelity" of the Irish (*Ibid.*, 112-113. July 31, 1689). He disarmed the Irish in Nevis and sent them to Jamaica (*Ibid.*, 123. Aug. 15, 1689).

51. H. J. Ford, *The Scotch-Irish in America* (New York, 1941), 208.

52. *Calendar of State Papers, Colonial Series*, V, 495. Petition of Barbados, Sept. 5, 1667.

53. Stock, *op. cit.*, I, 288 n, 321 n, 327.

54. Harlow, *op. cit.*, 297-298.

55. Mittelberger, *op. cit.*, 19.

56. Stock, *op. cit.*, I, 249. March 25, 1659.

57. Geiser, *op. cit.*, 57.

58. E. W. Andrews (ed.), *Journal of a Lady of Quality; Being the Narrative of a Journey from Scotland to the West Indies, North Carolina and Portugal, in the years 1774-1776* (New Haven, 1923), 33.

59. Jeaffreson, *op. cit.*, II, 4.

60. J. A. Doyle, *English Colonies in America—Virginia, Maryland, and the Carolinas* (New York, 1889), 387.

61. MacInnes, *op. cit.*, 164-165; S. Seyer, *Memoirs Historical and Topographical of Bristol and its Neighbourhood* (Bristol, 1821-1823), II, 531; R. North, *The Life of the Rt. Hon. Francis North, Baron Guildford* (London, 1826), II, 24-27.

62. Seyer, *op. cit.*, II, 532.

63. *Cambridge History of the British Empire*, I, 563-565.

64. Ballagh, *op. cit.*, 42.

65. McCormac, *op. cit.*, 75.

66. *Ibid.*, 111.

67. C. A. Herrick, *White Servitude in Pennsylvania* (Philadelphia, 1926), 3.

68. Stock, *op. cit.*, I, 249.

69. Harlow, *op. cit.*, 306.

70. Stock, *op. cit.*, I, 250. March 25, 1659.

71. *Calendar of State Papers, Colonial Series*, IX, 394. May 30, 1676.

72. Sir W. Besant, *London in the Eighteenth Century* (London, 1902), 557.

73. *Calendar of State Papers, Colonial Series*, V, 229. Report of Committee of Council for Foreign Plantations, Aug., 1664 (?).

74. G. S. Callender, *Selections from the Economic History of the United States, 1765-1860* (New York, 1909), 48.

75. *Calendar of State Papers, Colonial Series*, X, 574. July 13, 1680.

76. H. J. Laski, *The Rise of European Liberalism* (London, 1936), 199, 215, 221.

77. Daniel Defoe, *Moll Flanders* (Abbey Classics edition, London, n.d.), 71.

78. T. J. Wertenbaker, *The Planters of Colonial Virginia* (Princeton, 1922), 61.

79. Herrick, *op. cit.*, 278.

80. *Ibid.*, 12.

81. *Calendar of State Papers, Colonial Series*, V, 220. Petition of Merchants, Planters and Masters of Ships trading to the Plantations, July 12, 1664.

82. Harlow, *op. cit.*, 307.

83. *Calendar of State Papers, Colonial Series*, IX, 445. Aug. 15, 1676.

84. U. B. Phillips, *Life and Labor in the Old South* (Boston, 1929), 25.

85. J. S. Bassett, *Slavery and Servitude in the Colony of North Carolina* (Baltimore, 1896), 77. On the docility of the Negro slave, see *infra*, pp. 201-208.

86. Flanders, *op. cit.*, 14.

87. Cairnes, *op. cit.*, 35 n.

88. Callender, *op. cit.*, 764 n.

89. Cairnes, *op. cit.*, 36.

90. Ortíz, *op. cit.*, 6, 84.

91. A. G. Price, *White Settlers in the Tropics* (New York, 1939), 83.

92. *Ibid.*, 83, 95.

93. *Ibid.*, 92.

94. *Ibid.*, 94.

95. E. T. Thompson, "The Climatic Theory of the Plantation," *Agricultural History* (Jan., 1941), 60.

96. H. L. Wilkinson, *The World's Population Problems and a White Australia* (London, 1930), 250.

97. *Ibid.*, 251.

98. R. Guerra, *Azúcar y Población en Las Antillas* (La Habana, 1935), 20.

99. Williamson, *op. cit.*, 157-158.

100. *Calendar of State Papers, Colonial Series*, X, 503. Governor Atkins, March 26, 1680.

101. *Ibid.*, VII, 141. Sir Peter Colleton to Governor Codrington, Dec. 14, 1670. A similar suggestion came from Jamaica in 1686. Permission was requested for the introduction of cotton manufacture, to provide employment for the poor whites. The reply of the British Customs authorities was that "the more such manufactures are encouraged in the Colonies

the less they will be dependent on England." F. Cundall, *The Governors of Jamaica in the Seventeenth Century* (London, 1936), 102-103.

102. *Calendar of State Papers, Colonial Series*, XIV, 446-447. Governor Russell, March 23, 1695.

103. C. S. S. Higham, *The Development of the Leeward Islands under the Restoration, 1660-1688* (Cambridge, 1921), 145.

104. Harlow, *op. cit.*, 44.

105. Callender, *op. cit.*, 762.

106. Merivale, *op. cit.*, 62.

107. Harlow, *op. cit.*, 293.

108. *Ibid.*, 41.

109. *Calendar of State Papers, Colonial Series*, V, 529. "Some Observations on the Island of Barbadoes," 1667.

110. Harlow, *op. cit.*, 41.

111. *Ibid.*, 43.

112. Merivale, *op. cit.*, 81.

113. F. W. Pitman, *The Settlement and Financing of British West India Plantations in the Eighteenth Century*, in *Essays in Colonial History by Students of C. M. Andrews* (New Haven, 1931), 267.

114. *Ibid.*, 267-269.

115. *Calendar of State Papers, Colonial Series*, I, 79. Governor Sir Francis Wyatt and Council of Virginia, April 6, 1626.

116. Wertenbaker, *op. cit.*, 59, 115, 122-123, 131, 151.

117. R. B. Vance, *Human Factors in Cotton Culture: A Study in the Social Geography of the American South* (Chapel Hill, 1929), 36.

118. J. A. Saco, *Historia de la Esclavitud de la Raza Africana en el Nuevo Mundo y en especial en los Países America-Hispanos* (La Habana, 1938), I, Introduction, p. xxviii. The Introduction is by Fernando Ortíz.

119. T. Blanco, "El Prejuicio Racial en Puerto Rico," *Estudios Afrocubanos*, II (1938), 26.

120. Saco, *Historia de la Esclavitud de la Raza Africana* ... Introduction, p. xxx.

121. *Immigration of Labourers into the West Indian Colonies and the Mauritius*, Part II, *Parliamentary Papers*, Aug. 26, 1846, 60. Henry Light to Lord Stanley, Sept. 17, 1845: "As labourers they are invaluable, as citizens they are amongst the best, and rarely are brought before the courts of justice or the police."

122. *Papers Relative to the West Indies, 1841-1842, Jamaica-Barbados*, 18. C. T. Metcalfe to Lord John Russell, Oct. 27, 1841.

123. *Immigration of Labourers into the West Indian Colonies* ..., 111. William Reynolds to C. A. Fitzroy, August 20, 1845.

124. These figures are taken from tables in I. Ferenczi, *International Migrations* (New York, 1929), I, 506-509, 516-518, 520, 534, 537.

125. The following table illustrates the use of Chinese labor on Cuban sugar plantations in 1857:

Plantation	Negroes	Chinese
Flor de Cuba	409	170
San Martín	452	125
El Progreso	550	40
Armonía	330	20
Santa Rosa	300	30
San Rafael	260	20
Santa Susana	632	200

The last plantation was truly cosmopolitan; the slave gang included 34 natives of Yucatan. These figures are taken from J. G. Cantero, *Los Ingenios de la Isla de Cuba* (La Habana, 1857). The book is not paged. There was some opposition to this Chinese labor, on the ground that it increased the heterogeneity of the population. "And what shall we lose thereby?" was the retort. *Anales de la Real Junta de Fomento y Sociedad Económica de La Habana* (La Habana, 1851), 187.

126. Ferenczi, *op. cit.*, I, 527.

CHAPTER 2

1. *Calendar of State Papers, Colonial Series*, V, 167. Renatus Enys to Secretary Bennet, Nov. 1, 1663.

2. C. Whitworth (ed.), *The Political and Commercial Works of Charles Davenant* (London, 1781), V, 146.

3. G. F. Zook, *The Company of Royal Adventurers trading into Africa* (Lancaster, 1919), 9, 16.

4. M. Postlethwayt, *Great Britain's Commercial Interest Explained and Improved* (London, 1759), II, 148-149, 236; Postlethwayt, *The African Trade, the Great Pillar and Support of the British Plantation Trade in North America* (London, 1745), 38-39; Postlethwayt, *The National and Private Advantages of the African Trade Considered* (London, 1746), 113, 122.

5. J. Gee, *The Trade and Navigation of Great Britain Considered* (Glasgow, 1750), 25-26.

6. Whitworth, *op. cit.*, II, 37-40.

7. *Ibid.*, V, 140-141. The whole essay, "Reflections upon the Constitution and Management of the African Trade," will repay reading.

8. E. Donnan (ed.), *Documents Illustrative of the History of the Slave Trade to America* (Washington, D. C., 1930-1935), II, 129-130.

9. *Ibid.*, I, 265. In 1681 these debts were estimated at £271,000. E. D. Collins, *Studies in the Colonial Policy of England, 1672-1680* (Annual Report of the American Historical Association, 1900), 185.

10. J. Latimer, *Annals of Bristol in the Eighteenth Century* (Bristol, 1893), 271.

11. Higham, *op. cit.*, 158.

12. Latimer, *op. cit.*, 272.

13. Anonymous, *Some Matters of Fact relating to the present state of the African Trade* (London, 1720), 3.

14. Pitman, *The Development of the British West Indies, 1700-1763* (New Haven, 1917), 67.

15. *Ibid.*, 69-70, 79.

16. Postlethwayt, *Great Britain's Commercial Interest* . . ., II, 479-480. See also pp. 149-151, 154-155.

17. H. H. S. Aimes, *A History of Slavery in Cuba, 1511 to 1868* (New York, 1907), 33, 269.

18. W. E. H. Lecky, *A History of England in the Eighteenth Century* (London, 1892-1920), II, 244.

19. *Report of the Lords of the Committee of Privy Council appointed for the consideration of all matters relating to Trade and Foreign Plantations, 1788*. Part VI, Evidence of Messrs. Baillie, King, Camden and Hubbert. The following figures, taken from the same report (Part IV, No. 4 and No. 15, Supplement No. 6, and Papers received since the date of the report), give some indication of the extent of the re-export trade:

Colony	Years	Imports	Re-Exports
Jamaica	1784-1787	37,841	14,477
St. Kitts	1778-1788	2,784	1,769
Dominica	1784-1788	27,553	15,781
Grenada	1784-1792	44,712	31,210

According to Dundas, the total British West Indian importation for 1791 amounted to 74,000, the re-exports to 34,000. *Cobbett's Parliamentary History of England* (referred to hereafter as *Parl. Hist.*), XXIX, 1206. April 23, 1792.

20. B. Edwards, *The History, Civil and Commercial, of the British Colonies in the West Indies* (London, 1801), I, 299.

21. J. Ramsay, A Manuscript entirely in his own hand mainly concerned with his activities towards the Abolition of the Slave Trade, 1787 (Rhodes House Library, Oxford), f. 23(v). "Memorial on the Supplying of the Navy with Seamen."

22. W. Enfield, *An Essay towards the history of Liverpool* (London, 1774), 67.

23. Donnan, *op. cit.*, II, 630. Liverpool's progress is seen from the following table:

Year	Liverpool	London	Bristol
1720	21	60	39
1753	64	13	27
1771	107	58	23

Between 1756 and 1786 Bristol sent 588 ships to Africa, Liverpool 1,858; between 1795 and 1804 Liverpool sent 1,099 vessels to Africa, London 155, Bristol 29. (The figures for 1720 come from *Some Matters of Fact* . . ., 3; the others from MacInnes, *op. cit.*, 191.)

24. *Cobbett's Parliamentary Debates* (Referred to hereafter as *Parl. Deb.*), IX, 127. George Hibbert, March 16, 1807.

25. Correspondence between Robert Bostock, master mariner and merchant, and others, giving particulars of the slave trading of Liverpool ships in the West Indies, 1789-1792 (MS. Vol., Liverpool Public Library). Bostock to Capt. James Fryer, July 17, 1790.

26. MacInnes, *op. cit.*, 202.

27. T. Clarkson, *History of the Rise, Progress, and Accomplishment of the Abolition of the African Slave Trade by the British Parliament* (London, 1839), 197.

28. Donnan, *op. cit.*, I, 132. The Guinea Company to Francis Soane, Dec. 9, 1651.

29. Journals of Liverpool Slave Ships ("Bloom" and others); with correspondence and prices of slaves sold (MS. Vol., Liverpool Public Library). Bostock to Knowles, June 19, 1788.

30. E. Martin (ed.), *Journal of a Slave Dealer*. "A View of some Remarkable Axcedents in the Life of Nics. Owen on the Coast of Africa and America from the year 1746 to the year 1757*" (London, 1930), 77-78, 97-98.

31. Latimer, *op. cit.*, 144-145.

32. A. P. Wadsworth and J. de L. Mann, *The Cotton Trade and Industrial Lancashire* (Manchester, 1931), 228-229.

33. Donnan, *op. cit.*, II, 625-627.

34. *Ibid.*, II, 631.

35. Latimer, *op. cit.*, 476; Wadsworth and Mann, *op. cit.*, 225.

36. Quoted from Sir Thomas Mun in J. E. Gillespie, *The Influence of Oversea Expansion on England to 1700* (New York, 1920), 165.

37. Donnan, *op. cit.*, II, 627.

38. J. Wallace, *A General and Descriptive History of the Ancient and Present State of the Town of Liverpool . . . together with a Circumstantial Account of the True Causes of its Extensive African Trade* (Liverpool, 1795), 229-230. For instances of subdivision see also Wadsworth and Mann, *op. cit.*, 224-225.

39. Edwards, *op. cit.*, II, 72, 74, 87-89; J. Atkins, *A Voyage to Guinea, Brasil, and the West-Indies* (London, 1735), 179. For an authoritative modern discussion, see M. J. Herskovits, *The Myth of the Negro Past* (New York, 1941), 34-50.

40. Correspondence between Robert Bostock . . . Bostock to Fryer, Jan. 1790; Bostock to Flint, Nov. 11, 1790.

41. W. Sypher, *Guinea's Captive Kings, British Anti-Slavery Literature of the XVIIIth Century* (Chapel Hill, 1942), 170. The slaves were inspected as carefully as cattle in the Smithfield market, the chief qualities

emphasized being height, sound teeth, pliant limbs, and lack of venereal disease. Atkins, *op. cit.*, 180.

42. E. F. Gay, "Letters from a Sugar Plantation in Nevis, 1723-1732," *Journal of Economic and Business History* (Nov., 1928), 164.

43. Donnan, *op. cit.*, II, 626.

44. Correspondence between Robert Bostock . . ., Bostock to Cleveland, Aug. 10, 1789.

45. T. Clarkson, *Essay on the Impolicy of the African Slave Trade* (London, 1788),29.

46. W. Roscoe, *A General View of the African Slave Trade demonstrating its Injustice and Impolicy* (London, 1788), 23-24.

47. A. Mackenzie-Grieve, *The Last Years of the English Slave Trade* (London, 1941), 178.

48. F. Caravaca, *Esclavos! El Hombre Negro: Instrumento del Progreso del Blanco* (Barcelona, 1933), 50.

49. This was the Brandenburg Company, sometimes called, from its headquarters, the Emden Company. Incorporated in 1682, the company established two settlements on the African coast and unsuccessfully tried to obtain West Indian possessions. Donnan, *op. cit.*, I, 103-104.

50. Zook, *op. cit.*, 11-12, 19.

51. R. I. and S. Wilberforce, *The Life of William Wilberforce* (London, 1838), I, 343. George III had once whispered jestingly to the abolitionist at a levée: "How go on your black clients, Mr. Wilberforce?" In 1804 Wilberforce wrote to Muncaster that "it was truly humiliating to see, in the House of Lords, four of the Royal Family come down to vote against the poor, helpless, friendless slaves." *Ibid.*, III, 182. July 6, 1804.

52. Correspondence between Robert Bostock . . ., Bostock to Fryer, May 24, 1792. The Duke was the recipient of a service of plate as "the poor but honourable testimony of the gratitude of the people of Jamaica." G. W. Bridges, *The Annals of Jamaica* (London, 1828), II, 263 n.

53. *Parl. Hist.*, XXX, 659. April 11, 1793.

54. Andrews, *op. cit.*, IV, 61.

55. C. M. Andrews, "Anglo-French Commercial Rivalry, 1700-1750," *American Historical Review* (April, 1915), 546.

56. Donnan, *op. cit.*, II, 45.

57. *H. of C. Sess. Pap., Accounts and Papers, 1795-1796*. A. & P. 42, Series No. 100, Document 848, 1-21.

58. Add. MSS. 12433 (British Museum), ff. 13, 19. Edward Law, May 14, 1792.

59. P. Cunningham (ed.), *The Letters of Horace Walpole* (London, 1891), II, 197. To Sir H. Mann, Feb. 25, 1750.

60. *Parl. Hist.*, XVII, 507-508. May 5, 1772.

61. R. Terry, *Some Old Papers relating to the Newport Slave Trade* (Bulletin of the Newport Historical Society, July, 1927), 10.

62. *Calendar of State Papers, Colonial Series*, X, 611. Evidence of

Barbados planters before the Lords of Trade and Plantations, Oct. 8, 1680. For a vigorous dissent from the view that the slaves had no means of communication except in the language of their masters, see Herskovits, *op. cit.*, 79-81.

63. *Calendar of State Papers,* XIV, 448. Governor Russell, March 23, 1695.

64. See *infra,* p. 198. The governor of Barbados opposed the building of churches on the ground that permission to the Negroes thus to assemble would turn their minds to plots and insurrections. C. O. 28 92 (Public Record Office), Nov. 4, 1823. The planters justified their attitude by the plea that the missionaries instilled dangerous notions into the heads of the slaves which were subversive of plantation discipline.

65. Lecky, *op. cit.*, II, 249.

66. Sypher, *op. cit.*, 14.

67. V. T. Harlow, *Christopher Codrington* (Oxford, 1928), 211, 215.

68. Sypher, *op. cit.*, 65.

69. Latimer, *op. cit.*, 100.

70. *Ibid.*, 478.

71. S. H. Swinny, *The Humanitarianism of the Eighteenth Century and its results,* in F. S. Marvin (ed.), *Western Races and the World* (Oxford, 1922), 130-131.

72. L. Strachey, *Eminent Victorians* (Phoenix ed., London, 1929), 3.

73. Mackenzie-Grieve, *op. cit.*, 162.

74. G. R. Wynne, *The Church in Greater Britain* (London, 1911), 120.

75. *H. of C. Sess. Pap.,* 1837-8, Vol. 48. The exact figure was £12,729.4.4 (pp. 19, 22).

76. Wynne, *op. cit.*, 120; C. J. Abbey and J. H. Overton, *The English Church in the Eighteenth Century* (London, 1878), II, 107.

77. Abbey and Overton, *op. cit.*, II, 106.

78. A. T. Gary, *The Political and Economic Relations of English and American Quakers, 1750-1785* (Oxford University D. Phil. Thesis, 1935), 506. The copy examined was deposited in the Library of Friends' House, London.

79. H. J. Cadbury, *Colonial Quaker Antecedents to British Abolition of Slavery* (Friends' House, London, 1933), 1.

80. Gary, *op. cit.*, 173-174.

81. See Liverpool Papers, Add. MSS. 38227 (British Museum), f. 202, for an undated letter of Lord Hawkesbury, President of the Privy Council, to Lord Rodney, agreeing to use Rodney's proxy. Hawkesbury promised to "make the best use of it in defending the island of Jamaica and the other West India islands which his Lordship so gloriously defended against a foreign enemy on the memorable 12th. April," and he expressed his sorrow that only a severe fit of the gout prevented Rodney from "attending Parliament and affording his personal support to those who are in so much want of it."

82. *Parl. Deb.,* VIII, 669. Feb. 5, 1807.

83. F. J. Klingberg, *The Anti-Slavery Movement in England* (New Haven, 1926), 127.

84. *H. of C. Sess. Pap.,* 1837-8, Vol. 48. The exact figure is £6,207.7.6 (pp. 49, 62).

85. Bready, *op. cit.,* 341.

86. Zook, *op. cit.,* 18.

87. Swinny, *op. cit.,* 140.

88. G. Williams, *History of the Liverpool Privateers, with an Account of the Liverpool Slave Trade* (Liverpool, 1897), 473-474.

89. Latimer, *op. cit.,* 147.

90. M. Steen, *The Sun is My Undoing* (New York, 1941), 50.

91. M. D. George, *London Life in the Eighteenth Century* (London, 1925), 137-138.

92. H. T. Catterall, *Judicial Cases concerning Negro Slavery* (Washington, D. C., 1926-1927), I, 9, 12.

93. Bready, *op. cit.,* 104-105.

94. R. Coupland, *The British Anti-Slavery Movement* (London, 1933), 55-56.

95. Sypher, *op. cit.,* 63.

96. Catterall, *op. cit.,* I, 19-20; W. Massey, *A History of England during the Reign of George the Third* (London, 1865), III, 178-179.

97. Anonymous, *Recollections of Old Liverpool, by a Nonagenarian* (Liverpool, 1863), 10.

98. Ramsay, MS. Vol., f. 65. "An Address on the Proposed Bill for the Abolition of the Slave Trade."

99. G. Williams, *op. cit.,* 586.

100. *Hansard, Third Series,* CIX, 1102. Hutt, March 19, 1850.

101. H. W. Preston, *Rhode Island and the Sea* (Providence, 1932), 70, 73. The author was Director of the State Bureau of Information.

102. Latimer, *op. cit.,* 142.

103. J. W. D. Powell, *Bristol Privateers and Ships of War* (London, 1930), 167.

104. H. R. F. Bourne, *English Merchants, Memoirs in Illustration of the Progress of British Commerce* (London, 1866), II, 63; J. B. Botsford, *English Society in the Eighteenth Century as Influenced from Oversea* (New York, 1924), 122; Enfield, *op. cit.,* 48-49. For Blundell's slave trading, see Donnan, *op. cit.,* II, 492.

105. For Cunliffe, see Bourne, *op. cit.,* II, 57; Botsford, *op. cit.,* 122; Enfield, *op. cit.,* 43, 49; Donnan, *op. cit.,* II, 492, 497.

106. Donnan, *op. cit.,* II, 631; J. Hughes, *Liverpool Banks and Bankers, 1760-1817* (Liverpool, 1906), 174.

107. L. H. Grindon, *Manchester Banks and Bankers* (Manchester, 1878), 55, 79-80, 187-188; Bourne, *op. cit.,* II, 64, 78; Botsford, *op. cit.,* 122; Donnan, *op. cit.,* II, 492.

108. Donnan, *op. cit.,* I, 169-172.

109. *Ibid.,* II, 468.

110. Latimer, *op. cit.*, 476-477.

111. For examples, see Wadsworth and Mann, *op. cit.*, 216 n; Hughes, *op. cit.*, 109, 139, 172, 174, 176; Donnan, *op. cit.*, II, 492 n.

112. L. B. Namier, "Antony Bacon, an Eighteenth Century Merchant," *Journal of Economic and Business History* (Nov., 1929), 21.

113. Donnan, *op. cit.*, II, 642-644, 656-657 n.

114. *Parl. Deb.*, IX, 170. March 23, 1807.

115. *Ibid.*, VII, 230. May 16, 1806.

116. Wilberforce, *Life of Wilberforce*, III, 170. Wilberforce to John Newton, June, 1804.

117. C. O. 137/91. Petition of Committee of Jamaica House of Assembly on the Sugar and Slave Trade, Dec. 5, 1972.

118. Sypher, *op. cit.*, 157-158, 162-163, 186-188, 217-219.

119. *Ibid.*, 59; Bready, *op. cit.*, 341.

120. *Parl. Hist.*, XIX, 305. May 23, 1777.

121. Bready, *op. cit.*, 102.

122. Postlethwayt, *Great Britain's Commercial Interest* ..., II, 217-218; Savary des Bruslons, *The Universal Dictionary of Trade and Commerce. With large additions and improvements by* M. Postlethwayt (London, 1751), I, 25. It is not true to say, as Sypher does (*op. cit.*, 84), that Postlethwayt "takes a dark view" of the slave trade.

123. W. Snelgrave, *A New Account of Guinea and the Slave Trade* (London, 1754), 160-161.

CHAPTER 3

1. Adam Smith, *op. cit.*, 415-416, 590-591.

2. W. Wood, *A Survey of Trade* (London, 1718), Part III, 193.

3. J. F. Rees, "The Phases of British Commercial Policy in the Eighteenth Century," *Economica* (June, 1925), 143.

4. Gee, *op. cit.*, III.

5. Postlethwayt, *The African Trade, the Great Pillar* ..., 4, 6.

6. *Cambridge History of the British Empire*, I, 565.

7. Whitworth, *op. cit.*, II, 20.

8. J. Bennett, *Two Letters and Several Calculations on the Sugar Colonies and Trade* (London, 1738), 55.

9. Wood, *op. cit.*, 156.

10. Sir D. Thomas, *An Historical Account of the Rise and Growth of the West India Colonies, and of the Great Advantages they are to England, in respect to Trade* (London, 1690). The essay is printed in the Harleian Miscellany, II, 347.

11. Pitman, *The Settlement ... of British West India Plantations* ..., 271.

12. *Report of the Committee of Privy Council, 1788*, Part IV, No. 18, Appendix.
13. J. H. Rose, *William Pitt and the Great War* (London, 1911), 370.
14. Adam Smith, *op. cit.*, 366.
15. Whitworth, *op. cit.*, II, 18.
16. The following tables have been compiled from Sir C. Whitworth, *State of the Trade of Great Britain in its imports and exports, progressively from the year 1697-1773* (London, 1776), Part II, pp. 1-2, 47-50, 53-72, 75-76, 78, 82-91. Trade figures are in pounds sterling.

In the general percentages given in the text for West Indian and mainland trade, I have included in the West Indies figures for 1714-1773 trade with minor places, such as St. Croix, Monte Christi, St. Eustatius, and also trade with islands conquered by Britain in war but later restored —e.g., Cuba, Guadeloupe, etc. Similarly figures for the mainland, 1714-1773, include Canada, Florida, etc. For the comparative importance of these different areas, see Chapter VI, pp. 114-115, and note 36.

In order to see these statistics in their proper perspective, general British trade figures must be included. They are as follows (*Ibid.*, Part I, pp. 78-79.)

Year	British Imports	British Exports
1697	3482586	3525906
1773	11406841	14763252
1714-1773	492146670	730962105

Colony	Year	British Imports from	% of Total British Imports	British Exports to	% of Total British Exports	% of Total British Trade
West Indies..	1697	326536	9.3	142795	4	7
Mainland....	1697	279852	8	140129	3.9	6
Africa.......	1697	6615	...	13435	...	...
West Indies..	1773	2830853	24.8	1270846	8.6	15.5
Mainland....	1773	1420471	12.5	2375797	16.1	14.5
Africa.......	1773	68424	...	662112	...	...
West Indies..	1714 – 1773	101264818	20.5	45389988	6.2	12.
Mainland....	1714 – 1773	55552675	11.3	69903613	9.6	10.2
Africa.......	1714 – 1773	2407447	0.5	15235829	2.1	1.4

Imports from and exports to the individual colonies are as follows:

Colony	British Imports from		British Exports to		British Imports from	
	1697	1773	1697	1773	1714–1773	1714–1773
Antigua......	28209	112779	8029	93323	12785262	3821726
Barbados.....	196532	168682	77465	148817	14506497	7442652
Jamaica......	70000	1286888	40726	683451	42259749	16844990
Montserrat...	14699	47911	3532	14947	3387237	537831
Nevis.........	17096	39299	13043	9181	3636504	549564
Carolina......	12374	456513	5289	344859	11410480	8423588
New England.	26282	124624	68468	527055	4134392	16934316
New York....	10093	76246	4579	289214	1910796	11377696
Pennsylvania.	3347	36652	2997	426448	1115112	9627409
Virginia and Maryland...	227756	589803	58796	328904	35158481	18391097
Georgia......		85391		62932	622958*	746093*
St. Kitts.....		150512		62607	13305659	3181901
Tobago.......		20453		30049	49587†	122093†
Grenada......		445041		102761	3620504‡	1179279‡
St. Vincent...		145619		38444	672991	235665
Dominica.....		248868		43679	1469704§	322294§
Spanish West Indies......		35941		15114		
Tortola.......		48000		26927	863931‖	220038‖
Anguilla......					29933¶	1241¶
West Indies in general..					220448**	7193829**
Hudson's Bay.					583817	211336

*1732–1773
†1764–1773
‡1762–1773
§1763–1773
‖1748–1773
¶1750–1770
**1714–1768

17. Bennett, *op. cit.*, 50, 54.
18. Stock, *op. cit.*, IV, 329. Sir John Barnard, March 28, 1737.
19. Postlethwayt, *The African Trade, the Great Pillar...,* 13-14.

20. E. D. Ellis, *An Introduction to the History of Sugar as a Commodity* (Philadelphia, 1905), 82.

21. Whitworth, *Works of Davenant,* II, 10.

22. H. See, *Modern Capitalism, its Origin and Evolution* (New York, 1928), 104.

23. L. A. Harper, *The English Navigation Laws* (New York, 1939), 242.

24. Andrews, *The Colonial Period* . . ., IV, 9.

25. *Ibid.,* IV, 65, 71, 126, 154-155.

26. See the study by G. P. Insh, *The Company of Scotland Trading to Africa and the Indies* (London, 1932).

27. Collins, *op. cit.,* 143.

28. *Ibid.,* 157. In 1697 the governor of Jamaica asked for a relaxation of the Navigation Laws for seven years to ensure recovery. *Calendar of State Papers, Colonial Series,* XV, 386. Beeston to Blathwayt, Feb. 27, 1697.

29. *Calendar of State Papers, Colonial Series,* IX, 474-475. Oct. 26, 1676.

30. Stock, *op. cit.,* IV, 828. May 30, 1739.

31. Andrews, *The Colonial Period* . . ., II, 264.

32. *Parl. Hist.,* XXIX, 343. Alderman Watson, April 18, 1791; Donnan, *op. cit.,* II, 606.

33. Holt and Gregson Papers (Liverpool Public Library), X, 429. Letter entitled "Commerce," in Gregson's handwriting, undated.

34. G. L. Beer, *The Old Colonial System* (New York, 1933), I, 17.

35. *Ibid.,* I, 43 n.

36. Stock, *op. cit.,* III, 355.

37. This proportion is obtained by taking the average of the 122,000 tons for the West Indies in the five years 1710-1714, and comparing it with the figure of 243,600 tons engaged in foreign trade in 1709, given in A. P. Usher, "The Growth of English Shipping, 1572-1922," *Quarterly Journal of Economics* (May, 1928), 469.

38. Usher, *op. cit.,* 469. In 1787, 998,637 tons.

39. Pitman, *Development of the British West Indies,* 66.

40. R. Stewart-Browne, *Liverpool Ships in the Eighteenth Century* (Liverpool, 1932), 117, 119, 126-127, 130. For Baker and Dawson's slave trading with the Spanish colonies, see Donnan, *op. cit.,* II, 577 n; Aimes, *op. cit.,* 36; *Report of the Committee of Privy Council, 1788,* Part VI.

41. Enfield, *op. cit.,* 26, gives 5,967 seamen in 1771. Gregson says 3,000 were employed in the slave trade. Holt and Gregson Papers, X, 434. Undated letter to T. Brooke, M.P.

42. The shipping trades of London petitioned in 1708 in favor of the monopoly. Against the monopoly came two petitions from the shipowners of Whitehaven in 1709 and 1710; three petitions from the shipwrights of London and its environs in 1708 and 1710; and a petition from the shipwrights of several cities in 1709. Stock, *op. cit.,* III, 204 n, 207 n, 225 n, 226, 249, 250 n, 251.

43. Holt and Gregson Papers, X, 375, 377.

44. Enfield, *op. cit.*, 89.

45. Holt and Gregson Papers, X, 435. Gregson to Brooke.

46. MacInnes, *op. cit.*, 337.

47. *Parl. Hist.,* XXIX, 343. Alderman Watson, April 18, 1791.

48. J. G. Broodbank, *History of the Port of London* (London, 1921), I, 76-82, 89-108; W. S. Lindsay, *A History of Merchant Shipping and Ancient Commerce* (London, 1874-1876), II, 415-420.

49. Latimer, *op. cit.*, 6.

50. W. N. Reid and J. E. Hicks, *Leading Events in the History of the Port of Bristol* (Bristol, n.d.), 106; J. Latimer, *Annals of Bristol in the Seventeenth Century* (Bristol, 1900), 334; W. Barrett, *The History and Antiquities of the City of Bristol* (Bristol, 1780), 186; J. A. Fraser, *Spain and the West Country* (London, 1935), 254-255.

51. J. F. Nicholls and J. Taylor, *Bristol Past and Present* (Bristol, 1881-1882), III, 165.

52. MacInnes, *op. cit.*, 335.

53. *Ibid.*, 202.

54. *Ibid.*, 233.

55. Barrett, *op. cit.*, 189.

56. *Ibid.* Incoming ships from the West Indies amounted to 16,209 out of a total of 48,125 tons; outgoing ships to the West Indies represented 16,913 out of a total of 46,729 tons.

57. MacInnes, *op. cit.*, 236, 367.

58. *Ibid.*, 358, 370.

59. *Ibid.*, 228, 230, 235, 363, 370.

60. *H. of C. Sess. Pap.,* 1837-8, Vol. 48. The exact figure was £62,335.0.5. The family owned 954 slaves outright, and was part owner of another 456 (pages 117, 120, 132, 168).

61. MacInnes, *op. cit.*, 371.

62. Enfield, *op. cit.*, 11-12.

63. P. Mantoux, *The Industrial Revolution in the Eighteenth Century* (London, 1928), 108.

64. Enfield, *op. cit.*, 67.

65. Fraser, *op. cit.*, 254-255.

66. Enfield, *op. cit.*, 69.

67. Mantoux, *op. cit.*, 109.

68. Clarkson, *Essay on the Impolicy ...*, 123-125.

69. J. Corry, *The History of Lancashire* (London, 1825), II, 690.

70. H. Smithers, *Liverpool, Its Commerce, Statistics and Institutions* (Liverpool, 1825), 105.

71. Mackenzie-Grieve, *op. cit.*, 4.

72. G. Williams, *op. cit.*, 594.

73. Holt and Gregson Papers, X, 367, 369, 371, 373.

74. J. A. Picton, *Memorials of Liverpool* (London, 1873), I, 256.

75. MacInnes, *op. cit.*, 191.

76. J. Touzeau, *The Rise and Progress of Liverpool from 1551 to 1835* (Liverpool, 1910), II, 589, 745.

77. "Robin Hood," "The Liverpool Slave Trade," *The Commercial World and Journal of Transport* (Feb. 25, 1893), pp. 8-10; (March 4, 1893), p. 3.

78. G. Eyre-Todd, *History of Glasgow* (Glasgow, 1934), III, 295.

79. Donnan, *op. cit.*, II, 567-568.

80. Stock, *op. cit.*, II, 109.

81. Donnan, *op. cit.*, I, 267.

82. Stock, *op. cit.*, II, 179.

83. Donnan, *op. cit.*, I, 413, 417-418; Stock, *op. cit.*, II, 162 n, 186 n, III, 207 n, 302 n.

84. Donnan, *op. cit.*, I, 379.

85. *Ibid.*, I, 411, 418 n.

86. Stock, *op. cit.*, II, 29 n, 89 n, 94, 186 n.

87. *Ibid.*, II, 20; III, 90, 224 n, 298; IV, 293-297.

88. *Ibid.*, IV, 161 n-162 n.

89. *Ibid.*, III, 45.

90. J. James, *History of the Worsted Manufacture in England from the Earliest Times* (London, 1857), appendix, p. 7.

91. A. S. Turberville, *Johnson's England* (Oxford, 1933), I, 231-232.

92. Wadsworth and Mann, *op. cit.*, 147-166.

93. Holt and Gregson Papers, X, 422-423.

94. *Report of the Committee of Privy Council, 1788*, Part VI. Evidence of Mr. Taylor.

95. Holt and Gregson Papers, X, 423.

96. Donnan, *op. cit.*, II, 337 n, 521-522 n.

97. Wadsworth and Mann, *op. cit.*, 149, 156-157, 231, 233, 243-247, 447.

98. *Ibid.*, 229 n, 231, 231 n.

99. *Cambridge History of the British Empire*, II, 224; Wadsworth and Mann, *op. cit.*, 190.

100. The British import figures are given in J. Wheeler, *Manchester, its Political, Social and Commercial History, Ancient and Modern* (Manchester, 1842), 148, 170; the West Indian imports in L. J. Ragatz, *Statistics for the Study of British Caribbean History, 1763-1833* (London, n.d.), 15, Table VI.

101. Wadsworth and Mann, *op. cit.*, 169.

102. Fraser, *op. cit.*, 241.

103. Latimer, *Annals of Bristol in the Eighteenth Century*, 302; Pitman, *Development of the British West Indies*, 340.

104. Nicholls and Taylor, *op. cit.*, III, 34.

105. Latimer, *Annals of Bristol in the Seventeenth Century*, 280-281, 318-320.

106. *The New Bristol Guide* (Bristol, 1799), 70.

107. Donnan, *op. cit.*, II, 602-604.

108. Reid and Hicks, *op. cit.*, 66; MacInnes, *op. cit.*, 371.

109. Latimer, *Annals of Bristol in the Seventeenth Century*, 44-45, 88.

110. Bourne, *op. cit.*, II, 17-18; Botsford, *op. cit.*, 120, 123.

111. *H. of C. Sess. Pap.*, 1837-8, Vol. 48. The exact sum was £17,868.16.8 (pages 68-69, 167-168).

112. Eyre-Todd, *op. cit.*, III, 39-40, 150-154.

113. Enfield, *op. cit.*, 90; T. Kaye, *The Stranger in Liverpool; or, an Historical and Descriptive View of the Town of Liverpool and its environs* (Liverpool, 1829), 184. For the Branckers and the slave trade, see Donnan, *op. cit.*, II, 655 n.

114. Stock, *op. cit.*, I, 385, 390.

115. Whitworth, *Works of Davenant*, II, 37.

116. C. W. Cole, *French Mercantilism, 1683-1700* (New York, 1943), 87-88. The prohibition is still in operation today. See J. E. Dalton, *Sugar, A Case Study of Government Control* (New York, 1937), 265-274.

117. Bennett, *op. cit.*, Introduction, p. xxvii.

118. Anonymous, *Some Considerations humbly offer'd upon the Bill now depending in the House of Lords, relating to the Trade between the Northern Colonies and the Sugar-Islands* (London, 1732), 15.

119. F. Cundall, *The Governors of Jamaica in the First Half of the Eighteenth Century* (London, 1937), 178.

120. *Parl. Hist.*, XIV, 1293-1294. Jan. 26, 1753; Anonymous, *An Account of the Late Application to Parliament from the Sugar Refiners, Grocers, etc., of the Cities of London and Westminster, the Borough of Southwark, and of the City of Bristol* (London, 1753), 3-5, 43.

121. Stock, *op. cit.*, V, 559. March 23, 1753.

122. *H. of C. Sess. Pap., Reports, Miscellaneous, 1778-1782*, Vol. 35, 1781. *Report from the Committee to whom the Petition of the Sugar Refiners of London was referred*. See especially the evidence of Frances Kemble.

123. Stock, *op. cit.*, IV, 132 n; Ragatz, *Statistics . . .*, 17, Table XI.

124. Saugnier and Brisson, *Voyages to the Coast of Africa* (London, 1792), 285.

125. R. Muir, *A History of Liverpool* (London, 1907), 197.

126. Donnan, *op. cit.*, II, 529 n.

127. Stock, *op. cit.*, IV, 303, 306, 309.

128. Anonymous, *Short Animadversions on the Difference now set up between Gin and Rum, and Our Mother Country and Colonies* (London, 1769), 8-9.

129. Stock, *op. cit.*, IV, 310.

130. Windham Papers (British Museum), Add. MSS. 37886, ff. 125-128. "Observations on the proposal of the West India Merchants to substitute sugar in the distilleries instead of barley." Anonymous, probably 1807.

131. *Hansard, Third Series*, V, 82. July 20, 1831.

132. E. R. Johnson, et al., *History of Domestic and Foreign Commerce*

of the United States (Washington, D. C., 1915), I, 118. The exports to Africa were 292,966 gallons out of total exports of 349,281.

133. J. Corry and J. Evans, *The History of Bristol, Civil and Ecclesiastical* (Bristol, 1816), II, 307-308; Saugnier and Brisson, *op. cit.*, 296-299.

134. Saugnier and Brisson, *op. cit.*, 217.

135. Stock, *op. cit.*, II, 264 n.

136. Donnan, *op. cit.*, I, 234 n, 300 n.

137. *Ibid.*, I, 256, 262; II, 445.

138. *Ibid.*, I, 283.

139. Stock, *op. cit.*, III, 207 n, 225 n, 250 n, 278 n (Birmingham); 204 n, 228 n (London).

140. Donnan, *op. cit.*, II, 98.

141. W. H. B. Court, *The Rise of the Midland Industries* (Oxford, 1938), 145-146.

142. T. S. Ashton, *Iron and Steel in the Industrial Revolution* (Manchester, 1924), 195.

143. Stock, *op. cit.*, IV, 434.

144. R. K. Dent, *The Making of Birmingham: being a History of the Rise and Growth of the Midland Metropolis* (Birmingham, 1894), 147.

145. H. Hamilton, *The English Brass and Copper Industries to 1800* (London, 1926), 137-138, 149-151, 286-292.

146. E. Shiercliff, *The Bristol and Hotwell Guide* (Bristol, 1789), 16.

147. A. H. Dodd, *The Industrial Revolution in North Wales* (Cardiff, 1933), 156-157.

148. Donnan, *op. cit.*, I, 237.

149. Stewart-Browne, *op. cit.*, 52-53.

150. Donnan, *op. cit.*, II, 610-611.

151. *Ibid.*, II, 609.

152. H. Scrivenor, *A Comprehensive History of the Iron Trade* (London, 1841), 344-346, 347-355. The percentages have been computed from tables given.

CHAPTER 4

1. Adam Smith, *op. cit.*, 158.

2. R. Cumberland, *The West Indian: A Comedy* (London, 1775 edition), Act I, Scene III. A brief notice of the play is given in *Sypher, op. cit.,* 239.

3. Stock, *op. cit.*, V, 259. William Beckford, Feb. 8, 1747.

4. F. W. Pitman, "The West Indian Absentee Planter as a British Colonial Type" *(Proceedings of the Pacific Coast Branch of the American Historical Association,* 1927), 113.

5. Whitworth, *Works of Davenant,* II, 7.

6. Cumberland, *op. cit.*, Act I, Scene V. Quoted also in Pitman, *The West Indian Absentee Planter* . . ., 124.

7. Pitman, *The West Indian Absentee Planter* . . ., 125.

8. Merivale, *op. cit.*, 82-83.

9. L. J. Ragatz, *Absentee Landlordism in the British Caribbean, 1750-1833* (London, n.d), 8-20; Pitman, *The West Indian Absentee Planter* . . ., 117-121.

10. R. M. Howard (ed.), *Records and Letters of the Family of the Longs of Longville, Jamaica, and Hampton Lodge, Surrey* (London, 1925), I, 11-12; Cundall, *The Governors of Jamaica in the Seventeenth Century*, 26.

11. J. Britton, *Graphical and Literary Illustrations of Fonthill Abbey, Wiltshire, with Heraldical and Genealogical Notices of the Beckford Family* (London, 1823), 25-26.

12. *Ibid.*, 26-28, 35, 39.

13. *H. of C. Sess. Pap.*, 1837-38, Vol. 48. The exact amount was £15,160.2.9 (pp. 20-21, 64-65).

14. J. Murch, *Memoir of Robert Hibbert, Esquire* (Bath, 1874), 5-6, 15, 18-19, 97, 99, 104-105.

15. Broodbank, *op. cit.*, I, 102-103; A. Beaven, *The Aldermen of the City of London* (London, 1908-1913), II, 203.

16. *H. of C. Sess. Pap.*, 1837-38, Vol. 48. The precise figure was £31,-121.16.0 (pp. 20, 22, 46, 52, 67, 79).

17. See inside cover page of the first issue of the Hibbert Journal. The family mansion, in Duke Street, Kingston, Jamaica, was erected by Thomas Hibbert who arrived in the island in 1734. Called at first "Hibbert's House," it served for some time as the headquarters of the Commander-in-Chief of the armed forces and was popularly known as Headquarters House. It later housed the Colonial Secretary's office and the Legislative Council Chamber. See *Papers relating to the Preservation of Historic Sites and Ancient Monuments and Buildings in the West Indian Colonies, Cd. 6428* (His Majesty's Stationery Office, 1912), 13.

18. Howard, *op. cit.*, I, 67, 71.

19. *Ibid.*, I, 177.

20. C. De Thierry, "Distinguished West Indians in England," *United Empire* (Oct., 1912), 831.

21. Anonymous, *Fortunes made in Business* (London, 1884), II, 117-119, 122-124, 130, 134; Bourne, *op. cit.*, II, 303.

22. *Correspondence between John Gladstone, M.P. and James Cropper, on the present state of Slavery in the British West Indies and in the United States of America, and on the Importation of Sugar from the British Settlements in India* (Liverpool, 1824).

23. *H. of C. Sess. Pap.*, 1837-38, Vol. 48. The exact sum was £85,606.0.2 (pp. 23, 58, 120-121).

24. Harlow, *Christopher Codrington*, 210, 242.

25. A. Warner, *Sir Thomas Warner, Pioneer of the West Indies* (London, 1933), 119-123, 126, 132.

26. Edwards, *op. cit.*, I, Introduction, p. ix.

27. MacInnes, *op. cit.*, 308-310.

28. C. Wright and C. E. Fayle, *A History of Lloyd's, from the Founding of Lloyd's Coffee House to the Present Day* (London, 1928), 286.

29. Eyre-Todd, *op. cit.*, III, 151-152.

30. L. J. Ragatz, *The Fall of the Planter Class in the British Caribbean, 1763-1833* (New York, 1928), 51.

31. *Parl. Hist.*, XXXIV, 1102. Duke of Clarence, July 5, 1799.

32. Ragatz, *Fall of the Planter Class . . .*, 50.

33. Botsford, *op. cit.*, 148; A. Ponsonby, *English Diaries* (London, 1923), 284.

34. MacInnes, *op. cit.*, 236.

35. Bready, *op. cit.*, 157.

36. G. W. Dasent, *Annals of an Eventful Life* (London, 1870), I, 9-10.

37. Sypher, *op. cit.*, 255.

38. L. B. Namier, *The Structure of Politics at the Accession of George III* (London, 1929), I, 210.

39. L. M. Penson, *The Colonial Agents of the British West Indies* (London, 1924), 185-187.

40. A. S. Turberville, *English Men and Manners in the Eighteenth Century* (Oxford, 1926), 134.

41. Lecky, *op. cit.*, I, 251, quoting Bolingbroke.

42. Cumberland, *op. cit.*, Act I, Scene V. Also quoted in Pitman, *The West Indian Absentee Planter . . .*, 124.

43. J. Latimer, *Annals of Bristol in the Nineteenth Century* (Bristol, 1887), 137-138.

44. *Recollections of Old Liverpool,* 76-82. Significant of the new trend, the West Indian's rival, William Ewart, who was to play a prominent part in destroying West Indian slavery and monopoly, was supported among others by such names as Brancker and Earle, whose connections with slavery and the slave trade have already been noted. John Bolton received £15,391.17.11 for 289 slaves in British Guiana. *H. of C. Sess. Pap.*, 1837-8, Vol. 48 (page 131). In 1798 Bolton had six ships which sailed to Africa and transported 2,534 slaves. Donnan, *op. cit.*, II, 642-644.

45. Penson, *op. cit.*, 176.

46. Enfield, *op. cit.*, 92.

47. C. De Thierry, "Colonials at Westminster," *United Empire,* (Jan., 1912), 80.

48. Beaven, *op. cit.*, II, 139.

49. Reid and Hicks, *op. cit.*, 57.

50. *Fortunes made in Business,* II, 127, 129-131.

51. *Hansard, Third Series,* LXXVIII, 469. John Bright, March 7, 1845.

52. De Thierry, "Colonials at Westminster," 80.

53. *Hansard, Third Series,* XVIII, 111. May 30, 1833.

54. *H. of C. Sess. Pap.,* 1837-8, Vol. 48. The compensation paid was £4,866.19.11 (page 19).

55. Ragatz, *Fall of the Planter Class* . . ., 53.

56. De Thierry, "Colonials at Westminister," 80.

57. *Hansard, Third Series,* X, 1238. March 7, 1832.

58. *H. of C. Sess. Pap.,* 1837-8, Vol. 48. The sum paid was £12,281.5.10 (pages 24, 53).

59. C. O.137/100. Balcarres to Portland, Sept. 16, 1798.

60. Anonymous, *A Report of the Proceedings of the Committee of Sugar Refiners for the purpose of effecting a reduction in the high prices of sugar, by lowering the bounty of refined sugar exported, and correcting the evils of the West India monopoly* (London, 1792), 34.

61. Anonymous, *A Merchant to his Friend on the Continent: Letters Concerning the Slave Trade* (Liverpool, n.d.). To Lord Hawkesbury, "as a patron to the trade of this country in general, and a favorer of that, the subject of these letters."

62. Liverpool Papers, Add. MSS. 38223, ff. 170, 175. Sept. 8, and 12, 1788.

63. *Ibid.,* Add. MSS. 38231, f. 59. Thomas Naylor, Mayor, to Hawkesbury, July 10, 1796; f. 60, Minutes of the Common Council, July 6, 1796; f. 64, Hawkesbury to Naylor, July 16, 1796.

64. Bourne, *op. cit.,* II, 135 n. Macaulay described him as "a noisy, purse-proud, illiterate demagogue, whose Cockney English and scraps of mispronounced Latin were the jest of the newspapers." *Ibid.* To Horace Walpole he was "a noisy vapouring fool." *The Letters of Horace Walpole,* V, 248. Walpole to Earl of Stratford, July 9, 1770. Beckford's Latin scholarship is illustrated by his famous "omnium meum mecum porto." Beaven, *op. cit.,* II, 211. This was only to be expected from a product of a society which talked only of planting and to which Dryden was nothing but a name. Steen, *op. cit.,* 430, 433.

65. *Guide to the Guildhall of the City of London* (London, 1927), 58-59.

66. Beaven, *op. cit.,* II, 139.

67. R. Pares, *War and Trade in the West Indies, 1739-1763* (Oxford, 1936), 509.

68. E. J. Stapleton (ed.), *Some Official Correspondence of George Canning* (London, 1887), I, 134. To Liverpool, Jan. 9, 1824. "This most fearful question. . . . There are knots which can not be suddenly disentangled, and must not be cut. . . . Care should be taken not to confound . . . what is morally true with what is historically false. . . . We cannot legislate in this House as if we were legislating for a new world." *Hansard, New Series,* IX, 275, 278, 282. May 15, 1823.

69. *Despatches, Correspondence and Memoranda of Field Marshal Arthur, Duke of Wellington* (London, 1867-1880), V, 603. Memorandum for Sir George Murray, May 16, 1829.

70. Huskisson Papers (British Museum), Add. MSS. 38745, ff. 182-183. To Joseph Sandars, Jan. 22, 1824. See also *Ibid.*, f. 81: "It appears to me not immaterial that the President of the Board of Trade and member for Liverpool should get out as soon as he can." Huskisson to Canning on his membership in the Anti-Slavery Society, Nov. 2, 1823.

71. *Ibid.*, Add. MSS. 38752, f. 26. Huskisson to Horton, Nov. 7, 1827. For Canning's letter of resignation from the Board of Governors of the African Institution, see *Ibid.*, Add. MSS. 38745, ff. 69-70. Oct. 26, 1823.

72. *Ibid.*, Add. MSS. 38752, ff. 26-27.

73. W. Smart, *Economic Annals of the Nineteenth Century* (London, 1910-1917), II, 545.

74. *The Right in the West India Merchants to a Double Monopoly of the Sugar-Market of Great Britain, and the Expedience of all Monopolies, examined* (London, n.d.), 59-60.

75. Stock, *op. cit.*, V, 261. Feb. 8, 1747.

76. Cundall, *The Governors of Jamaica in the Seventeenth Century,* 100.

77. *Parl. Hist.*, XIII, 641. Feb. 13, 1744.

78. *Ibid.*, 652, 655. Feb. 20, 1744.

79. Pares, *op. cit.*, 508-509.

80. Penson, *op. cit.*, 228.

CHAPTER 5

1. Hughes, *op. cit.*, 56-57, 217.

2. *Ibid.*, 91-97, 101; Grindon, *op. cit.*, 42, 54, 79-82, 185-189; Botsford, *op. cit.*, 122; Bourne, *op. cit.*, II, 78-79; Donnan, *op. cit.*, II, 493, 656.

3. Hughes, *op. cit.*, 170-174. In 1799 Leyland had four ships in the slave trade, which carried 1,641 slaves. Donnan, *op. cit.*, II, 646-649.

4. Hughes, *op. cit.*, 74-79, 84-85, 107-108, 111, 133, 138-141, 162, 165-166, 196-198, 220-221. For the Earles see Botsford, *op. cit.*, 123; Bourne, *op. cit.*, II, 64. In 1799 the Earles had three ships in the slave trade, which carried 969 slaves; Ingram, in 1798, three ships, with 1,005 slaves; Bold, in 1799, two ships, with 539 slaves. Donnan, *op. cit.*, II, 642-649.

5. Latimer, *Annals of Bristol in the Eighteenth Century,* 297-298, 392, 468, 507; *Annals of Bristol in the Nineteenth Century,* 113, 494; Bourne, *op. cit.*, II, 18.

6. C. W. Barclay, *A History of the Barclay Family* (London, 1924-1934), III, 235, 242-243, 246-247, 249; Gary, *op. cit.*, 194, 221, 455, 506; Bourne, *op. cit.*, II, 134-135; Botsford, *op. cit.*, 120-121, 295. Another prominent banking name in London associated with the slave trade was Baring. Gary, *op. cit.*, 506.

7. Eyre-Todd, *op. cit.*, III, 151, 218-220, 245, 372; J. Buchanan, *Banking in Glasgow during the olden time* (Glasgow, 1862), 5-6, 17, 23-26, 30-34.

8. J. Lord, *Capital and Steam-Power, 1750-1850* (London, 1923), 113.

9. *Ibid.*, 192.

10. Liverpool Papers, Add. MSS. 38227, ff. 43, 50, 140, 141. Sept. 7 and 14, Nov. 15 and 17, 1791.

11. Namier, "Antony Bacon . . .," 25-27, 32, 39, 41, 43; Ashton, *op. cit.*, 52, 136, 241-242; J. H. Clapham, *An Economic History of Modern Britain, The Early Railway Age, 1820-1850* (Cambridge, 1930), 187-188.

12. Beaven, *op. cit.*, II, 131.

13. Ashton, *op. cit.*, 157.

14. F. Martin, *The History of Lloyd's and of Marine Insurance in Great Britain* (London, 1876), 62.

15. Wright and Fayle, *op. cit.*, 19, 91, 151, 212, 218-219, 243, 293, 327. Other prominent names associated with Lloyd's were Baring, and the abolitionists, Richard Thornton and Zachary Macaulay. *Ibid.*, 196-197.

16. *H. of C. Sess. Pap.*, 1837-8, Vol. 48. The exact figure was £15,095.4.4 (pp. 12, 165, 169).

17. Clapham, *op. cit.*, 286.

18. Wright and Fayle, *op. cit.*, 240-241.

19. Callender, *op. cit.*, 78-79.

20. Dodd, *op. cit.*, 37, 91, 125, 204-208, 219. See also C. R. Fay, *Imperial Economy and its place in the formation of Economic Doctrine* (Oxford, 1934), 32.

21. Huskisson Papers, Add. MSS. 38745, ff. 182-183. Huskisson to Sandars, Jan. 22, 1824, agreeing with his withdrawal. See also J. Francis, *A History of the English Railway; its Social Relations and Revelations, 1820-1845* (London, 1851), I, 93.

22. See *Hansard*, VI, 919, where Gascoyne opposed the prohibition of the British slave trade to new colonies conquered during the Napoleonic wars as a violation of faith. April 25, 1806. For Gladstone, see Francis, *op. cit.*, I, 123; F. S. Williams, *Our Iron Roads: their history, construction, and social influences* (London, 1852), 323-324, 337. For Moss, see Francis, *op. cit.*, I, 123; Hughes, *op. cit.*, 197-198.

23. V. Sommerfield, *English Railways, their beginnings, development and personalities* (London, 1937), 34-38; Latimer, *Annals of Bristol in the Nineteenth Century*, III, 189-190. Three of the directors were connected with the West Indies, and subscribed £51,800 out of £217,500.

24. Lord, *op. cit.*, 166.

25. Scrivenor, *op. cit.*, 86-87. In 1740: 17,350 tons in 89 furnaces; in 1788: 68,300 tons in 85 furnaces.

26. Wheeler, *op. cit.*, 148, 170. Imports: from 1,985,868 to 6,700,000 pounds; exports: from £23,253 to £355,060.

27. W. T. Jackman, *The Development of Transportation in Modern England* (Cambridge, 1916), II, 514 n. From 19,837 to 27,246.

28. Butterworth, *op. cit.*, 57; Wheeler, *op. cit.*, 171. From 20,000 to 80,000.

29. Lord, *op. cit.*, 143.

30. Mantoux, *op. cit.*, 102-103.

31. Adam Smith, *op. cit.*, 549, 555, 558-559, 567, 573, 576, 579, 581, 595, 625-626.

32. *Ibid.*, 577.

CHAPTER 6

1. Johnson, *op. cit.*, I, 118-119. The proportions have been computed from the table of exports given.

2. Pitman, *Development of the British West Indies,* Preface, p. vii.

3. *Calendar of State Papers, Colonial Series,* V, 382. Governor Willoughby, May 12, 1666; *Ibid.,* V, 414. John Reid to Secretary Arlington, 1666(?)

4. Postlethwayt, *Universal Dictionary* ..., II, 767.

5. Callender, *op. cit.*, 96, quoting *American Husbandry* (1775).

6. *Ibid.*, 96.

7. *Cambridge History of the British Empire,* I, 572.

8. Andrews, *The Colonial Period* ..., I, 72.

9. *Cambridge History of the British Empire,* I, 564.

10. Andrews, *The Colonial Period* ..., I, 497-499.

11. *Calendar of State Papers, Colonial Series,* I, 429-430. Sept. 26, 1655. Governor Winthrop opposed emigration as "displeasing" to God. R. C. Winthrop, *Life and Letters of John Winthrop* (Boston, 1864-1867), II, 248.

12. Whitworth, *Works of Davenant,* II, 9, 21, 22.

13. H. A. Innis, *The Cod Fisheries, the History of an International Economy* (New Haven, 1940), 78.

14. Stock, *op. cit*, V, 259. William Beckford, Feb. 8, 1747.

15. Callender, *op. cit*, 78.

16. P. W. Bidwell and J. I. Falconer, *History of Agriculture in the Northern United States, 1620-1820* (New York, 1941), 43.

17. Harlow, *A History of Barbados* ..., 272.

18. *Ibid.*, 268.

19. Andrews, *The Colonial Period* ..., IV, 347.

20. Harlow, *A History of Barbados* ..., 287.

21. *Calendar of State Papers, Colonial Series,* VII, 4. John Style to Secretary Morrice, Jan. 14, 1669.

22. *Ibid.*, X, 297. "Narrative and Disposition of Capt. Breedon concerning New England," Oct. 17, 1678.

23. Stock, *op. cit*, II, 269. Jan. 27, 1698.

24. A. M. Whitson, "The Outlook of the Continental American Colonies on the British West Indies, 1760-1775," *Political Science Quarterly* (March, 1930), 61-63.

25. Innis, *op. cit.*, 134-135.

26. *Calendar of State Papers, Colonial Series*, V, 167. Renatus Enys to Secretary Bennet, Nov. 1, 1663: "The sworn enemies of the colony are the Dons of Barbadoes . . .; they use the utmost means to disparage the country."

27. *Ibid.*, XI, 431. Governor Lynch to Governor Stapleton of the Leeward Islands, May 16, 1683.

28. *Parl. Hist.*, XVII, 482-485. April 29, 1772. The question is discussed in C. Wilson, *Anglo-Dutch Commerce and Finance in the Eighteenth Century* (Cambridge, 1941), 182-183.

29. Pares, *op. cit.*, 220.

30. *Calendar of State Papers, Colonial Series*, V, 167. Governor Willoughby, Nov. 4, 1663.

31. Pitman, *Development of the British West Indies*, 70-71; Stock, *op. cit.*, IV, 97.

32. Bennett, *op. cit.*, 22-25.

33. Postlethwayt, *Great Britain's Commercial Interest* . . ., I, 494; Postlethwayt, *Universal Dictionary* . . ., I, 869; *An Account of the late application . . . from the Sugar Refiners*, 4; Stock, *op. cit.*, IV, 101.

34. Pares, *op. cit.*, 180.

35. J. Almon, *Anecdotes of the Life of the Right Honourable William Pitt, Earl of Chatham, and of the principal events of his time* (London, 1797), III, 222, 225. The quotations came from a contemporary pamphlet. *Letter from a Gentleman in Guadeloupe to his Friend in London* (1760), which is reproduced by Almon.

36. Whitworth, *State of the Trade of Great Britain* . . ., Part II, pp. 85-86. The figures for Canada and Florida are as follows:

	British Imports from	British Exports to
Canada	£448563	£2383679
Florida	£ 7999	£ 375068

For Grenada and Dominica, see Chapter III, note 16, *supra*.

37. Pares, *op. cit.*, 219.

38. Almon, *op. cit.*, III, 225.

39. Pares, *op. cit.*, 224.

40. Stock, *op. cit.*, V, 461. March 7, 1750.

41. Whitson, *op. cit.*, 73.

42. Stock, *op. cit.*, V, 537 n.

43. Anonymous, *The Importance of the Sugar Colonies to Great Britain Stated* (London, 1731), 7.

44. Stock, *op. cit.*, IV, 136. Thomas Winnington, Feb. 23, 1731.

45. *Ibid.*, V, 462.

46. Postlethwayt, *Universal Dictionary* . . ., I, 871-872, II, 769; Postlethwayt, *Great Britain's Commercial Interest* . . ., I, 482, 485, 489-490, 493.

47. Almon, *op. cit.*, III, 16. Circular Letter to the Governors of North America, Aug. 23, 1760.

48. Stock, *op. cit.*, V, 478. April 16, 1751.

49. Anonymous, *A Letter to a Noble Peer, relating to the Bill in favour of the Sugar-Planters* (London, 1733), 18.

50. Whitson, *op. cit.*, 76.

51. A. M. Schlesinger, *The Colonial Merchants and the American Revolution, 1763-1776* (New York, 1918), 42-43.

52. *Some Considerations Humbly offer'd ...*, 11.

53. *A Letter to a Noble Peer ...*, 20.

54. Whitson, *op. cit.*, 70.

55. Stock, *op. cit.*, V, 477. April 16, 1751.

56. *Ibid.*, IV, 161 n, 162 n, 163 n.

57. *Ibid.*, V, 482. April 19, 1751.

58. Donnan, *op. cit.*, III, 203-205. Jan. 24, 1764.

59. W. S. McClellan, *Smuggling in the American Colonies at the Outbreak of the Revolution* (New York, 1912), 37.

60. Wood, *op. cit.*, 136-141.

61. Stock, *op. cit.*, IV, 143. Feb. 23, 1731.

62. *Ibid.*, IV, 125. Jan. 28, 1731.

63. *Ibid.*, IV, 185. Feb. 21, 1732.

64. *Ibid.*, IV, 139. Feb. 23, 1731.

65. E. Donnan, "Eighteenth Century English Merchants, Micajah Perry," *Journal of Economic and Business History* (Nov., 1931), 96. Perry to Cadwallader Colden of New York.

66. Pitman, *Development of the British West Indies, 272.*

67. C. W. Taussig, *Rum, Romance and Rebellion* (New York, 1928), 39.

68. Stock, *op. cit.*, V, 477. April 16, 1751.

69. Callender, *op. cit.*, 133.

70. Innis, *op. cit.*, 212.

71. Arthur Young, *Annals of Agriculture* (London), IX, 1788, 95-96; X, 1788, 335-362. The whole essay, on "West Indian Agriculture," should be read.

72. Whitson, *op. cit.*, 77-78.

73. MacInnes, *op. cit.*, 295.

74. Edwards, *op. cit.*, II, 515.

75. Whitson, *op. cit.*, 86.

76. Ragatz, *Fall of the Planter Class ...*, 174.

77. G. Chalmers, *Opinions on Interesting Subjects of Public Law and Commercial Policy; arising from American Independence* (London, 1784), 60.

78. Ragatz, *Fall of the Planter Class ...*, 176.

79. C. P. Nettels, *The Roots of American Civilization* (New York, 1939), 655.

80. Petitions from the various islands that the ports should be opened were so numerous that Lord Hawkesbury was "apprehensive that every port in our West India islands will apply to be made a free port from a sense of the great advantages to be derived therefrom." Liverpool Papers, Add. MSS. 38228, f. 324. Feb. 1793. On Feb. 20, 1784, Governor Orde wrote from Dominica: "The people look with uncommon anxiety for the arrival of a free port act." B.T.6/103 (Public Record Office).

81. W. H. Elkins, *British Policy in its Relation to the Commerce and Navigation of the U.S.A., 1794-1807* (Oxford University D. Phil. Thesis, c. 1935), 96. Dr. Vincent Harlow, who supervised the thesis, kindly permitted me to read it.

82. Innis, *op. cit.*, 221, 251.

83. T. Pitkin, *A Statistical View of the Commerce of the United States* (Hartford, 1817), 167.

84. *Report of the Committee of Privy Council, 1788,* Part V, Question 1. Evidence of Messrs. Fuller, Long and Chisholme of Jamaica.

85. Pitman, *The Settlement ... of British West India Plantations ...,* 276.

86. *Report of the Committee of Privy Council, 1788.* See note 84 *supra.*

87. Pitman, *The Settlement ... of British West India Plantations ...,* 280.

88. *Parl. Hist.,* XXIX, 260. Wilberforce, April 18, 1791.

89. Klingberg, *op. cit.*, 13-14, 103; H. Brougham, *An Inquiry into the Colonial Policy of the European Powers* (Edinburgh, 1803), I, 522.

90. Chatham Papers (Public Record Office), G.D.8/349. West Indian Islands, Papers relating to Jamaica (1783-1804) and St. Domingo (1788-1800). Extracts from "Considerations on the State of St. Domingo," by Hilliard d'Auberteuil, 303.

91. *Report of the Committee of Privy Council, 1788,* Part V. See note 84 *supra.*

92. Brougham, *op. cit.*, I, 539-540.

93. In the Chatham Papers, G.D.8/102, there is this curious letter of Pitt's, dated Nov. 25, 1783, probably to the Governor of the East India Company: "It has occurred to me to be a very material part of the Company's case to show that the bill-holders are willing to allow the company all convenient time before they call for payment. I have in general understood that they are inclined to do so; but it would add a great weight if a public declaration could be obtained from them *as a body* to that effect. For that purpose it might be desirable to convene a public meeting of them; tho' such a measure ought not undoubtedly to be proposed without a certainty of success, I could not forbear suggesting this to your consideration. I must beg the favour of you, however, not to mention the idea as from me, and to excuse the liberty I take in troubling you."

94. R. Coupland, *Wilberforce* (Oxford, 1923), 93.

95. Sugar: Various MSS. (in the writer's possession). Adamson to Ferguson, March 25, 1787.

96. *East India Sugar, Papers respecting the Culture and Manufacture of Sugar in British India* (London, 1822), Appendix I, p. 3.

97. Clarkson, *Essay on the Impolicy* . . ., 34.

98. Pitkin, *op. cit.*, 30, 200-201. Pitkin gives the figures for 1784-1790 in pounds, 1792-1801 in dollars. The proportions given in the text are based on the tables as given in Pitkin. It seemed a more satisfactory way to show the increase of the trade than to attempt the conversion of pounds into dollars.

99. Merivale, *op. cit.*, 230.

100. Anonymous, *The Speeches of the Right Honourable William Huskisson with a Biographical Memoir* (London, 1831), II, 312. March 21, 1825.

CHAPTER 7

1. *Parl. Hist.*, XXIII, 1026-1027. June 17, 1783.

2. Mantoux, *op. cit.*, 340.

3. Clapham, *op. cit.*, Chap. V.

4. Lord, *op. cit.*, 176.

5. Clapham, *op. cit.*, 156.

6. Mantoux, *op. cit.*, 257.

7. Clapham, *op. cit.*, 184-185, 196.

8. Lord, *op. cit.*, 174.

9. A. Redford, *The Economic History of England, 1760-1860* (London, 1931), 22.

10. Mantoux, *op. cit.*, 258.

11. N. S. Buck, *The Development of the Organization of Anglo-American Trade, 1800-1850* (New Haven, 1925), 166.

12. *Ibid.*, 164.

13. Wheeler, *op. cit.*, 175.

14. Butterworth, *op. cit.*, 112.

15. Buck, *op. cit.*, 169.

16. Mantoux, *op. cit.*, 368. The phrase is Arthur Young's.

17. *Ibid.*, 367-368.

18. Jackman, *op. cit.*, II, 514 n. From 27,246 to 163,888.

19. Butterworth, *op. cit.*, 37.

20. Mantoux, *op. cit.*, 258.

21. C. H. Timperley, *Annals of Manchester; Biographical, Ecclesiastical, and Commercial, from the earliest period to the close of the year 1839* (Manchester, 1839), 89.

22. Buck, *op. cit.*, 36 n.

23. Scrivenor, *op. cit.*, 87 (68,300 tons in 1788); Clapham, *op. cit.*, 149 (650,000-700,000 tons in 1830).

24. Scrivenor, *op. cit.*, 87 (85 furnaces in 1788); Clapham, *op. cit.*, 149 (250-300 furnaces in 1830).

25. Scrivenor, *op. cit.*, 123-124, 293-294.

26. Clapham, *op. cit.*, 240.

27. *Cambridge History of the British Empire*, II, 223. The whole essay, "The Industrial Revolution and the Colonies, 1783-1822," by J. H. Clapham, should be read as an indispensable aid to an appreciation of the destruction of the West Indian monopoly.

28. Clapham, *op. cit.*, 431; F. Engels, *The Condition of the Working Class in England in 1844* (London, 1936 edition), 13. The number of mines increased from 40 to 76.

29. Scrivenor, *op. cit.*, 297.

30. Redford, *op. cit.*, 41-42.

31. Clapham, *op. cit.*, 152, 154; A. P. Usher, *A History of Mechanical Inventions* (New York, 1929), 332.

32. Clapham, *op. cit.*, 189.

33. Scrivenor, *op. cit.*, 421. The figures are as follows: 1815—exports, 79,596 tons; to B.W.I., 7,381; to U.S.A., 21,501; 1833—exports, 179,312 tons; to B.W.I., 5,400; to U.S.A., 62,253.

34. Mantoux, *op. cit.*, 276.

35. Clapham, *op. cit.*, 144, 196; Buck, *op. cit.*, 163.

36. Engels, *op. cit.*, 9. From 75,000 to 490,000 pieces.

37. Clapham, *op. cit.*, 243, 478.

38. James, *op. cit.*, 286; Mantoux, *op. cit.*, 106 n.; Clapham, *op. cit.*, 249. The cotton export for 1830 was £31,810,474. Buck, *op. cit.*, 166.

39. Mantoux, *op. cit.*, 369; Engels, *op. cit.*, 9.

40. Merivale, *op. cit.*, 120.

41. *Cambridge History of the British Empire*, II, 231.

42. Merivale, *op. cit.*, 121.

43. Redford, *op. cit.*, 45.

44. L. H. Jenks, *The Migration of British Capital to 1875* (London, 1927), 64.

45. Hansard, *New Series*, XV, 385. Lord Redesdale, April 19, 1825.

46. Jenks, *op. cit.*, 67.

47. Customs 8 (Public Record Office), Vols. 14 and 35. The figures are: 1821—£6,422,304; 1832—£7,017,048.

48. Jenks, *op. cit.*, 75-76.

49. *The Cambridge History of British Foreign Policy* (Cambridge, 1923), II, 74. Canning to Granville, Dec. 17, 1824.

50. Customs 8, Vols. 14 and 35. In 1821—£2,114,329; in 1832—£5,298,596.

51. *Ibid.*, In 1821—£3,239,894; in 1832—£9,452,822.

52. Jenks, *op. cit.*, 47.

53. Customs 8, Vols. 14 and 35. In 1821—£43,113,855; in 1832—£65,025,278.

54. *Ibid.*, In 1821—£19,082,693; in 1832—£29,908,964.

55. *Ibid.* In 1821—£3,639,746; in 1832—£6,377,507.

56. *Ibid.* To the B.W.I.: 1821—£4,704,610; 1832—£3,813,821. To Jamaica: 1821—£3,214,364; 1832—£2,022,435.

57. W. L. Burn, *Emancipation and Apprenticeship in the British West Indies* (London, 1937), 52.

58. *Hansard, Third Series,* LXXVII, 1062. Milner Gibson, Feb. 24, 1845.

59. Merivale, *op. cit.*, 203.

60. Burn, *op. cit.*, 73. Burn denies that they were an inferno.

61. W. L. Mathieson, *British Slavery and its Abolition, 1823-1838* (London, 1926), 222.

62. A. Prentice, *History of the Anti-Corn Law League* (London, 1853), I, 5.

63. E. Halévy, *A History of the English People, 1830-1841* (London, 1927), 42-43, 47, 56-58.

64. F. M. Eden, *Eight Letters on the Peace; and on the Commerce and Manufactures of Great Britain* (London, 1802), 129.

65. *Cambridge History of the British Empire,* II, 239.

CHAPTER 8

1. Merivale, *op. cit.*, 238-239.

2. *Ibid.*, 93.

3. Liverpool Papers, Add. MSS. 38295, f. 102. An anonymous correspondent to Lord Bexley, July, 1823.

4. C. O. 137/166. Hibbert to Horton, April 2, 1827.

5. *Hansard, New Series,* XIV, 1164. Lord Dudley and Ward, March 7, 1826.

6. *Ibid., Third Series,* III, 354. Mr. Robinson, March 11, 1831.

7. Bready, *op. cit.*, 308.

8. The statement is Dr. Bowring's. The date I have been unable to find.

9. Prentice, *op. cit.*, I, 75.

10. *The Right in the West India Merchants* . . ., 17, 18-19, 26-27, 50-51, 53, 74-75.

11. *Hansard, New Series,* VIII, 339. Petition of merchants, shipowners, etc., concerned in the trade to the East Indies, March 3, 1823.

12. *Report of a Committee of the Liverpool East India Association, appointed to take into consideration the restrictions of the East India Trade* (Liverpool, 1822), 21-22.

13. Z. Macaulay, *East and West India Sugar; or a Refutation of the Claims of the West India Colonists to a Protecting Duty on East India Sugar* (London, 1823), 37.

14. *Debates at the General Court of Proprietors of East India Stock on the 19th and 21st March 1823 on the East India Sugar Trade* (London, 1823), 12. Mr. Tucker.

15. *Ibid.*, 40-41.

16. *Cambridge Modern History* (Cambridge, 1934), X, 771-772.

17. *Hansard, New Series*, I, 424-425, 429. May 16, 1820.

18. *Ibid.*, XXII, 111, 118. March 23, 1812. The compliment to Pitt is in *Cambridge Modern History*, X, 771.

19. W. Naish, *Reasons for using East India Sugar* (London, 1828), 12.

20. *Hansard, Third Series*, LXXV, 438. Mr. Villiers, June 10, 1844.

21. *Ibid.*, 444.

22. Merivale, *op. cit.*, 225.

23. *Ibid.*, 205.

24. J. B. Seely, *A Few Hints to the West Indians on their Present Claims to Exclusive Favour and Protection at the Expense of the East India Interests* (London, 1823), 89.

25. *The Speeches of . . . Huskisson . . .*, II, 198. May 22, 1823.

26. *Ibid.*, III, 146. May 15, 1827.

27. *Hansard, Third Series*, LVII, 920. Villiers, April 5, 1841.

28. *Ibid.*, 162-163. Labouchere, March 12, 1841.

29. *Ibid., Third Series*, LXXVII, 1056. Milner Gibson, Feb. 24, 1845.

30. *Ibid., Third Series*, LVII, 920. Villiers, April 5, 1841.

31. *Ibid., Third Series*, LXXVII, 1078. Feb. 24, 1845.

32. P. Guedalla, *Gladstone and Palmerston* (London, 1928), 30.

33. *Hansard, Third Series*, CXI, 592. May 31, 1850.

34. *Ibid., Third Series*, XCVI, 123. Feb. 4, 1848.

35. *Ibid., Third Series*, CXXIV, 1036. March 3, 1853.

36. Pitman, *The Settlement . . . of British West India Plantations . . .*, 282-283.

37. Penson, *op. cit.*, 208.

38. T. Fletcher, *Letters in Vindication of the Rights of the British West India Colonies* (Liverpool, 1822), 27; Anonymous, *Memorandum on the Relative Importance of the West and East Indies to Great Britain* (London, 1823), 30; C. O. 137/140. Report from a Committee of the Honourable House of Assembly, appointed to inquire into various matters relative to the state of commerce and agriculture of the island; the probable effects thereon of opening the trade to the East Indies; and the operation of the present maximum on the exportation of sugar. Jamaica, 1813.

39. C. O. 137/140. Report from a Committee of the Honourable House of Assembly . . ., Jamaica, 1813.

40. K. Bell and W. P. Morrell, *Select Documents on British Colonial Policy, 1830-1860* (Oxford, 1928), 414. Russell to Light, Feb. 15, 1840.

41. Merivale, *op. cit.*, 84.

42. *Hansard, Third Series*, III, 537. Mr. Fitzgerald, March 18, 1831; *Ibid., Third Series*, XVIII, 111. Henry Goulburn, May 30, 1833.

43. *Ibid., New Series*, IV, 947. Marryat, Feb. 28, 1821.

44. *Ibid., Third Series*, C, 356. Bentinck, July 10, 1848.

45. *Ibid., Third Series*, LXXV, 213. Stewart, June 3, 1844; *Ibid., Third Series*, XCIC, 1094. Miles, June 23, 1848.

46. *Ibid., Third Series,* LVI, 616. Viscount Sandon, Feb. 12, 1841.

47. *Ibid., Third Series,* XCIX, 1098. Miles, June 23, 1848; *Ibid.,* 1466. Nugent, June 30, 1848. They argued that when the Africans, at the end of their contract, returned home, they would introduce civilization into Africa. *Ibid., Third Series,* LXXXVIII, 91. Hogg, July 27, 1846. On the request for convicts, see *Ibid., Third Series,* LXXV, 1214. Mr. James, June 21, 1844.

48. *Ibid., Third Series,* LXXVII, 1269. Feb. 26, 1845.

49. *Ibid., Third Series,* CXI, 581. May 31, 1850.

50. *Ibid., Third Series,* LXXV, 198. June 3, 1844.

51. *Ibid., Third Series,* CXV, 1440. April 10, 1851.

52. *Ibid.,* 1443.

53. *The Political Writings of Richard Cobden* (London, 1878), 12, 14.

54. *Ibid.,* 257. Cobden was prepared to let the United States seize Cuba. —*Hansard, Third Series,* CXXXII, 429-430. April 4, 1854.

55. *Hansard, Third Series,* CVI, 942, 951-952, 958. June 26, 1849; *Ibid., Third Series,* C, 825. July 25, 1848.

56. *Ibid., Third Series,* C, 831, 834, 849. July 25, 1848.

57. *Ibid., New Series,* XXII, 855. Feb. 23, 1830.

58. *Ibid., Third Series,* XI, 834. March 23, 1832.

59. *Ibid., Third Series,* XCIX, 875. June 19, 1848.

60. W. P. Morrell, *British Colonial Policy in the Age of Peel and Russell* (Oxford, 1930), 286.

61. Bell and Morrell, *op. cit.,* Introduction, pp. xiii, xxiv.

62. Merivale, *op. cit.,* 78.

63. *Hansard,* XXXIV, 1192. Barham, June 19, 1816.

64. *Addresses and Memorials to His Majesty from the House of Assembly at Jamaica, voted in the years 1821 to 1826, inclusive, and which have been presented to His Majesty by the Island Agent* (London, 1828), 22.

65. *Hansard, Third Series,* XCIX, 872. Seymer, June 19, 1848.

66. *Ibid., Third Series,* XCVI, 75. Robinson, Feb. 3, 1848.

67. *Ibid., Third Series,* LXIII, 1218-1219. June 3, 1842.

68. *Ibid., Third Series,* LXXV, 462. June 10, 1844.

69. *Ibid., Third Series,* LXXXVIII, 164. July 28, 1846.

70. E. L. Woodward, *The Age of Reform, 1815-1870* (Oxford, 1938), 351. Morrell, *op. cit.,* 519, speaks of this as "the famous indiscretion" of Disraeli's, though it is not clear just how it is indiscreet. The phrase "damnosa hereditas" is Taylor's of the Colonial Office. Bell and Morrell, *op. cit.,* Introduction, p. XXVI.

71. J. Morley, *The Life of William Ewart Gladstone* (London, 1912), I, 268.

72. Penson, *op. cit.,* 209.

73. Chatham Papers, G.D. 8/352. West India Planters and Merchants, Resolutions, May 19, 1791.

74. *Calendar of State Papers, Colonial Series,* XIII, 719. Petition of Jamaica Merchants, Oct. 11, 1692.

75. A. M. Arnould, *De la Balance du Commerce et des Relations Commerciales Extérieures de la France, dans Toutes les Parties du Globe, particulièrement à la fin du Règne de Louis XIV, et au Moment de la Révolution* (Paris, 1791), I, 263, 326-328.

76. *Hansard,* IX, 90-91. Hibbert, March 12, 1807.

77. *Parl. Hist.,* XXIX, 1147. April 2, 1792.

78. Ragatz, *The Fall of the Planter Class* ..., 211.

79. See Chatham Papers, G.D. 8/102. Pitt to Eden, Dec. 7, 1787: "The more I reflect on it, the more anxious and impatient I am that the business should be brought as speedily as possible to a point." Pitt refused to consider temporary suspension of the trade and to compromise "the principle of humanity and justice, on which the whole rests." *The Journal and Correspondence of William, Lord Auckland* (London, 1861), I , 304. Pitt to Eden, Jan. 7, 1788. Pitt thought that one good result of the new constitution in France (1788) would be that "our chance of settling something about the slave trade" would be improved. *The Manuscripts of J. B. Fortescue Esq. preserved at Dropmore* (Historical Manuscripts Commission, London, 1892-1927), I , 353. Pitt to Grenville, Aug. 29, 1788.

80. Ragatz, *The Fall of the Planter Class* ..., 213-214.

81. Liverpool Papers, Add. MSS. 38409, ff. 151, 155. Written probably in 1789.

82. *Ibid.,* ff. 147-148.

83. *Ibid.,* Add. MSS. 38349, f. 393. Written probably after 1791.

84. *Correspondence, Despatches and other Papers of Viscount Castlereagh* (London, 1848-1853), XI, 41. Liverpool to Castlereagh, Oct. 2, 1815. See too Liverpool Papers, Add. MSS. 38578, f. 28. Liverpool to Castlereagh, Nov. 20, 1818. Coming from a West Indian slaveowner, the phrase is amusing.

85. See Liverpool Papers, Add. MSS. 38224, f. 118. Lord Dorset, British Ambassador in Paris, wrote to Lord Hawkesbury on May 7, 1789, that the flattering references to British humanitarianism "seem'd only meant to compliment us and to keep us quiet and in good humour." Sir James Harris, from Holland, wrote that the principles of humanity were not likely to make much impression on the Dutch merchants and that it would be difficult to obtain their acquiescence. *The Manuscripts of J. B. Fortescue* ..., III, 442-443. Harris to Grenville, Jan. 4, 1788.

86. Gaston-Martin, *La Doctrine Coloniale de la France en 1789* (Cahiers de la Révolution Française, No. 3, Bordeaux, 1935), 25, 39.

87. J. Ramsay, *An Inquiry into the Effects of Putting a Stop to the African Slave Trade* (London, 1784), 24.

88. Chatham Papers, G.D. 8/349. West Indian Islands, Papers relating to Jamaica and St. Domingo. The offer was made by De Cadusey, President of the Island Assembly, on Oct. 29, 1791. He stated that necessity

justified a step which would normally be treason, for obvious reasons the offer could not be "official," and begged Pitt in the name of policy as well as of humanity to accept "the expression of the general will." The offer was not unexpected in England. On May 13, 1791, the British Ambassador in Paris reported that the French colonists were talking of "throwing themselves into the arms of England." F.O. 27/36. (Public Record Office). Gower to Grenville.

89. F.O. 27/40. De Curt to Hawkesbury, Dec. 18, 1792. De Curt begged to be considered in all respects as an Englishman, and later formally asked for protection "in the name of humanity and English loyalty." Liverpool Papers, Add. MSS. 38228, f. 197. Jan. 3, 1793.

90. *Parl. Hist.*, XXXII, 752. Dundas, Feb. 18, 1796.

91. J. W. Fortescue, *A History of the British Army* (London, 1899-1930), IV, Part I, 325.

92. *Ibid.*, 565.

93. Wilberforce, *Life of Wilberforce*, I , 341.

94. *Ibid.*, II, 147, 286; A. M. Wilberforce, *The Private Papers of William Wilberforce* (London, 1897), 31. Pitt to Wilberforce, May 31, 1802.

95. Klingberg, *op. cit.*, 116, quoting Lecky.

96. Wilberforce, *Life of Wilberforce*, II, 225. Stephen to Wilberforce, July, 1797.

97. Liverpool Papers, Add. MSS. 38227, f. 5. Aug. 7, 1791. An anonymous writer from Jamaica to one Mr. Brickwood.

98. Chatham Papers, G.D. 8/334. Miscellaneous Papers relating to France, 1784-1795. James Chalmers to Pitt, Dec. 24, 1792.

99. Eden, *op. cit.*, 18.

100. Ragatz, *The Fall of the Planter Class* . . ., 308.

101. *H. of C. Sess. Pap. Report on the Commercial State of the West India Colonies*, 1807, 4-6; *Hansard*, IX, 98. Hibbert, March 12, 1807.

102. *Hansard*, VIII, 238-239. Dec. 30, 1806.

103. *Ibid.*, 985. Hibbert, Feb. 23, 1807. The greater need of slaves in the newer colonies explains that peculiar migration from the old to the new colonies between 1807 and 1833 under the guise of "domestics" in attendance on their master. See Eric Williams, "The Intercolonial Slave Trade after its Abolition in 1807," *Journal of Negro History* (April, 1942).

104. *Hansard*, II, 652. June 13, 1804. Lord Sheffield replied that this would be a breach of faith. *Ibid.*, VII, 235. May 16, 1806.

105. *Ibid.*, VIII, 658-659. Feb. 5, 1807.

106. *Ibid.*, IX, 101. March 12, 1807.

107. Merivale, *op. cit.*, 303, 313-317.

108. Ragatz, *Statistics* . . ., 20 (Table XVII).

109. *Ibid.*, 20 (Tables XVII, XIX and XX). Antigua, 162,573 and 115,-932 cwt.; Mauritius, 155,247 and 524,017 cwt.

110. *Ibid.*, 20 (Tables XIX and XXI). From 4,000 to 111,000 cwt.

111. Customs 5 (Public Record Office), Vols. 16 and 22. Singapore's increased from 5,000 to 33,000 cwt.; Philippines' from 8,800 to 32,500; Java's from 950 to 21,700.

112. J. de la Pezuela, *Diccionario Geográfico, Estadístico, Histórico de la Isla de Cuba* (Madrid, 1862), I, 59; *Anuario Azucarero de Cuba* (Habana, 1940), 59. From 14,500 to 620,000 tons.

113. Customs, 5, Vols. 6, 20 and 21. From Brazil 50,800 and 362,600 cwt.; from Cuba 35,500 and 210,800 cwt.

114. Pitman, *The Settlement . . . of British West India Plantations. . .*, 262.

115. Pezuela, *op. cit.*, I, 59. Alava plantation, another "monster" comprised 4,933 acres, employed 600 slaves, and produced 3,570 tons of sugar. *Ibid.*

116. *Hansard, Third Series*, LXX, 212. Cobden, June 22, 1843.

117. *Ibid., Third Series*, LVII, 610. Ellenborough, March 26, 1841.

118. *Ibid., Third Series*, II, 790. Poulett Thomson, Feb. 21, 1831.

119. *Statements, Calculations and Explanations submitted to the Board of Trade relative to the Commercial, Financial and Political State of the British West India Colonies, since the 19th of May, 1830. (H. of C. Sess. Pap., Accounts and Papers, 1830-1831, IX, No. 120)*, 58. Imports into Hamburg rose from 68,798 to 75,441 boxes; into Prussia from 207,801 to 415,134. Russian imports of Cuban sugar rose from 616,542 to 935,395 poods (36 pounds), of Brazilian from 331,584 to 415,287 poods.

120. *Hansard, Third Series*, XVII, 1209, 1211-1212. May 14, 1833.

121. Burn, *op. cit.*, 367 n.

122. C. O. 295/93, n.d. The Council's petition was enclosed in Governor Grant's despatch of Aug. 29, 1832.

CHAPTER 9

1. H. Richard, *Memoirs of Joseph Sturge* (London, 1864), 84. Cropper to Sturge, Oct. 14, 1825.

2. Auckland Papers (British Museum), Add. MSS. 34427, ff. 401-402 (v). Wilberforce to Eden, Jan. 1788.

3. Coupland, *Wilberforce*, 422.

4. Bready, *op. cit.*, 302, 341.

5. Prentice, *op. cit.*, I, 3-4.

6. T. P. Martin, "Some International Aspects of the Anti-Slavery Movement 1818-1823," *Journal of Economic and Business History* (Nov., 1928), 146.

7. *Hansard, Third Series*, XVI, 290, March 6, 1833.

8. Wadsworth and Mann, *op. cit.*, 288, 289.

9. Murch, *op. cit.*, 76.

10. Report of the Speeches at the Great Dinner in the Theatre, Manchester, to celebrate the election of Mark Philips, Esq. and the Rt. Hon. C. P. Thomson (John Rylands Library), 2, 8.

11. *Hansard, Third Series,* XXXIII, 472. April 29, 1836.

12. *Ibid., Third Series,* XLVIII, 1029. June 28, 1839.

13. *Ibid., Third Series,* C, 54. Milner Gibson, July 3, 1848.

14. *Ibid., Third Series,* LXXVII, 1053. Gibson, Feb. 24, 1845.

15. *Ibid., Third Series,* LVI, 605. Hawes, Feb. 12, 1841.

16. *Ibid., Third Series,* LXXVII, 1053. Gibson, Feb. 24, 1845; *Ibid., Third Series,* C, 54. Gibson, July 3, 1848.

17. *Ibid., Third Series,* LXXVII, 1144. Feb. 24, 1845; *Ibid., Third Series,* XCIX, 1428. June 30, 1848.

18. *Ibid., Third Series,* C, 324. Bentinck, July 10, 1848, quoting Bright. Bentinck emphasized the previous protection against Indian textiles.

19. *Ibid., Third Series,* LXXVIII, 930. March 14, 1845.

20. *Ibid., Third Series,* LXXVI, 37. June 27, 1844.

21. *Ibid., Third Series,* XCIX, 1420. June 30, 1848.

22. *Ibid.,* 747. June 16, 1848.

23. Auckland Papers, Add. MSS. 34427, ff. 401-402 (v). Wilberforce to Eden, Jan., 1788.

24. J. A. Langford, *A Century of Birmingham Life: or a Chronicle of Local Events* (Birmingham, 1870), I, 434.

25. Ashton, *op. cit.*, 223.

26. Langford, *op. cit.*, I, 436, 440.

27. *Ibid.*, I, 437.

28. Dent, *op. cit.*, 427.

29. *Ibid.*

30. N. B. Lewis, *The Abolitionist Movement in Sheffield, 1823-1833* (Manchester, 1934), 4-5.

31. Eng. MS., 743 (John Rylands Library). Auxiliary Society for the relief of Negro Slaves, f. 12. Jan. 9, 1827; f. 15. July 10, 1827. The plea to their townsmen is on a small card, undated, in the same library, in Box V.

32. Lewis, *op. cit.*, 6.

33. *Hansard, Third Series,* XIX, 1270. July 25, 1833.

34. *Ibid., Third Series,* XVI, 288. March 6, 1833; *Ibid., Third Series,* XVIII, 911. June 17, 1833.

35. *Ibid., Third Series,* LXXV, 446-447. June 10, 1844.

36. *Ibid., Third Series,* LXIII, 1174. June 3, 1842.

37. *Ibid.*, 1173.

38. *Ibid., Third Series,* LXX, 210. June 22, 1843.

39. J. Bright and J. T. Rogers (eds.), *Speeches on Questions of Public Policy by Richard Cobden, M. P.* (London, 1878), 91-92.

40. J. E. Ritchie, *The Life and Times of Viscount Palmerston* (London, 1866-1867), II, 743-744.

41. *Hansard, Third Series,* LXXVII, 1128. Feb. 24, 1845.

42. *Ibid., Third Series,* XCIX, 751-752. June 16, 1848.

43. Mackenzie-Grieve, *op. cit.,* 283.

44. *Hansard,* VI, 918. April 25, 1806.

45. *Ibid.,* VII, 612. Lord Howick, June 10, 1806.

46. *Ibid.,* VIII, 948. Lord Howick, Feb. 23, 1807.

47. Jackman, *op. cit.,* II, 515 n.

48. *Hansard,* VIII, 961-962. Feb. 23, 1807.

49. Buck, *op. cit.,* 31-32.

50. *Hansard, New Series,* XXIII, 180. March 11, 1830.

51. *The Speeches of . . . Huskisson . . .,* I, 115. Feb. 1826.

52. *Hansard, Third Series,* XIX, 793. July 17, 1833.

53. *Ibid., Third Series,* XVIII, 909-910. June 17, 1833.

54. *Ibid., Third Series,* XVI, 285. March 6, 1833.

55. *Ibid., Third Series,* XVIII, 910. June 17, 1833.

56. Eyre-Todd, *op. cit.,* III, 256, 263-264.

57. Donnan, *op. cit.,* II, 537 n, 564 n-565 n.

58. *Hansard, Third Series,* XVI, 291. March 6, 1833. In 1846 another Oswald went further: "When we wore slave-grown cotton, when we drank slave-grown coffee, and smoked slave-grown tobacco, he could not for the life of him conceive on what principle they might not also use slave-grown sugar. . . . They must look for the amelioration of this evil to some other quarter than the Custom-House." *Hansard, Third Series,* LXXXVIII, 122. July 28, 1846. It would be interesting to know whether this was a member of the same family.

59. Ragatz, *Statistics . . .,* 9 (Table IV).

60. *Report of the Proceedings of the Committee of Sugar Refiners,* 3, 8, 15.

61. *Ibid.,* 18 n.

62. Liverpool Papers, Add. MSS. 38227, 217. Chairman to Hawkesbury, Jan. 23, 1792; ff. 219-222. Chairman to Pitt, Jan. 12, 1792.

63. Indian cotton exports were 7 million pounds in 1816, 31 million in 1817, 67 million in 1818 but only 4 million in 1822. Exports from the United States were 50 million in 1816, 59 million in 1822; from Brazil 20 million in 1816 and 24 million in 1822. *Customs 5,* Vols. 5, 6, 7, 11. But Indian cotton was "the worst in the English market; owing to the negligent cultivation and packing." E. Baines, *History of the Cotton Manufacture in Great Britain* (London, 1835), 308. John Bright later used to tell a story of a Lancashire prayer meeting at which the following petition was offered up: "O Lord, we beseech Thee send us cotton;—but O Lord, not Shoorat." The reference is to Surat cotton and probably has to do with the American Civil War. G. M. Trevelyan, *The Life of John Bright* (Boston, 1913), 318 n.

64. T. P. Martin, *op. cit.,* 144. The phrase is M' Queen's.

65. *Debates . . . on the East India Sugar Trade,* 19.

66. *Hansard, Third Series,* VII, 764. John Wood, Sept. 28, 1831.

67. *Ibid., Third Series,* XIX, 1165-1167. William Clay, July 24, 1833.

68. *Ibid., Third Series,* VII, 764. Sept. 28, 1831.

69. *Ibid., Third Series,* VIII, 362. Oct. 7, 1831.

70. *The Speeches of . . . Huskisson . . .,* III, 454. May 25, 1829.

71. *Hansard, Third Series,* XVIII, 589. June 11, 1833.

72. *Ibid., Third Series,* XVII, 75. William Ewart, April 3, 1833; *Ibid., Third Series,* LVIII, 101. Ewart, May 10, 1841.

73. *Ibid., Third Series,* LVI, 608. B. Hawes, Feb. 12, 1841.

74. *Ibid., Third Series,* LXXXVIII, 517. Aug. 10, 1846.

75. Ramsay, MS. Vol., f. 64. "An Address on the proposed bill for the Abolition of the Slave Trade."

76. Auckland Papers, Add. MSS. 34227, f. 123. Wilberforce to Eden, Nov. 23, 1787.

77. *Parl. Hist.,* XXIX, 270. April 18, 1791.

78. *Ibid.,* 322.

79. *Hansard,* VIII, 948-949. Feb. 23, 1807.

80. Proceedings of the Committee for Abolition of the Slave Trade, 1787-1819 (British Museum), Add. MSS. 21255, f. 100 (v). April 14, 1789.

81. J. Newton, *Thoughts upon the African Slave Trade* (Liverpool, 1788), 8.

82. Ramsay, MS. Vol., f. 64.

83. *Hansard,* VIII, 947-948. Lord Howick, Feb. 23, 1807.

84. *Report of a Committee of the Liverpool East India Association . . .,* 56.

85. *The Speeches of . . . Huskisson . . .,* III, 442. May 12, 1829.

86. *Hansard, Third Series,* VII, 755. Sept. 28, 1831.

87. *Ibid., Third Series,* XVI, 881-882. March 20, 1833.

88. *Ibid.,* 290. March 6, 1833.

89. *Ibid., Third Series,* XIX, 1169. July 24, 1833.

90. Lindsay, *op. cit.,* III, 85-86.

91. Bell and Morrell, *op. cit.,* Introduction, p. xli.

CHAPTER 10

1. *Hansard, Third Series,* XCIX, 1223. G. Thompson, June 26, 1848. Thompson was a prominent abolitionist speaker.

2. *Ibid., Third Series,* LXXV, 170. Lord John Russell, June 3, 1844.

3. *Despatches . . . of Wellington,* I, 329. Canning to Wellington, Sept. 30, 1822.

4. *Ibid.,* I, 453. Wellington to Canning, Oct. 28, 1822.

5. *Correspondence . . . of Canning,* I, 62. Memorandum for the Cabinet, Nov. 15, 1822.

6. *Hansard, Third Series,* XCVI, 1096. Hutt, Feb. 22, 1848.

7. *Despatches . . . of Wellington,* I, 329. Canning to Wellington, Sept. 30, 1822.

8. *Correspondence . . . of Canning,* I, 62. Memorandum for the Cabinet, Nov. 15, 1822.

9. R. I. and S. Wilberforce, *The Correspondence of William Wilberforce* (London, 1840), II, 466. Oct. 24, 1822.

10. *Despatches . . . of Wellington,* I, 474-475. Oct. 31, 1822.

11. *Hansard,* XXX, 657-658. April 18, 1815; *Ibid.,* XXXI, 174. May 5, 1815. For the Barings and Latin America, see Jenks, *op. cit.,* 48.

12. Hansard, XXXI. See pages 557, 606, 850-851, 1064. June 1, 5, 16, and 30, 1815.

13. *Ibid., New Series,* XI, 1345. June 15, 1824.

14. *Ibid.,* 1475-1477. June 23, 1824.

15. *Ibid., New Series,* XXV, 398. June 15, 1830.

16. *Ibid.,* 405. General Gascoyne, June 15, 1830; *Ibid.,* New Series, XX, 495. Gascoyne, Feb. 23, 1829.

17. *Correspondence . . . of Castlereagh,* X, 112. Castlereagh to Liverpool, Sept. 9, 1814.

18. *Hansard, Third Series,* LIX, 609. Brougham, Sept. 20, 1841.

19. *Ibid., Third Series,* XCVI, 1101-1102. Jackson, Feb. 22, 1848.

20. *Ibid., Third Series,* CII, 1084. Bishop of Oxford, Feb. 22, 1849.

21. *Ibid., Third Series,* XCVI, 1095. Quoted by Hutt, Feb. 22, 1848.

22. *Ibid., Third Series,* XCVIII, 1168. Palmerston, May 17, 1848; *Ibid.,* 1198. Cardwell, May 18, 1848.

23. *Ibid., Third Series,* LXV, 938, 942, 945. Aug. 2, 1842.

24. *Ibid., Third Series,* LXXI, 941. Aug. 18, 1843.

25. A. K. Manchester, *British preëminence in Brazil, Its Rise and Decline* (Chapel Hill, N. C., 1933), 315.

26. *Hansard, Third Series,* LXXVII, 1066. Ewart, Feb. 24, 1845; *Ibid.,* LXX, 224. June 22, 1843.

27. *Ibid., Third Series,* XCIX, 1121. Hawes, June 23, 1848.

28. *Ibid., Third Series,* XCVI, 1100. Hutt, Feb. 22, 1848.

29. *Ibid., Third Series,* LXXXI, 1170. Hutt, June 24, 1845.

30. *Ibid., Third Series,* XCIX, 748. June 16, 1848.

31. *Ibid., Third Series,* CXIII, 40. July 19, 1850.

32. *Ibid., Third Series,* XCVII, 988. Urquhart, March 24, 1848.

33. *Ibid., Third Series,* LXXXI, 1169-1170. Hutt, June 24, 1845.

34. *Ibid., Third Series,* LXXV, 170. Russell, June 3, 1844.

35. *Ibid., Third Series,* CVII, 1036. Gibson, July 27, 1849.

36. *Ibid., Third Series,* XCVI, 1101. Hutt, Feb. 22, 1848.

37. *Ibid., Third Series,* LXXXI, 1158-1159. June 24, 1845.

38. *Ibid., Third Series,* XCVI, 1092, 1096. Hutt, Feb. 22, 1848.

39. *Ibid.,* 1092.

40. *Ibid., Third Series,* XCVII, 986-987. Urquhart, March 24, 1848.

41. *Ibid., Third Series,* CI, 177. Urquhart, Aug. 16, 1848.

42. *Ibid., Third Series,* LXXXI, 1156, 1158. Hutt, June 24, 1845.

43. *Ibid., Third Series,* XCVII, 987. Urquhart, March 24, 1848.

44. *Ibid., Third Series,* LXXXI, 1165, 1170. Hutt, June 24, 1845.

45. *Ibid., Third Series,* CIX, 1109. Hutt, March 19, 1850.

46. *Ibid., Third Series,* CXIII, 61. Hutt, July 19, 1850.

47. *Ibid., Third Series,* LXXXI, 1158. Hutt, June 24, 1845.

48. W. L. Mathieson, *Great Britain and the Slave Trade, 1839-1865* (London, 1929), 90 n. The phrase is Carlyle's.

49. *Hansard, Third Series,* LXXVI, 947, 963. Peel, July 16, 1844.

50. *Ibid., Third Series,* LXXX, 482. Peel, May 16, 1845.

51. *Ibid., Third Series,* LXXXII, 1058-1064. July 24, 1845.

52. *Ibid., Third Series,* XCVI, 1125. Feb. 22, 1848.

53. *Ibid., Third Series,* LVIII, 648, 653. May 18, 1841.

54. *Ibid., Third Series,* LXXXII, 550, 552. July 15, 1845.

55. *Ibid., Third Series,* XCVIII, 994-996. March 24, 1848.

56. *Ibid., Third Series,* L, 383. Aug. 19, 1839.

57. *Ibid., Third Series,* LVIII, 167, 169. May 10, 1841.

58. *Ibid., Third Series,* CIX, 1162. March 19, 1850.

59. *The Manuscripts of J. B. Fortescue . . .,* IX, 14-19. Edmund Lyon to Grenville, Jan. 16, 1807.

60. *Hansard,* XXVIII, 349. Lord Holland, June 27, 1814.

61. *Ibid.,* XXX, 657-658. April 18, 1815.

62. *Statements, Calculations and Explanations submitted to the Board of Trade . . .,* p. 84. Letter from Keith Douglas, Oct. 30, 1830.

63. C. O. 137/186. Memorial of Jamaica deputies, Nov. 29, 1832.

64. D. Turnbull, *The Jamaica Movement, for promoting the enforcement of the Slave-Trade Treaties, and the Suppression of the Slave Trade* (London, 1850), 65, 94-95, 99, 120, 201, 249, 267.

65. *Times,* Jan. 30, 1857.

66. Guedalla, *op. cit.,* 64-66.

CHAPTER 11

1. R. Coupland, *The Empire in These Days* (London, 1935), 264. Professor Coupland understands the history of the abolition movement as little as his hero. "How popular abolition is, just now," wrote Wilberforce in 1807. "God can turn the hearts of men." Wilberforce, *Life of Wilberforce,* III, 295. Feb. 11, 1807.

2. *Hansard,* VIII, 679-682. Feb. 6, 1807.

3. K. Farrer (ed.), *The Correspondence of Josiah Wedgwood* (London, 1906), I, 215-216. June 17, 1793.

4. See Proceedings of the Committee for Abolition of the Slave

Trade, Add. MSS., 21254, ff. 12-12 (v). Samuel Hoare to Clarkson, July 25, 1787: "I hope the zeal and animation with which thou hast taken up the cause will be accompanied with temper and moderation, which alone can insure its success."

5. Wilberforce, *Life of Wilberforce*, IV, 240-241. Written in 1811.

6. Bell and Morrell, *op. cit.*, 376. Memorandum of Stephen, October, 1831.

7. C. O. 295/93. Stephen to Howick, Aug. 25, 1832.

8. Bell and Morrell, *op. cit.*, 420. Minute of Stephen, Sept. 15, 1841.

9. Ramsay, MS. Vol., f. 28. Dec. 27, 1787.

10. Klingberg, *op. cit.*, 60-61. Ramsay's evidence before the Privy Council in 1788 is well worth reading.

11. Sir G. Stephen, *Anti-Slavery Recollections* (London, 1854), 77; Richard, *op. cit.*, 78. Stephen and Richard actually were discussing the African Institution and Anti-Slavery Society.

12. Stephen, *op. cit.*, 79.

13. Coupland, *Wilberforce*, 417.

14. *Hansard, New Series*, XI, 1413. Wilberforce, June 15, 1824.

15. Coupland, *Wilberforce*, 406-408, 411-417. For his opposition to feminine anti-Slavery associations, see Wilberforce, *Life of Wilberforce*, V, 264-265. Wilberforce to Babington, Jan. 31, 1826. For his views on the First Reform Bill, see Wilberforce, *Correspondence of Wilberforce*, II, 265. Wilberforce to his son Samuel, March 4, 1831.

16. Proceedings of the Committee for Abolition of the Slave Trade, Add. MSS. 21255, f. 50 (v). Aug. 12, 1788; Add. MSS. 21256, ff. 40 (v), 96 (v). Jan. 31, 1792, March 29, 1797.

17. *Hansard*, IX, 143-144. March 17, 1807.

18. *Parl. Hist.*, XXXIII, 1119. July 5, 1799.

19. *Hansard, New Series*, XIX, 1469. Quoted by Lord Seaford, June 23, 1828.

20. *Ibid., New Series*, IX, 265-266. May 15, 1823.

21. Richard, *op. cit.*, 79.

22. Stephen, *op. cit.*, 120-122.

23. Richard, *op. cit.*, 101-102. March 28, 1833.

24. A. Cochin, *L'Abolition de L'Esclavage* (Paris, 1861), Introduction, pp. xiv-xv.

25. Proceedings of the Committee for Abolition of the Slave Trade, Add. MSS., 21256, f. 95. June 25, 1795.

26. W. Fox, *Address to the People of Great Britain on the Propriety of Abstaining from West India Sugar and Rum* (London, 1791), *passim*.

27. R. K. Nuermberger, *The Free Produce Movement, A Quaker Protest against Slavery* (Durham, N. C., 1943), 9-10.

28. (Anonymous), *Remarkable Extracts and Observations on the Slave Trade with Some Considerations on the Consumption of West India Produce* (Stockton, 1792), 9. Copy in Wilberforce Museum, Hull.

29. Naish, *op. cit.*, 3.

30. Undated sheet, in Wilberforce Museum.

31. Anonymous, *The Ladies' Free Grown Cotton Movement* (John Rylands Library). Undated.

32. Gurney to Scoble, Dec. 5, 1840. In Wilberforce Museum. There is a reference number, D.B. 883, given with some hesitation, as the heterogeneous papers were not well arranged.

33. "The Principles, Plans, and Objects of *The Hibernian Negro's Friend Society*, contrasted with those of the previously existing Anti-Slavery Societies, being a circular, in the form of a letter to Thomas Pringle, Esq., Secretary of the London Anti-Slavery Society," 3. Jan. 8, 1831 (John Rylands Library).

34. *Hansard, Third Series,* XX, 315, 323, 324. Aug. 5, 1833; *Ibid.,* 446. Aug. 9, 1833.

35. *Ibid., Third Series,* XXXVIII, 1853. Hobhouse, July 10, 1837.

36. *Ibid., Third Series,* LVI, 218. O'Connell, Feb. 2, 1841.

37. *Ibid.,* 619. Feb. 12, 1841.

38. *Ibid., Third Series,* LXV, 1075. Baring, Aug. 5, 1842.

39. *Ibid., Third Series,* LXX, 1294. July 21, 1843.

40. *Ibid., Third Series,* LXVIII, 753. April 10, 1843.

41. Eng. MS. 741. Clarkson to L. Townsend, Aug. 1825.

42. Clarkson Papers (British Museum), Add. MSS. 41267 A, ff. 178-179.

43. *Debates . . . on the East India Sugar Trade,* 35.

44. *Hansard, Third Series,* XXXVIII, 1853-1854. July 10, 1837.

45. *Ibid., Third Series,* LXX, 1294. July 21, 1843.

46. Bell and Morrell, *op. cit.,* Introduction, p. xxx.

47. East India Company Subscription Journals to £800,000 additional stock, July 1786; East India Company Stock Ledgers, 1783-1791, 1791-1796. These records are kept in the Bank of England Record Office, Roehampton, London. Henry Thornton subscribed £500 and John Thornton £3,000 to the stock issued in 1786. At his death John left £2,000 to each of the others, which left Henry with £3,000, Robert with £4,000 and Samuel with £3,000.

48. *Debates on the expendiency of cultivating sugar in the territories of the East India Company* (East India House, 1793).

49. *Debates . . . on the East India Sugar Trade,* 5. Only Ragatz, *The Fall of the Planter Class . . .,* 363, mentions this important fact.

50. Macaulay, *op. cit.,* 29.

51. *Debates . . . on the East India Sugar Trade,* 36. Hume.

52. *Correspondence between . . . Gladstone . . . and Cropper . . .,* 15; F. A. Conybeare, *Dingle Bank, the home of the Croppers* (Cambridge, 1925), 7; Ragatz, *The Fall of the Planter Class . . .,* 364.

53. J. Cropper, *Letters to William Wilberforce, M.P., recommending the encouragement of the cultivation of sugar in our dominions in the East Indies, as the natural and certain means of effecting the total and*

general abolition of the Slave Trade (Liverpool, 1822), Introduction, p. vii.

54. *Correspondence between . . . Gladstone . . . and Cropper . . .,* 16. Cropper replied that this connection had ceased, to which Gladstone retorted: "It would be rather a curious coincidence were we to find that this cessation was coeval with his becoming a public writer against slavery: and in that case is it not rather remarkable that he should not have been induced to turn author until his slave cotton agency had ceased?" *Ibid.,* 37.

55. *Correspondence between . . . Gladstone . . . and Cropper . . .,* 55.

56. J. Cropper, "Slave Labour and Free Labour." *The substance of Mr. Cropper's address on Wednesday November 22 (1825) at the respectable meeting at the King's Head, Derby* (Derby, 1825), 3. John Rylands Library.

57. J. Cropper, *A Letter addressed to the Liverpool Society for promoting the abolition of Slavery, on the injurious effects of high prices of produce, and the beneficial effects of low prices, on the condition of slaves* (Liverpool, 1823), 8-9.

58. *Ibid.,* 22.

59. J. Cropper, *Relief for West Indian distress, shewing the inefficiency of protecting duties on East India sugar, and pointing out other modes of certain relief* (London, 1823), 9.

60. *Ibid.,* 30.

61. Conybeare, *op. cit.,* 25, 56-57.

62. *The Liverpool Mercury and Lancashire General Advertiser,* June 7, 1833.

63. Coupland, *The British Anti-Slavery Movement,* 124; Mathieson, *British Slavery and Its Abolition,* 125.

64. Wilberforce, *Life of Wilberforce,* V, 180.

65. *Hansard, New Series,* IX, 467. May 22, 1823.

66. *Ibid., New Series,* VII, 698. May 17, 1822.

67. Coupland, *The British Anti-Slavery Movement,* 124.

68. Klingberg, *op. cit.,* 203.

69. Burn, *op. cit.,* 88.

70. Ragatz, *The Fall of the Planter Class . . .,* 436.

71. *Hansard, New Series,* IX, 349. Baring, May 15, 1823.

72. Klinberg, *op. cit.,* 146.

73. *Ibid.,* 147-148.

74. Wilberforce later admitted that "we have had the religious character of Alexander the Great represented to us. . .in too favourable colours." To Lady Olivia Sparrow, May 31, 1814. In Wilberforce Museum, D.B. 25 (60). He wrote a strong letter to the Tsar on the subject. Wilberforce, *Life of Wilberforce,* V, 136-137. Wilberforce to Macaulay, Nov. 20, 1822. Wilberforce regarded the Tsar's importation of Brazilian produce after his promise to boycott it as "a breach of faith of which any private

man who should be guilty would forfeit for ever the character of a man of honor." Liverpool Papers, Add. MSS. 38578, ff. 31-32. Wilberforce to Liverpool, Sept. 4, 1822.

75. *Correspondence . . . of Castlereagh,* XII, 4-35. Memorandum of James Stephen, Sept. 8, 1818, "relative to Africa and colonial discussions that may have place in the Congress at Aix-la-Chapelle."

76. Wilberforce, *Life of Wilberforce,* IV, 133.

77. *Hansard,* XXVIII, 279, 284. June 27, 1814.

78. *Ibid.,* 393. June 28, 1814.

79. Wilberforce, *Life of Wilberforce,* IV, 209. Sept. 7, 1814.

80. *Despatches . . . of Wellington,* V, 15. Sept. 4, 1828.

81. *Hansard, Third Series,* XCVI, 37. Bentinck, Feb. 3, 1848.

82. Pamphlets in the John Rylands Library.

83. *The Liverpool Mercury and Lancashire General Advertiser,* July 23, 1832, reporting a meeting of the Liverpool West India Association.

84. *Ibid.,* Aug. 24, 1832. Letter of "Another Elector" to "An Elector."

85. Anonymous, *The Tariff of Conscience. The Trade in Slave Produce considered and condemned* (Newcastle Anti-Slavery Series, No. 11, n.d.). John Rylands Library.

86. Anonymous, *Conscience versus Cotton; or, the Preference of Free Labour Produce* (Newcastle Anti-Slavery Series, No. 10, n.d.). John Rylands Library.

87. *Hansard, Third Series,* XIX, 1177. July 24, 1833.

88. *Ibid., Third Series,* VI, 1353. Sept. 12, 1831.

89. *Ibid.,* 1355. Hume.

90. Eng. MS. 415. Buxton to Mrs. Rawson, Oct. 6, 1833.

91. *Hansard, Third Series,* XCIX, 1022. June 22, 1848.

92. Eng. MS. 415. Buxton to Mrs. Rawson, Oct. 6, 1833.

93. Gurney to Scoble, Dec. 5, 1840. Wilberforce Museum, D.B. 883.

94. *Hansard, Third Series,* LXXXI, 1159. Quoted by Hutt, June 24, 1845.

95. *Ibid., Third Series,* CIX, 1098. Quoted by Hutt, March 19, 1850. In 1858, Wilberforce stated: "We had no right to put ourselves forward to the world as the suppressors of the slave trade unless we were prepared honestly and firmly to enforce those treaties for its suppression which our allies had made with us." *Ibid., Third Series,* CL, 2200. June 17, 1858.

96. *Ibid., Third Series,* XCIX, 849. June 19, 1848. In 1850 Buxton called for the exclusion of slave-grown sugar, though not of slave-grown cotton and tobacco, arguing that "he saw no reason why he should not oppose an evil that he could successfully oppose, because there were other evils that it was impossible for him to oppose." *Ibid., Third Series,* CXI, 533. May 31, 1850. In 1857, he moved an address to the Queen praying that all efforts be used to put down the Slave Trade. *Ibid., Third Series,* CXLVI, 1857. July 14, 1857. This change of opinion coincided with a change in the viewpoint of the capitalists. Hutt was chairman of a committee in 1849 which described the efforts to suppress the slave trade as

impracticable and hopeless. Another committee in 1853, of which both Hutt and Bright were members, declared that "these efforts in the cause of humanity, continued through so many years, must be considered as honourable to the nation, and the results afforded a strong inducement to persevere until this iniquitous trade shall be entirely abolished." Mathieson, *Great Britain and the Slave Trade,* 133-134.

97. *Hansard, Third Series,* CXXXIX, 116. June 26, 1855.

98. *Ibid., Third Series,* LXXVI, 187. July 2, 1844.

99. *Ibid., Third Series,* CL, 2205. June 17, 1858.

100. *Ibid., Third Series,* LXXVII, 1290, 1292, 1300, 1302. Feb. 26, 1845.

101. *Ibid., Third Series,* LVIII, 193. May 11, 1841.

102. *Ibid., Third Series,* LXXVII, 1290. Feb. 26, 1845.

103. *Ibid., Third Series,* LXXXVIII, 4-5. July 27, 1846. This was a petition from Clarkson to the House of Lords presented by Brougham.

104. Mathieson, *Great Britain and the Slave Trade,* 34-35. The reference is to "head-money"—£4 a ton on every ship captured without slaves, £5 a head on slaves delivered alive, £2.10.0. on those who died after capture.

105. *Hansard, Third Series,* XCVI, 85. Feb. 4, 1848.

106. *Ibid., Third Series,* L, 131. Inglis, Aug. 8, 1839.

107. *Ibid., Third Series,* XCIX, 1324. Inglis, June 29, 1848.

108. *Ibid., Third Series,* LXXXVIII, 163. Quoted by Disraeli, July 28, 1846.

109. Merivale, *op. cit.,* 303-304.

110. *Hansard, Third Series,* XCVI, 133. Feb. 4, 1848.

111. Morley, *op. cit.,* I, 78.

112. Sypher, *op. cit.,* 217.

113. E. B. Dykes, *The Negro in English Romantic Thought* (Washington, D. C., 1942), 79-80.

114. Sypher, *op. cit.,* 215-216; Dykes, *op. cit.,* 70.

115. Lewis, *op. cit.,* 15, 17.

116. *Ibid.,* 13-14.

117. T. Caryle, "The Nigger Question," in *English and other Critical Essays* (Everyman's Edition, London, 1925). The whole essay, written in 1849, should be read.

118. *Hansard, Third Series,* XCVI, 1052. Feb. 22, 1848.

CHAPTER 12

1. See C. L. R. James, *The Black Jacobins* (London, 1938) for the slave revolution in Saint Domingue. H. Aptheker, *Negro Slave Revolts in the United States* (New York, 1943), should also be consulted. An admirable short summary, for the entire Western Hemisphere, is to be found in Herskovits, *op. cit.,* 86-109.

1a. C. O. 28/95. House of Assembly, Barbados, Nov. 15, 1825.

2. C. O. 28/92. Report of a Debate in Council on a despatch from Lord Bathurst to Sir H. Warde, Sept. 3, 1823. Mr. Hamden, pp. 21-22. See also C. O. 295/59, where the governor of Trinidad argued that this concession to the female slaves would be considered an injustice by the men. Woodford to Bathurst, Aug. 6, 1823; C. O. 295/60. Mr. Burnley, one of the leading planters of Trinidad: "I confess the idea appears to me so monstrous and extraordinary that I hardly know how to approach the subject."

3. C. O. 28/92. Report of a Debate in Council. . . . Mr. Hamden, p. 5.

4. C. O. 137/145. Shand to Bathurst, Nov. 26, 1817.

5. C. O. 137/148. Manchester to Bathurst, July 10, 1819.

6. C. O. 28/92. Report of a Debate in Council. . . . Mr. Hamden, p. 24.

7. C. O. 295/92. Edward Jackson to Governor Grant, Dec. 31, 1831.

8. C. O. 137/156. Manchester to Bathurst, Dec. 24, 1824.

9. C. O. 137/163. Manchester to Bathurst, Nov. 13, 1826.

10. C. O. 137/154. Manchester to Bathurst, Oct. 13, 1823.

11. C. O. 111/55. D'Urban to Bathurst, July 4, 1826.

12. C. O. 295/85. Oct. 29, 1830. The following is the number of manumissions, 1825-1830:

Year	Number Manumitted	Manumissions Paid for	Field Slaves	Domestic Slaves
1825	162	98	38	124
1826	167	108	46	121
1827	167	129	49	118
1828	128	84	33	95
1829	87	41	15	72
1830	32	22	6	26
(to Oct. 29.)				

13. C. O. 295/72. Woodford to Bathurst, Aug. 8, 1826.

14. C. O. 295/73. Stephen to Horton, Oct. 5, 1826.

15. C. O. 295/67. Henry Gloster, Protector of Slaves, to Governor Woodford, July 7, 1825. Fitzgerald's returns are as follows: Slave John Philip—"7 stripes on that part where if the foot be hostilely applied is considered in all civilized countries an act of the vilest indignity"; Slave Philip—"23 stripes on that part which my Lord Chesterfield strongly recommends to be the last to enter and the first to retire on all presentations at levies and to name which in the presence of ladies is considered a great breach in the laws of politeness"; Slave Simon Mind— "23 stripes on that particular part of the body corporate which is rarely guilty of a crime but which pays for transgressions committed by other members."

16. Bell and Morrell, op. cit., p. 382.

17. C. O. 28/99. Carrington, Agent for Barbados, to Bathurst, March 2, 1826.

18. C. O. 28/93. Warde to Bathurst, Oct. 21, 1824.

19. C. O. 28/92. Report of a Debate in Council. . ., p. 33.

20. C. O. 137/165. Message of House of Assembly, Dec. 1827.

21. C. O. 137/143. Oct. 31, 1815.

22. Bell and Morrell, *op. cit.*, 405. Protest of Assembly of Jamaica, June, 1838.

23. C. O. 137/183. Manchester to Goderich, Nov. 13, 1832.

24. *Ibid.* Manchester to Goderich, Dec. 16, 1832.

25. C. O. 137/186. Memorial of the Jamaica deputies to Britain, Nov. 29, 1832.

26. C. O. 137/183. Manchester to Goderich, secret and confidential, Dec. 16, 1832.

27. *Hansard,* XXXI, 781-782. Marryat, June 13, 1815.

28. C. O. 137/183. Manchester to Goderich, secret and confidential, Dec. 16, 1832.

29. C. O. 137/187. Z. Jones to Goderich, Feb. 22, 1832.

30. C. O. 137/187. Goderich to Manchester, secret, March 5, 1832.

31. The phrase is Canning's.

32. C. O. 137/154. Manchester to Bathurst, Dec. 24, 1823.

33. C. O. 28/111. Smith to Stanley, July 13, 1833.

34. C. O. 295/92. Memorial for ourselves and in behalf of all our fellow subjects of African descent (enclosed in Governor Grant's despatch to Goderich, March 26, 1832).

35. *Ibid.* Grant to Goderich, March 26, 1832.

36. *Ibid.* William Clunes to Goderich, Jan. 27, 1832.

37. C. O. 28/111. Smith to Stanley, May 23, 1833.

38. C. O. 28/88. Combermere to Bathurst, Jan. 15, 1819.

39. C. O. 111/69. D'Urban to Murray, April 20, 1830. See also C. O. 295/87. Smith to Goderich from Trinidad, July 13, 1831: "The slaves have an unaccountable facility in obtaining partial, and generally distorted, information whenever a public document is about to be received which can in any way affect their condition or station."

40. C. O. 295/92. Grant to Goderich, March 26, 1832.

41. *Ibid. Gazette Extraordinary*, March 25, 1832.

42. C. O. 295/93. Extract from a Trinidad paper, n.d.

43. C. O. 295/92. Grant to Howick, April 30, 1832.

44. C. O. 137/119. Coote to Castlereagh, June 27, 1807; C. O. 137/120. Edmund Lyon, Agent for Jamaica, to Castlereagh, July 17, 1807.

45. C. O. 137/142. Manchester to Bathurst, Jan. 26, 1816.

46. C. O. 137/143. Extract of a letter from Jamaica, May 11, 1816.

47. C. O. 295/39. John Spooner, of Barbados, to Governor Woodford, April 18, 1816.

48. C. O. 28/85. Col. Codd to Governor Leith, April 25, 1816; *Ibid.*, Rear Admiral Harvey to J. W. Croker, April 30, 1816.

49. C. O. 295/60. A commandant of Trinidad to Governor Woodford, Aug. 30, 1823.

50. C. O. 137/145. Shand to Bathurst, Nov. 26, 1817.

51. C. O. 111/44. D'Urban to Bathurst, May 5, 1824.

52 C. O. 295/89. Grant to Howick, Dec. 10, 1831.

53. C. O. 137/183. Mulgrave to Howick, Aug. 6, 1832.

54. C. O. 28/111. Smith to Stanley, May 23, 1833.

55. C. O. 111/8. Nicholson to Castlereagh, June 6, 1808.

56. C. O. 137/156. Manchester to Bathurst, July 31, 1824.

57. C. O. 28/85. Leith to Bathurst, April 30, 1816.

58. *Ibid.* Codd to Leith, April 25, 1816.

59. *Ibid.* Leith to Bathurst, April 30, 1816.

60. C. O. 137/143. Alexander Aikman, Jr. to Bathurst, May 2, 1816.

61. C. O. 137/142. Manchester to Bathurst, May 4, 1816.

62. C. O. 111/39. Murray to Bathurst, Aug. 24, 1823.

63. *Ibid.* Murray to Bathurst, Sept. 27, 1823.

64. C. O. 28/92. Warde to Bathurst, Aug. 27, 1823.

65. C. O. 137/156. Manchester to Bathurst, July 31, 1824.

66. C. O. 111/44. D'Urban to Bathurst, May 5, 1824.

67. *Ibid.* D'Urban to Bathurst, May 5, 1824. (This was the second letter in one day.)

68. *Ibid.* D'Urban to Bathurst, May 15, 1824.

69. C. O. 28/107. Lyon to Goderich, March 28, 1831.

70. *Ibid.* Lyon to Goderich, April 2, 1831.

71. C. O. 137/181. Belmore to Goderich, Jan. 6, 1832.

72. C. O. 137/182. Belmore to Goderich, May 2, 1832.

73. C. O. 295/92. Grant to Howick, April 30, 1832.

74. C. O. 137/188. Mulgrave to Goderich, April 26, 1833.

75. *Hansard, Third Series*, XIII, 77. May 24, 1832.

76. C. O. 137/191. F. B. Zuicke to Governor Belmore, May 23, 1832.

77. C. O. 28/111. Smith to Goderich, May 7, 1833.

78. *Ibid.*

79. *Ibid.* Smith to Stanley, May 23, 1833.

CHAPTER 13

1. Gaston-Martin, L'*Ère des Négriers*, *1714-1774* (Paris, 1931), 424.

BIBLIOGRAPHY

This book is based on a doctoral dissertation, "The Economic Aspect of the Abolition of the British West Indian Slave Trade and Slavery," submitted to the Faculty of Modern History of Oxford University in September, 1938. Manuscript sources have been consulted chiefly for the years 1783-1833, the period covered by the dissertation.

I. PRIMARY SOURCES (MANUSCRIPT)

A. PUBLIC RECORD OFFICE, LONDON

1. Colonial Office Papers. There is no need to stress the value of this source. While quotations have been reduced to a minimum, those selected for the text have been based on a thorough investigation of more than 230 volumes, embracing Jamaica, Barbados, Trinidad and Demerara (British Guiana), and covering the period 1789-1796 (the early years of the Abolition Movement) and 1807 to 1833. The call numbers are C. O. 27 (Barbados), C. O. III (Demerara, that is, British Guiana), C. O. 295 (Trinidad), C. O. 137 (Jamaica).

2. Chatham Papers, G.D./8. These were tapped only for the correspondence and records of the younger Pitt and not of his father. Much information on Chatham is scattered in the work of Pares. The papers consulted yielded much valuable material on the British islands, Saint Domingue and India, and as Pitt dominated the British parliamentary scene from 1784 until his death in 1806, the collection is of cardinal importance.

3. Foreign Office Papers. These were used especially for the years 1787 to 1793 and with specific reference to the British government's attitude to French Saint Domingue; a few important items have been included in the text. The call number is F.O. 27 (France).

4. Customs Records. The records consulted were *Customs 8, British exports*, for the years 1814 to 1832; and *Customs 5*, British imports.

B. BRITISH MUSEUM

1. Liverpool Papers. This is the most important of the collection of Additional Manuscripts for this study. The papers run into many volumes; specific references on each occasion will be found in the Notes. As a West Indian proprietor and President of the Board of Trade, Lord Hawkesbury, later first Earl of Liverpool, occupied a prominent position in the period of the Abolition Movement. His correspondence includes many valuable letters and memoranda relative to the slave trade, the British and French colonies, British negotiations with the rebellious French colonists during the war with France, and the question of East India Sugar.

2. Minute Books of the Committee for the Abolition of the Slave Trade—three volumes containing much useful and pertinent material.

3. Auckland Papers. These are the papers of the British envoy sent to persuade the French in 1787 to abolish the slave trade; they contain five very valuable letters from William Wilberforce to supplement the biographies of the abolitionist.

4. Huskisson Papers. These papers contain some excellent material on Huskisson's views of emancipation, the West Indians, and the abolitionists.

C. LIVERPOOL PUBLIC LIBRARY

This library possesses three important manuscripts for this study. They are Vol. 10 of the Holt and Gregson Papers, full of statistics on Liverpool's dependence on the slave trade and letters from Matthew Gregson on the same subject; correspondence of a slave trader, Robert Bostock, with his captains for the years 1789-1792; and the *Journals of Liverpool Slave Ships, 1779-1788.*

D. JOHN RYLANDS LIBRARY, MANCHESTER

In this famous provincial library, in a key town for the development of British Capitalism and its relation to Negro slavery, there are the hitherto unused English Manuscripts. The collection contains much material on East India sugar and the boycott of West Indian slave produce; the letter of Buxton offering Christianity to the Negroes as compensation for slavery; and an interesting letter from T. B. Macaulay pleading pressure of business as the reason for his inability to contribute to a projected anthology to celebrate the Emancipation Act.

E.   Wilberforce Museum, Hull

This institution contains very little material. A few letters here and there, such as Gurney's on the value of Evangelization to Africa, are quoted in the text, with such call numbers as existed at the time of my visit (June 1939). The value of the Museum lies not in its literary records but in its exhibit of the gruesome instruments used in the slave trade. In one of the rooms there is a framed list of slaves on "Orange Hill Estate" (location not given) which, among the classifications according to labor, age and color, has one interesting category into which fall five of the slaves, varying in age from 1 year and 8 months to 20 years—"mongrels." Just what constituted a mongrel, on a plantation with the more familiar divisions of black, mulatto, etc., is not clear.

F.   Rhodes House Library, Oxford

In the possession of Rhodes House there is a manuscript volume in the hand-writing of the abolitionist, James Ramsay. It is an interesting collection of notes, memoranda and speeches useful not only for a study of the abolition movement in general but for the light they throw on an abolitionist too little known from his few pamphlets and the evidence he gave before the Privy Council in 1788.

G.   Bank of England Record Office, Roehampton, London

The Stock Ledgers of the East India Company are kept here. The volumes examined were the East India Company Subscription journals to £800,000 additional stock, July, 1786, and East India Company Stock Ledgers, 1783-1791, 1791-1796. They were consulted for the connection between East Indians and abolitionists.

II.   PRIMARY SOURCES (PRINTED)

1. *Hansard.* The importance of the Parliamentary Debates for this period needs to be emphasized, for with the exception of one British writer, W. L. Mathieson, no real attempt has been made to utilize a source whose value, it might be thought, would be readily ap-

parent. The debates have been thoroughly covered, for the years 1650 to 1860. For the earlier period ending roughly at 1760, the speeches are widely scattered, but, fortunately for the student, they have been collected and compiled in an easily consulted form by a painstaking worker, L. F. Stock, under the title of *Proceedings and Debates in the British Parliament respecting North America*, and published, in five volumes to date, under the auspices of the Carnegie Institution.

For the years 1760 to 1860 the parliamentary debates appear under the following different titles: 1760 to 1803, *Cobbett's Parliamentary History of England*; 1803 to 1812, *Cobbett's Parliamentary Debates*; 1812 to 1820, *Hansard*; 1820 to 1830, *Hansard, New Series*; 1830 to 1860, *Hansard, Third Series*. I have kept this official division to facilitate checking or consultation. This seemed more satisfactory than the use of the single word *Hansard* to cover entirely different series, which would entail serious confusion as far as different volumes are concerned. In the earlier period many years' debates are included in a single volume; for the debates for 1845 and later years in general, a single year means usually four separate volumes.

2. *Documents Illustrative of the Slave Trade to America*. This remarkable four-volume work, another publication of the Carnegie Institution, puts the student of Negro slavery eternally in the debt of the late Professor Elizabeth Donnan and her able assistants. For present purposes the most important volume was Volume II, which deals with the eighteenth century and the West Indies. But Volume I, the seventeenth century, is also very useful especially for the period after 1688, while, where necessary, Volumes III and IV, dealing with the Northern and Middle, and the Southern Colonies of the mainland respectively, have been consulted.

3. *Parliamentary Papers*. Under this heading I include the papers submitted to Parliament and evidence collected by Parliamentary Committees. A detailed list is unnecessary in view of references given in the Notes, but from 1784 to 1848 there are many useful reports which cannot be ignored for a study of the West Indies. If only because its existence is little known and its vast possibilities are still to be explored, special mention should be made of Volume 48 of the Sessional Papers for the Years 1837-1838, which gives a detailed list of the claims for compensation of slaves in accordance with the Emancipation Act of 1833. The only complete collection of the Parliamentary Papers in existence is in the British Museum.

4. *Report of the Committee of the Lords of the Privy Council*

for all Matters Relating to Trade and Foreign Plantations, 1788. This is an indispensable document for anyone who seeks to understand the situation of the sugar colonies after the American Revolution. It is certain that it was this report which explains the attitude of Pitt to the slave trade. Running into many pages, its most important sections are Part III, dealing with the conditions of the slaves; Part V, French competition in the sugar trade; and Part VI, Miscellaneous Papers received in the late stages of publication of the Report.

5. The correspondence and memoranda of various leading statesmen of the period have been published, at least in part—Canning, Castlereagh, Wellington and Grenville (the last by the Historical Manuscripts Commission under the title of *The Manuscripts of J. B. Fortescue Esq., preserved at Dropmore*). In this category might well be included the *Correspondence of William Wilberforce* and the *Private Papers of William Wilberforce*, published by his sons.

6. *Calendar of State Papers, Colonial Series, America and West Indies*. Equipped with an excellent index, these volumes include many items, generally in condensed form, relative to the West Indies, sugar cultivation, the slave trade, and economic relations between islands and mainland, while they also contain much useful information on the white servants in the islands. The volumes consulted cover the period 1611 to 1697.

III.   SECONDARY SOURCES

A.   CONTEMPORARY

The contemporary material is voluminous. The writings of the leading mercantilists, Postlethwayt, Davenant, Gee, Sir Dalby Thomas, Wood, have been carefully examined; so has *The Wealth of Nations*, the anti-mercantilist classic. Contemporary information on the indentured servants is limited, but what exists is useful. The bitter polemical warfare between West Indians and East Indians, of great importance, has been thoroughly investigated; in addition to the material in the British Museum, there were the resources of the India Office Library and the pamphlet series of the John Rylands Library. Bryan Edwards' well-known *History of the British West Indies* deserves some notice, not only for its intrinsic value, but as one of those rare cultural landmarks in a slave society which, unlike the slave society of Greece, despised education and did not reproduce any of the great gifts of Greece to the world. In addition numerous local histories, especially of the great seaport towns and industrial centers, and contemporary accounts of the growth of British commerce and industry, have been examined. The writings of the abolitionists themselves have been used to a large extent, especially the well-known five-volume, rambling but informative biography of Wilberforce by his sons.

B. MODERN

The listing of authorities and sources is unnecessary in any study of the British West Indies which covers the years 1763-1833. There is a story to the effect that in the abolitionist circle, whenever a point was in dispute, someone would remark, "Look it up in Macaulay." "Look it up in Ragatz" would not be an exaggeration for Caribbean history during the period 1763-1833. Ragatz' *The Fall of the Planter Class in the British Caribbean* is a comprehensive study of the original sources. His *Guide for the Study of British Caribbean History, 1763-1834* (Washington, D. C., 1932) is an indispensable aid to the student of the Caribbean, who will find in it not only a complete list of works of all sorts but also a succinct précis of the leading ideas advanced in each work. The same writer's *Statistics for the Study of British Caribbean History, 1763-1833* gives valuable statistical data. The *Check Lists of House of Commons and House of Lords Sessional Papers, 1763-1834* should be consulted by all students baffled by apparently conflicting ways of referring to such papers in this period. Professor Ragatz' three bibliographies: *A List of Books and Articles on Colonial History and Overseas Expansion published in the United States*, for the years 1900-1930, 1931-1932, 1933-1935, respectively, cite numerous books and articles which treat of the position of the white indentured servant. Finally his most recent bibliography: *A Bibliography for the Study of European History, 1815 to 1939* (Ann Arbor, 1942) gives, on pages 140-158, an exhaustive list of works on the United Kingdom, which contains many useful titles for the development of Britain in the nineteenth century.

After Professor Ragatz comes yet another American scholar whose work on the Caribbean deserves especial mention, more so as it actually supplements, in the period of which it treats, the research of Ragatz. Professor Frank Pitman's *The Development of the British West Indies, 1700-1763* is another outstanding piece of work based, like Ragatz', on a careful analysis of original materials. The same author's essay on *The Settlement and Financing of British West India Plantations in the Eighteenth Century*, one of many essays written by students of C. M. Andrews in his honor, is nothing short of a masterpiece.

Two English studies deserve to be separated from the idealistic and garbled versions of slavery familiar in England. Richard Pares' *War and Trade in the West Indies, 1739-1763*, while inevitably full of war and diplomacy, none the less contains vital information on the West Indies, and is of great importance for the attitude of the West Indian planters to the foreign sugar colonies. Where the social and economic with Pares are subordinate, they dominate with W. L. Burn. The latter's *Emancipation and Apprenticeship in the British West Indies* is a scholarly analysis of the apprenticeship system, 1833-1838, though the first three chapters of the book, which deal with emancipation, are of less value, partly because the author was content with secondary sources. Among the lesser English writers, W. L. Mathieson is entitled to some mention if only because while, like Coupland, he used only secondary sources, unlike Coupland, he used them well and remembered that England has a Parliament, where debates are held. With a better index, his four works on slavery would be useful references. Coupland represents the sentimental conception of history; his works help us to understand what the abolition movement was not. Compared with his earlier venture into the field of slavery, *England and Slavery* (London, 1934), C. M. MacInnes' *Bristol, a Gateway of Empire* is a healthy departure from emotional to scientific history; the latter work is based on unpublished materials in the Bristol archives. American historical idealism is represented by F. J. Klingberg's *The Anti-Slavery Movement in England*.

Special mention must be made of two studies which present in a general way the relationship between capitalism and slavery. The first is a Master's essay by W. E. Williams: *Africa and the Rise of Capitalism*, published by the Division of the Social Sciences of Howard University in 1938. The second and more important is C. L. R. James, *The Black Jacobins, Toussaint L'Ouverture and the San Domingo Revolution* (London, 1938). On pages 38-41 the thesis advanced in this book is stated clearly and concisely and, as far as I know, for the first time in English.

In the field of colonial policy in general, two books are indispensable. C. M. Andrews, *The Colonial Period of American History*, not merely includes excellent chapters on Barbados and

Jamaica; it puts the sugar islands in their proper perspective in the mercantilist picture, while his description and analysis of the laws of trade and the colonial system in general are an essential introduction to any student of the first British Empire. Less broad in scope, but just as pertinent, is G. L. Beer's *The Old Colonial System*. Merivale's lectures at Oxford during the years 1839 to 1841 on *Colonization and Colonies* is Oxford scholarship at its best, while Bell and Morrell's *Select Documents on British Colonial Policy, 1830-1860* includes some very valuable reproductions of original documents for a vital period. For special studies of the West Indies under the old colonial system the works of Harlow, Williamson, and Higham are very important, Harlow's *History of Barbados* being the best of the three as showing an understanding of the fact that Barbadian—for that matter, British West Indian—problems of the twentieth century have their roots in the economic and social changes of the seventeenth, represented by sugar and slavery.

Works on the growth and development of individual British industries are indicated in the Notes to the respective chapters. For the best general treatment of the development of capitalism in England, only two names need be mentioned—Mantoux and Clapham. Chapter V of Clapham's *Economic History of Modern Britain, The Early Railway Age*, is the best short analysis of the Industrial Revolution, while his essay on *"The Industrial Revolution and the Colonies, 1783-1822"* in Vol. II of the *Cambridge History of the British Empire* shows a more intelligent understanding of the abolition movement and the destruction of West Indian slavery than is to be found in all the works of the "official" British historians.

In the field of literature Professor Sypher's *Guinea's Captive Kings: British Anti-Slavery Literature of the XVIIIth Century* is one of those excellent studies on Negro slavery which we have learned to associate with the University of North Carolina Press. While the book is very weak—in some respects unpardonably weak—from the political angle, it is an intelligent and comprehensive analysis of the literature of the period, and as such, a useful aid for the social sciences. It can profitably be supplemented by a recent publication of one of my colleagues, Dr. Eva Dykes' *The Negro in English Romantic Thought* (Associated Publishers, Washington, D. C., 1942). Marguerite Steen's best-seller novel, *The Sun is My Undoing*, reveals a profound understanding of the triangular trade and its importance to British capitalism.

Such sources as have been used for the development of French Saint Domingue and Spanish Cuba during the period under review have necessarily been secondary sources. For France the most important writer is Gaston-Martin. A Rosenwald Fellowship in the summer of 1940 permitted me to work in the archives and libraries of Cuba. Pezuela's comprehensive *Diccionario* of the Island includes excellent material under the heading "Azúcar" (Sugar), while *Los Ingenios de la Isla de Cuba*, by a contemporary sugar baron, Cantero, is a lyrical, profusely illustrated, valuable and rare work.

I have, in three published articles, treated in greater detail some of the issues currently raised: "The Golden Age of the Slave System in Britain" (*Journal of Negro History*, Jan. 1940); "The Intercolonial Slave Trade after its Abolition in 1807" (*Journal of Negro History*, April 1942); "Protection, Laisser-Faire and Sugar" (*Political Science Quarterly*, March 1943).

INDEX

Abolitionists, hypocrisy of, 34; significance of attack on W. I., 135-36; strength of in industrial centers, 154; in Manchester, 155; in Birmingham, 157-58; in Sheffield, 159; boycott of slave-grown produce by, 159, 183-84, 190; support of Cobden by, 161; A. Committee, 166, 182-83; portraits of, 179-82; and emancipation, 182-83; on East India sugar, 183-88; relations with East Indians, 183-88; on Brazilian sugar, 188-91, 193-94; on universal abolition of slave trade, 189; on reconquest of Saint Domingue, 189

Absentee planters, and Deficiency Laws, 25, 86-87; consequences of absenteeism, 85-86; Merivale on, 86; social position in England, 91

Adams, John, 120-21

Africa, British trade with, 54-55, 171; trade compared with American mainland colonies, 54-55; shipping and trade with, 58; Bristol's trade with, 61; exports of wool to, 65-68; Manchester's trade with, 68-70; exports of rum to, 78-80; iron exports to, 81-82; exports of guns to, 82; exports of brass to, 83

Agricultural Revolution, 98, 120

American mainland colonies, trade with Britain compared with W. I. trade, 53-55; shipping and trade with, 58; triangular trade of, 78, 80, 116; molasses and, 80-81, 115-16, 118-20; exports to W. I., 108; attitude of mercantilists to, 109-11; personal contacts with West Indians, 112; economic relations with W. I., 108-22; trade with foreign W. I., 115-20; mercantilists on trade of with foreign W. I., 116-19; William Wood on trade of with foreign W. I., 118-19; effect of Molasses Act on, 119; effect of Sugar Duties Act on, 119-20

American Revolution, 50, 130; effect on slave trade, 38; effect on cotton trade, 69, 72; effect on sugar trade, 77-78; effect on mercantilism, 96, 107, 120; molasses an essential ingredient of, 120; effect on W. I., 120-25; effect on W. I. slave system, 123-24; effect on old colonial system, 124-26; British reaction to, 209-10

Andrews, C. M., 56

Anglo-French rivalry, rival mercantilisms, 40; in sugar trade, 77-78, 116, 122-23, 145-48

Anti-Corn Law League, 137, 155, 160

Antigua, trade of compared with

American mainland colonies, 54-55; decline of sugar production in, 150-51; emancipation in, 191; slave revolt in, 206

Apprenticeship, Birmingham on, 158; Sheffield on, 159

Asiento, importance of, 33; Postlethwayt on, 33; to Portugal, 39; Anglo-French struggle for, 40; Bishop Robinson and, 42

Attwood, Thomas, 158

Auckland, Earl of, 184-85

Australia, labor problem in, 5; convict labor in, 12; white labor in, 22-23; woolen production of, 131; Molesworth on, 143

Bacon, Antony, 103-4

Baillie family, 62

Baptists, 43

Barbados, 7; governor on weakness of Spain, 4; Monmouth's followers sent to, 13; conditions of servants, 16-17; cheapness of black labor in, 19; decline of white population, 23; increase of black population, 23; ex-servants, 24; Redlegs, 25; sugar and increase of wealth, 25; growth of Latifundia, 25; on Christianity for slaves, 42; trade of compared with American mainland colonies, 54-55; on free trade in sugar, 56-57; woolen imports, 67; Codrington family in, 90; Charles II on importance of, 108; governor on trade with New England, 110; soil exhaustion in, 112-13; attitude to new settlements, 113; compared with French islands, 113-14; sugar production in, 151; emancipation in, 191; on policy of amelioration, 197-99; attitude of planters to slaves, 201; free people of color in, 201; misconceptions of

slaves in, 203-4; slave revolts in, 204-6; governor on slave revolt in British Guiana, 205; governor on cruelty of suspense, 207-8

Barclay family, slave trading of, 43; banking interests of, 101

Baring family, 43, 171

Beckford, William, Fonthill Mansion, 87-88; slave compensation to, 88; family dynasty in Parliament, 93; Mayor of London, 95; on increase of sugar duties, 96; master ironmonger, 104; role of in peace treaty of 1763, 115

Birmingham, in age of industry, 60; gun trade of, 82; W. I. trade of, 82-83; exports of brass of, 83; slave trade and, 82, 84; on abolition, 84; on Reform Bill, 134; opposition to W. I. monopoly, 154; abolition movement in, 157-58; interest in slave trade, 158

Blundell, Bryan, 47

Bolton, John, 93, 95

Boulton, Matthew, 102, 126-27, 131, 157

Brazil, slave trade, 47, 140, 170-75, 192; cotton exports, 71-72; British exports to, 132; restrictions on British trade with, 138; sugar cultivation in, 145, 150-52; sugar exports to Britain, 151; sugar exports to Europe, 151; importation of sugar of for refining, 155, 163, 167, 193-94; Manchester on sugar of, 155; Brazilian Association in Liverpool, 162; Glasgow on sugar of, 163; boycott of produce of, 170-71; British trade with, 172; abolitionists on importation of sugar of, 188-91

Bright, John, on W. I. monopoly, 156; on British capital in Brazilian slave trade, 172; on suppression of slave trade, 173

Bristol, trade in indentured servants, 10, 19; kidnaping, 11; Jeffreys' visitation to, 14-15; slave trade, 32, 61; Clarkson's investigations in, 35; profits of slave trade in, 36; Edmund Burke as representative of, 41; protest against colonial duties on slave imports, 41; enthusiasm over rejection of Wilberforce's abolition bill, 42; committee of 1789 to oppose abolition, 48, 61, 101; in age of trade, 60; popularity of trade in, 60-61; W. I. trade, 60-62; customs duties in, 61; wharfage dues in, 61; triangular trade of, 61; members of Parliament associated with W. I., 62, 74, 93; sugar refining industry, 73-74, 77-78; distilleries in, 79; pacotille trade, 81; brass industry in, 83; banking in, 101; on Reform Bill, 134

British Guiana, East Indian immigration to, 28; Gladstone plantations in, 89, 93; abolition in, 150-51; sugar production in, 151, 153; policy of amelioration in, 197-99; Bush Negroes in, 202; governor on alertness of slaves, 202; misconceptions of slaves in, 203; slave revolts in, 204-5

Brougham, Lord, 181; on absentee planters, 86; representative of York, 159; spokesman for woolen industry, 160; on British capital in Brazilian slave trade, 172; on Pownall amendment, 183; on slavery in India, 186; on equalization of sugar duties, 188; on slavery in sugar but not in cotton, 193

Burke, Edmund, 17, 41, 73

Burn, W. L., 132, 188

Buxton, Fowell, 49; on gradual emancipation, 182; on Pownall amendment, 183; on slavery in India, 185-86; on equalization of sugar duties, 188; on importation of Brazilian sugar, 191; on emancipation, 191-92; on suppression of slave trade, 192; son of, 193

Canada, a secure and certain investment, 4; Voltaire on, 114; British acquisition of, 114-15; compared with Grenada, 114; Disraeli on, 144

Canning, George, attitude to West Indians, 95-96; on independence of Latin America, 132; representative of Liverpool, 162; on Brazilian trade, 170-71

Capitalism, British, attack on W.I. system, 136; attack on monopoly, 139; opposed to colonies, 142-45; on overproduction of sugar in West Indies, 152; opposed to W. I. monopoly, 154-68; opposed to suppression of slave trade, 169-77; attitude to W. I. slavery, 169

Carlyle, Thomas, 195-96

Castlereagh, Lord, 189

Chatham, Earl of, on British slave trade, 40; on colonial manufactures, 56; attitude to West Indians, 95; influence of Beckford on, 95, 115; on mainland trade with foreign W. I., 117

Child, Sir Josiah, on emigration, 16; on value of labor in W. I., 52; on New England, 109

China, 20, 131; Chinese in Cuba, 29; British exports to, 132, 134

Church, the, and slavery, 42-44

Clapham, J. H., 127, 129

Clapham Sect, 181, 186

Clarkson, Thomas, on size of

slave ships, 35; on transportation of slaves, 35; on rise of Liverpool, 63; on American Revolution, 124; praised by Wordsworth, 136, 195; French translations of works of, 147; on mortality of white sailors in slave trade, 166; humanitarianism of, 179; on East India sugar, 185; sent to Aix-la-Chapelle, 189; on slave-grown produce, 194

Clay, William, 165, 167

Cobbett, William, 133, 155

Cobden, Richard, on colonies, 142-43; spokesman for woolen industry, 160-61; on W. I. monopoly, 160-61; on slave-grown sugar, 160-61; on suppression of slave trade, 173

Codrington, Christopher, legacy to Society for the Propagation of the Gospel, 42; slave plantations of, 90; bequest to All Souls College, 90; descendant in Parliament, 93

Coleridge, Samuel, 195

Colonial Office, 139, 143-44, 153, 180

Columbus, Christopher, 3, 8, 9

Company of Merchants trading to Africa, 32; Edmund Burke on, 41; Quakers in, 43; cotton manufacturers as members of, 70

Company of Royal Adventurers trading to Africa, incorporation, 30-31; superseded by Royal African Company, 31; royal patronage of, 39, 48

Convicts, 9, 11; Benjamin Franklin on, 12; in Australia, 12; Merivale on, 12; in Virginia, 12; in W. I., 12; after emancipation in W. I., 27, 141

Cotton, cotton gin, 20, 72, 124, 128, 155; Negro Slavery and, 23; superseded wool, 68, 130;

technological changes in, 68; triangular trade and, 68-73; manufacturers of and slave trade, 70; Lancashire cotton interest, 97; expansion of, 106, 127-29, 132; opposition of manufacturers to W. I. monopoly, 154-57; imports from America, 162

Coupland, Reginald, 45, 178, 188, 211n

Cowper, William, 45, 49

Cromwell, Oliver, transportation of Irish prisoners, 13; on acquisition of Jamaica, 108; on New England, 109

Cropper, James, controversy with Gladstone, 90; arrangements on slavery, 186-87

Cuba, 7; tobacco industry in compared with Virginia, 21; American capital in, 26; white labor in tobacco industry, 27; Chinese labor, 29; Haitian labor, 29; British W. I. labor, 29; British occupation, 33, 114; slave trade, 47; British restoration of, 114-15; restrictions on British trade with, 138; sugar production, 145, 149-52; British sugar imports from, 151; sugar exports to Europe, 152; growth of sugar plantations, 151-52

Cunliffe, family, 47-48

Davenant, Charles, on monopoly in slave trade, 31; on value of labor in W. I., 52; on British trade in seventeenth century, 53; on colonies, 55; on sugar refining in colonies, 76; on wealth of West Indians, 86; on Northern mainland colonies, 110

Declaration of Independence, 107, 120

Deficiency Laws, 24-25
Defoe, Daniel, 18, 48
Disraeli, Benjamin, on W. I. monopoly, 140; on W. I., 144; on colonies, 144; on suppression of slave trade, 175; on emancipation, 194-95
Dominica, compared with Florida, 114-15; sugar production in, 151
Dominican Republic, 26
Dumbell, Professor, 26
Dutch East Indies, 28
Dutch Guiana, 28

East India Company, compared with slave trading companies, 31; profits of, 37; mercantilists on trade of, 37; competition of Manchester with, 69; interest in slave trade of, 69; imports of guns by, 82; cultivation of sugar by, 123, 137-38, 140, 146, 151; monopoly of, 137; attack on W. I. monopoly by, 137-38; receive sugar protection, 153; renewal of charter of, 184
East India Company (Dutch), 37
East India Sugar, Manchester on, 155; Sheffield on, 159; refiners on, 164; shipowners on, 167; abolitionists on, 183-88; slave-grown, 184-86
Edwards, Bryan, 24, 90-91
Ewart, William, 163, 167
Exeter, Bishop of, 43; woolen industry of, 66

Fazackerly, Sir William, 70
Florida, 114-15
Fortescue, J. W., 147
Francis I, 4
Francklyn, Gilbert, 103
Franklin, Benjamin, 12, 45
Free Trade, in slaves, 31-32; West Indians on, 56, 141; struggle against monopoly, 57; Jesus Christ and, 136; movement for, 136-42; anti-imperialism and, 142-45
French Revolution, 147, 209

Garbett, Samuel, 157
Gascoyne, General, 105
Gaston-Martin, 147, 209
Gee, Joshua, 31
George III, opposition to abolition of, 39; Beckford and, 95; coronation procession of, 128
George IV, 128
Georgia, 5, 7, 20, 43
Gibson, Milner, 156
Gladstone, John, of Corrie and Company, 89; slave plantations of, 89; chairman of Liverpool West Indian Association, 90; controversy with Cropper, 90; slave compensation to, 90; member of Parliament, 93; friend of Canning, 95; banking connections of, 99; insurance connections of, 105; railway connections of, 105
Gladstone, Robertson, 99
Gladstone, William Ewart, election campaign in Newark, 89-90; defence of slavery by, 93; banking connections of, 99; on W. I. monopoly, 141-42; on parliamentary interest in colonies, 144-45; on suppression of slave trade, 175; on Civil War in the United States, 176-77; on protecting duty and Negroes, 191
Glasgow, in age of trade, 60; colonial trade of, 64; sugar refining in, 64, 75; tobacco industry in, 64, 75; Colonel Macdowall and, 75, 91; banking in, 101-2; steam power in, 127; on free trade, 138;

on importation of Brazilian sugar, 163
Glassford, John, 102
Goulburn, Henry, 93-94
Gregson, William, 99-100
Grenada, compared with Canada, 114; decline of sugar production, 151, 153
Guadeloupe, British occupation, 33; British slave trade to, 33; cotton exports of, 72; British restoration of, 114-15
Guinea (coin), 44
Gurney, Joseph, 158, 184, 192

Harlow, Vincent, 17, 25
Hatuey, 8
Hawkesbury, Lord, 94-95, 146, 178, 189
Hawkins, Sir John, 30, 39
Henry the Navigator, Prince, 9
Heywood family, slave trading of, 47; importers of slave-grown cotton, 47; humanitarianism of, 47-48; banking interests of, 99
Hibbert family, cotton manufacturers, 71; sugar planters, 88; Hibbert trust, 88, 156; and W. I. Docks, 88; slave compensation to, 88; Hibbert's House, 88; Hibbert Journal, 88-89; George Hibbert, 88, 93, 95, 136
Hogarth, William, 44, 79
Holland, rivalry with England, 40; trade with British Colonies, 56
House of Lords, opposition to abolition, 48; West Indians in, 94; rejected Reform Bill, 133; protest to against Corn Laws, 138
Howick, Lord, 166
Hume, Joseph, 138, 143, 177
Huskisson, William, attitude to West Indians, 95-96, 139; on lessons of American Revolution, 124-125; representative

of Liverpool, 162-63; on sugar refining in England, 165; on trade with India, 167
Hutt, William, 173

Jamaica, 7; English officialdom on, 17; German settlers in Seaford, 22; slave imports, 33; duties on slaves imported, 41, 46; trade of compared with American mainland colonies, 54-55; Bristol's trade with, 61-62; on woolen industry and monopoly in slave trade, 67; woolen imports of, 67; restriction of production in, 77, 112-13; compared with Leeward Islands, 77; Beckford family in, 87-88; Hibbert family in, 88; Long family in, 89; Gladstone plantations in, 90; governor on increased sugar duties, 96; effect of American Revolution in, 121-23; decline of British exports to, 132; anti-British feeling in, 144, 200; Roebuck on, 144; bankruptcies in, 149; decline of sugar production in, 149-53; on suppression of slave trade, 176; on policy of amelioration, 198-99; attitude of planters to slaves, 201; Maroons in, 202; misconceptions of slaves in, 203-4; slave revolts in, 204-7; violence of planters in, 207
Java, 150
Jefferson, Thomas, 7, 18, 107, 120
Jeffreys, Judge, 14-16
Jenks, Leland, 131
Klingberg, F. J., 188
Knight, James, 25
Lansdowne, Lord, 166
Lascelles family, 93-94
Latin America, export of British capital to, 131-32; British exports

to, 132; Canning on independence of, 132

Lauber, A. W., 8-9

Lecky, W. E. H., 13

Leeds, 130

Leeward Islands, 13; Bristol's trade with, 61; compared with Jamaica, 77

Leyland, Thomas, mayor of Liverpool, 47; slave trading of, 47; banking interests of, 99-100

Liverpool, slave trade, 32, 34; profits of slave trade, 36; popularity of slave trade, 37, 62-64, 95; profits of W. I. trade, 36-37; losses of slave trade, 38; protest against colonial duties on slave imports, 41; slave traders, 47; mayors engaged in slave trade, 47-48; members of Parliament engaged in slave trade, 48; on modification of Navigation Laws (1739), 57; shipbuilders and slave trade, 58-59; sailors in slave trade, 59; roperies in, 59; on regulation of slave trade, 59; in age of trade, 60; customs receipts in, 62-63; growth of population in, 63; dock duties in, 63, 162; Clarkson on rise of, 63; relationship with Manchester, 63, 68, 162; capital in slave trade, 63; opposition to abolition, 63; on woolen industry and monopoly in slave trade, 67; sugar refining in, 75; distilleries in, 79; heavy industry in, 83-84; banking in, 98-101; anti-slavery society of, 105; railway between Manchester and, 105; trade of with Latin America, 132; indifference of to W. I., 132; on East India Company's monopoly, 138; on free trade, 138; opposition to W. I. monopoly, 154, 161-63; slave trade, 161-62; connection

with slavery, 162; cotton imports of, 162; free trade sentiments in, 162-63; Brazilian slave trade and, 172

Lloyd family (banking), 157

Lloyd's (insurance), 104-5

London, kidnaping in, 11; slave trade and, 32; protest against colonial duties on slave imports, 41; W. I. Docks of, 60; woolen industry of, 66-67; sugar refining in, 74, 77; gun trade in, 82; banking in, 101; on free trade, 138; opposition to W. I. monopoly, 154; on independence of South America, 171

Long family, 89; on cost of sugar plantations, 25; Beeston Long, 89; Edward Long, historian of Jamaica, 89; Lord Farnborough, 89; steam engine and, 103; profits of sugar plantations of, 122

Louis XIV, 39

Louisiana, 9, 150

Luttrell, Temple, 49

Macdowall, William, 75, 91, 102, 163

Macaulay, T. B. (Lord), 193-94

Macaulay, Zachary, 181, 185-86

Manchester, in age of industry, 60; on woolen trade, 67; triangular trade and, 68-73; relationship with Liverpool, 63, 68; W. I. trade of, 68, 128-29, 133; trade with Africa, 68; competition with Indian textiles, 68-69, 71; relationship of cotton manufactures with slave traders, 70-71; raw cotton imports of, 71-73; sugar refining in, 75; banking in, 98; railway between Liverpool and, 105; growth of population in, 106, 128; development of cotton industry, 127-29; on monop-

oly, 133; on trade by "moral obligation," 134; on free trade, 136;
opposition to W. I. monopoly,
154-57; interest in slave trade,
155; opposition to slave system,
155-56; relations with Liverpool,
162; on South American market,
171; Brazilian slave trade and,
172, 174

Manning, Cardinal, 43

Mansfield, Chief Justice, 45-46

Mantoux, Paul, 127

Marryat, Joseph, 94; famous son
of, 91; connection with Lloyd's,
104-5; slave compensation to, 105

Maryland, 7, 16, 26

Massachusetts, 4-5

Mauritius, 49; equalization of sugar
duties of with W. I., 133; growth
of sugar production, 150-51

Mercantilism, favored emigration,
10; opposed to emigration, 15-
16; on danger of colonial manufactures from introduction of
white servants, 18; proposal to
manufacture dimity in Barbados
and, 24; on slave trade to foreign colonies, 33; on East India
trade, 37; rival mercantilisms,
40; effect of discovery of America on, 51; on triangular trade,
55; on W. I. colonies, 55; on
colonial system, 55-56; Navigation Laws and, 56-57, 133; on
woolen industry, 57, 67; struggle
against laissez faire, 57; on fisheries, 59; ban on sugar refining
in colonies, 75-76; in France, 76;
effect of American Revolution on,
96, 107; stimulated Industrial
Revolution, 98-105; brake on
ecomonic progress, 106-7, 133;
Adam Smith on, 107; attitude of
to Northern mainland colonies,
109-11; a system, however bad,

110; on mainland trade with foreign W. I., 116-19; slavery and,
136; Disraeli on, 140; Navigation
Laws and, 168

Merivale, Herman, on importance
of labor for commercial production, 4; on slavery, 5; on expensiveness of slave labor, 7; on
superiority of slave labor on fresh
soil, 7; value of convict labor, 12;
on industriousness of whites in
slave economy, 25; on absenteeism, 86; on free trade with U. S.,
124; on Australian wool, 131; on
W. I. monopoly, 133, 135, 138;
on colonies, 144; on abolition,
150; on slavery, 194

Metallurgical industries, triangular trade and, 81-84; technological innovations in, 84, 126-27;
expansion of iron industry, 103-
4, 106, 129-30; expansion of coal
industry, 129; ironmasters and
abolition, 157-59; ironmasters
and slave trade, 158

Methodists, 129, 155, 181

Middle Passage, 34-35

Miles family, representing Bristol
in Parliament, 62; sugar refining of, 74; slave compensation,
74-75; alderman of Bristol, 95;
banking interests of, 101

Mittelberger, G., 13

Molasses, embittered relations
between sugar planter and English landlord, 80; embittered
relations between sugar planter
and mainland colonist, 80; in
New England economy, 80-
81, 118; in French W. I., 80;
Molasses Act, 119

Molesworth, 143

Monk, General, 40

Monopoly, in slave trade, 30-32;
W. I. planters oppose, 31, 56; in

colonial system, 55-56; British merchants on, in eighteenth century, 57; struggle against free trade, 57; woolen industry on monopoly in slave trade, 66-67; Adam Smith on, 107; attack on West Indian, 126-27, 135-42, 153; attack on, 127, 137-39; Manchester on, 133; in corn, 137-38; in sugar, 137-39; of East India Company, 137-38; capitalists on West Indian, 154-68; Manchester on, 154-57; Liverpool on, 162-63; sugar refiners on, 163-66

Montserrat, an Irish colony, 13; need of white servants and Negroes, 17; decline of white population, 24; increase of black population, 24; trade of compared with American mainland colonies, 54-55

Moravians, 43

Moss, James, banking interests, of, 101; railway connections of, 105

Namier, L. B., 92, 113

Navigation Laws, and mercantilism, 56-57; modified, 57, 133; West Indians on, after American Revolution, 121; repealed, 167-68

Nelson, Horatio, 44

Nevis, white servants, 24; decline of white population, 24; increase of black population, 24; slaves in, 39; trade of compared with American mainland colonies, 54-55; Pinney family in, 91; of Alexander Hamilton, 112; decline of sugar production in, 150-51

New England, slavery in, 9; trade compared with West Indies and Africa, 54-55; distilling in, 80-81, 118; triangular trade of, 78, 80; exports of rum, 80; attitude of mercantilists to, 109-11;

food trade with West Indies of, 109-11

Newfoundland, 52; W. I. market of, 59

Newton, John, 42-43, 166

New York, trade of compared with West Indian colonies and Africa, 54-55; woolen imports, 67

New Zealand, 143

North, Lord, on American Revolution, 121; on abolition, 126

North Carolina, 19-20

O'Connell, Daniel, 207

Okill, John, 58

Oldham, 128

Oswald family, 163

Ortiz, Fernando, 8, 21

Pacotille, 81

Palmerston, Viscount, on protection, 139; on suppression of slave trade, 174-75

Peel, Sir Robert, protectionist in sugar, 140; on British participation in Brazilian slave trade, 172; on slavery in India, 185

Pennant, Richard, member of Parliament, 93; raised to the peerage, 94; on steam engine, 103; revolutionized state industry in Wales, 105

Pennsylvania, indentured servants, 10; treatment of indentured servants, 16; trade of compared with W. I. colonies and Africa, 54-55; woolen imports of, 67

Philippines, 150, 167

Philips, Mark, 155-156, 167

Phillips, V. B., 19, 27

Pinney family, in Nevis, 91; on American Revolution, 121

Pitman, Frank, on value of W. I. plantations, 53; on mainland trade with W. I., 108; on Jamaica plantations, 151

Pitt, William, on incomes from W. I., 53; on free trade between W. I. and America, 121; interest in India of, 123; encourages Wilberforce to sponsor abolition, 123, 148; compliment to Adam Smith, 138; on slave trade, 146; on East India sugar, 146; on abolition, 146-48; acceptance of Saint Domingue, 147-49

Plantation, climatic theory of, 20-25; decline of whites in W. I. and, 23-24; increase of blacks in W. I. and, 23-24; slavery and, 27

Pope, the, 3, 30, 33

Portugal, claimed ownership of Columbus' discoveries, 3; ownership of Brazil, 3; immigrants in W. I., 27; Asiento and, 39; slave trade, 39

Postlethwayt, Malachi, on danger of manufacturing in colonies from white servants, 18; on monopoly in slave trade, 31; on abolition of slave trade, 49-50; on slave trade, 51-52; on colonies, 55; on mainland trade with foreign W. I., 116-17

Price, Grenfell, 21-22

Privy Council Committee of 1788, 70; on British slave trade to foreign colonies, 34; on costs of sugar production, 145-46

Protection, Palmerston on, 139; unsound, 139; protectionists on, 140; West Indians on, 141

Puerto Rico, 21, 26-27

Quakers, transportation of, 13; participation in slave trade, 43-44; petition of against slave trade, 126

Queen Elizabeth, 39

Queensland, 22-23

Queen Victoria, 136

Ragatz, L. J., 188

Ramsay, James, on British slave trade to foreign colonies, 34; on character of slave traders, 46; on value of slave trade, 147; on mortality of white sailors in the slave trade, 167; personal experience of slavery of, 180-81

Rathbone, William, 58-59

Raynal, Abbé, 105-110

Reform Bill, 133-34, 158, 209

Ricardo, J. L., 139, 164, 168

Robinson, Bishop, 42

Rodney, Admiral, 44, 127

Roebuck, J., 144

Roscoe, William, 49, 100, 162

Royal African Company, patronage of Royal Family, 16, 39, 48; created, 31; abolition of monopoly of slave trade and, 31-32; slaves exported by, 32; war with Dutch West India Company, 40; woolen industry and, 66-67; Samuel Touchet and, 70; iron trade and, 81-82; gun trade and, 82

Rum, triangular trade and, 78-81; imports into Britain, 78; distilleries in New England, 78-80; distilleries in Bristol, 79; distilleries in Liverpool, 79; competition with gin, 79; competition with corn spirits, 80

Saba, 21

Saco, J. A., 18, 27

Saint Domingue, 7; refiners on, 78; British evacuation of, 94; necessity of Britain taking over, 103, 148; value of, 108; compared with Jamaica, 113, 122-23; sugar production in, 113, 122-23, 145-50; offered to England, 147-49, 200; effect of slave revolt on price of sugar, 164; abolitionists on reconquest of, 189; repercussions of slave revolt in, 202

St. Kitts (St. Christopher), European immigrants in, 28; decline of sugar production in, 151

St. Lucia, 151

St. Martin, 21

St. Thomas, 21

St. Vincent, 151, 153

St. Vincent, Earl, 44

Sandars, Joseph, 105

Scotland, attempt to set up independent African company, 56; Act of Union, 56, 64, 75

Servants, indentured, successors of Indian slaves, 9; reasons for, 10; passion for independence of, 10; traffic in, 10; kidnaping of, 10-11, 14; "newlanders," 11; transportation of Cromwell's Irish prisoners, 13; transportation of Cromwell's Scottish prisoners, 13; transportation of Quakers, 13; transportation of Morrmouth's followers, 13; transportation of Jacobites, 13; conditions of journey, 13-14; vested interest in system, 14; Jeffreys' treatment of kidnapers, 14-16; status became progressively worse, 16-17; English sensitiveness on, 17; Defoe on, 18; tended to democratic society, 18; Postlethwayt on, 18; compared with Negro slaves, 18-19; the historical base for Negro slavery, 19; climatic theory of plantation and, 20-23

Sharp, Granville, 45

Sheffield, in age of industry, 60; W. I. connections of, 104; opposition to W. I. monopoly, 154; abolition movement in, 159; on East India produce, 159; on apprenticeship, 159

Sheffield, Lord, 121

Shipping industry, stimulated by triangular trade, 57-58; on monopoly of slave trade, 59; on abolition, 59; ancillary trades, 59; interest in slave trade, 167; interest in free trade in sugar, 167; Navigation Laws and, 167-68

Sierra Leone, 43, 145, 163, 179

Singapore, 131, 151, 167

Slave compensation, to Bishop of Exeter, 43; to Earl St. Vincent, 44; to Baillie family, 62; to Miles family, 74-75; to Beckford family, 88; to Hibbert family, 88; to Gladstone family, 90; to Goulburn, 94; to Earl of Balcarres, 94; to Marryat family, 105; opposition of Sheffield to, 159; sugar refineries on, 165

Slavery, necessary to prevent dispersion of labor, 5; importance of as an economic institution, 5; expensiveness, 5-6, 7, 153; advantages and disadvantages of, 6; soil exhaustion and, 7, 113; expansion necessary, 7; racism and, 7-29; Indian slavery, 7-9; inefficiency of Indian slave, 9; economic origin of Negro slavery, 16, 19-29; climatic theory of, rejected, 20-23; sugar, cotton, tobacco and, 23; supported by Church, 42-44; in England, 44-45; law of slave production, 113, 145, 150-51; Manchester on, 156; in India, 184-86; changed attitude towards, 194-96; policy of amelioration, 197-201; attitude of slaves to, 201-8

Slave trade, Negro, demanded by slavery, 30; British foreign policy and, 30; Sir John Hawkins' expedition, 30, 39; monopoly in, 30-32; volume of British, 32, 33;

to foreign colonies in W.I., 33-34; Asiento, 33, 40; mortality of slaves, 34-35; profits of, 35-37; popularity in Liverpool, 37, 62-64; required discrimination, 37-38; risks of, 38; royal patronage of, 16, 39, 48; British Government's attitude to, 40; struggle for Asiento, 40; British Government's attitude to colonial duties on, 40-41, 46; insurance companies and, 46, 104-5; character of men engaged in, 46-48; a great education, 47; humanitarianism of men engaged in, 47-48; protests against in eighteenth century, 48-49; defence of in eighteenth century, 49-50; William Wood on, 51; Postlethwayt on, 51; importance to W. I. of, 52; merchant marine and, 58; woolen industry and, 66-67; Manchester's interest in, 68-73; rum in, 78-80; development of banks and, 98-101; effect of American Revolution on, 123-24; Lord North on abolition of, 126; Quaker petition against, 126; West Indians demand renewal of, 141; Pitt on, 146; attempt at international abolition of, 146-47; British abolition of, 149-50; W. I. planters support abolition of, 149-50; abolition movement in Manchester, 155; abolition movement in Birmingham, 157-58; Birmingham on, 158; mortality of white sailors in, 166-67; shipowners' interest in, 167; British attempts to secure abolition of by Spain and Portugal, 169; British capital in, 171-72; British policy of suppression of, 171-76; British goods in, 172; abolitionists on suppressing, 193-94; Gaston-Martin on, 209

Smith, Adam, on prosperity of new colonies, 4; on expensiveness of slave labor, 5-6; on importance of discovery of America, 51; on profits of sugar plantations, 53, 85; Wealth of Nations, 107, 120, 124; on colonial system, 107, 120; on free trade between West Indies and America, 121; "invisible hand" of, 136; complimented by Pitt, 138; quoted by Cobden, 142

Society for the Propagation of the Gospel, 42

South Africa, 143

Southey, Robert, 49, 195

Spain, Indian slavery in colonies, 8-9; colonial policy and white immigrants, 21, 27; Asiento and, 33, 39; smuggling trade to colonies, 34; monarchy and slave trade, 39

Steam engine, financed by capital from W. I. trade, 102; progress of, 106, 126-28, 131, 155

Steen, Marguerite, 44

Stephen, James, trusteeship of, 144, 180; on Pitt, 148; on manumissions in Trinidad, 199

Sturge, Joseph, 158, 161, 192

Sugar, Negro slavery and, 23; dispossession of small farmer by, 23-25; increase of black population and, 23-24; increase of wealth in Barbados and, 25; growth of latifundia in Barbados and, 25; a capitalist undertaking, 25; a lottery, 38; profits of, 53, 85, 110; importance of to England, 55; W. I. Docks and imports of, 60; refining industry in England, 73-78; refining in plantations, 75-76; iron industry and, 82-83; brass industry and, 83-84; increase of duties on, 96-97; involved monoculture, 110-11; superiority of French production, 113-14, 145-49; duties on, 123, 137-38; world production, 145-53; in Cuba, 145, 149-52; in Brazil, 145, 150-52; beet, 149-50; overproduction in W. I., 149, 152; in Mauritius, 151; decline of production in British W. I., 149-53; equalization of duties, 153; importation of Brazilian for refining, 155, 163; slave-grown, 156, 165; refiners of, 163-66; equalization of duties on, 164

Sugar planters, opposed to monopoly in slave trade, 31; clash with slave traders, 33-34, 40-41; clash with merchants, 40-41, 55-57, 92; opposed to monopoly in sugar trade, 56; on free ports, 56; clash with refiners, 76-78; restriction of production by, 76-78; clash with English agricultural interest, 80, 93, 97; wealth of, 85; opposed to increase of sugar duties, 96-97; to new settlements, 113, 149-50

Sugar refining, in Glasgow, 64, 75; in Britain, 73-78; in Bristol, 73-74, 77-78; in London, 74, 77; refiners on abolition, 74; in Liverpool, 75; clash of refiners with planters, 76-78; petitions of refiners, 74, 77, 164; refiners on high prices of sugar, 77; refiners on W. I. monopoly, 163-66; on East India sugar, 164; capital investment of, 165; on slave compensation, 165

Sypher, Wylie, 49

Tarleton family, 48, 162
"The West Indian," 86, 93
Thomas, Sir Dalby, on value of labor in the W. I., 53; on importance of sugar to England, 55

Thomson, James, 48-49
Thomson, Poulett, 167
Thornton family, 181, 186
Tobacco, comparison of in Cuba and Virginia, 21; small farming in Barbados, 23; Negro slavery and, 23; Negro slavery in Virginia and, 26; industry in Glasgow, 64, 75; compared with sugar, 85

Tobago, 150
Tordesillas, Treaty of, 3
Touchet, Samuel, 70-71
Toussaint, L'Ouverture, 195, 202, 204
Transportation, offences, 11-12; conditions of journey, 13-14
Triangular trade, organization of, 51-52; stimulus to British industry of, 52, 65-84, 98-107; profits from finance Industrial Revolution, 52, 98-105; stimulated shipping and shipbuilding, 57-59; stimulated growth of seaport towns, 60-64; woolen industry and, 65-68; cotton manufacture and, 68-73; sugar refining and, 73-78; rum and, 78-81; metallurgical industries and, 81-84, 102-4; banking and, 98-102; insurance and, 104-5

Trinidad, white servants, 24; East Indian migration to, 28, 90; Warner family in, 90; abolition in, 150-51; sugar production in, 151-53; on policy of amelioration, 197-99; free people of color in, 201; violence of planters of, 202-3, 207; misconceptions of slaves in, 203-4

Tucker, Josiah, 49

United States, trade with W. I., 121-22; transport of sugar to Europe, 122, 149; free trade with

Britain, 124-25, 131-32; Merivale on free trade with Britain, 124; Huskisson on free trade with Britain, 124-25; cotton exports to Britain, 128, 132; export of British capital to, 131; British imports of cotton from, 162; British government on Civil War in, 176-77
Utrecht, Treaty of, 40-42

Vasa, Gustavus, 158
Virginia, 7; Indian Slavery, 8; indentured servants, 10; convict labor, 12; Negro slavery, 26
Voltaire, F. M., 17, 114

Wakefield, Gibbon, 4, 6
Walpole, Horace, 41
Warner family, 90
Washington, George, 13, 107
Watt, James, 102, 126-27, 157
Wealth of Nations, 107, 120, 124, 142
Wedgwood, Josiah, 179
Wellington, Duke of, attitude to West Indians, 95-96; attitude to Reform Bill, 134; boycott of produce of slave trading countries and, 169-70; on suppression of slave trade, 175; on slavery in India, 184; and abolitionists, 189; on abolition, 189
Wertenbaker, T. J., 18, 26
Wesley, John, 181
West India Association, 90; of Liverpool, 100
West India Interest, clash with English agricultural interest, 80, 93, 97; social position of in England, 91; power of in eighteenth century, 92-97; members of, in Parliament, 92-94, 97; powerful friends of, 95-96; opposition

to increased sugar duties, 96-97; banking connections of, 100-2; insurance connections of, 105; railway connections of, 105; victory of with regard to peace treaty of 1763, 115; on their monopoly, 140-42; on East India sugar, 140; on Brazilian sugar, 140; on suppression of slave trade, 175-76

West Indies, white servants in, 11-14; convict labor in, 12; Irish servants in, 13; profits of trade with, 36-37; importance of Negroes to, 52; value of plantations in, 53; Adam Smith on profits of sugar cultivation in, 53, 85; trade with Britain compared with mainland colonies trade, 53-55; shipping and, 58; imports of fish in, 59; London docks and trade with, 60; Bristol's trade with, 61; Glasgow's trade with, 64; exports of wool to, 67-68; Manchester's trade with, 68-70; cotton exports of, 71-73, 128; refining in, 75-76; rum trade of, 78-81; iron exports to, 81-84, 130; exports of brass to, 83-84; legacy of plantation in, 92; profits of trade with, invested in heavy industry, 102-4; insurance companies and, 104-5; imports from mainland colonies of, 108; ecomonic relations with mainland colonies, 108-22; food imports of, 110-11, 121; monoculture in, 110-11; personal contacts with North Americans, 112; Stamp Act in, 121; effects of American Revolution in, 120-25; United States trade with after American Revolution, 121-22; decline of British trade with, 131-32; monopoly of, 126-27, 133, 135-42; unprofitable economy of, 135-36, 138-39; competi-

tion of East India sugar, 137-38,
153; Roebuck on, 144; decline of
sugar production in, 149-53; capitalists on monopoly of, 154-68;
Cobbett on monopoly of, 155; cotton manufacturers on monopoly of,
154-57; Bright on protecting duty
of, 156-57; boycott of produce of,
159, 183-84, 190; refiners of sugar
on, 164-65; attitude of planters towards slavery, 197-201; free
people of color in, 201; attitude
of slaves towards slavery, 201-8;
slave revolts in, 202-8
West Indies (French), British supply of slaves to, 33-34; sugar
refining in, 76; molasses in, 80;
superiority of, 113-14, 122-23;
American trade with, 115-20,
122; sugar cultivation in, 145
Westmoreland, Earl of, 48
West Riding, 130, 154, 160
Whitefield, George, 5, 43
Whitehaven, 103
Whitmore, Thomas, 187
Whitney, Eli, 20, 128
Whitworth, Sir Charles, 53-55
Wilberforce, William, on George
III's opposition to abolition, 39;
attacked by William IV, 39;
Bristol's enthusiasm over rejec-
tion of abolition bill of, 42;
attacked by Nelson, 44; fear of

House of Lords, 48; attacked
by Boswell, 49; encouraged by
Pitt to sponsor abolition, 123,
181; Pitt's support of, 148;
on abolition, 150; on abolition
movement in Manchester, 155;
Cobbett on, 155; representative of York, 159; spokesman for
woolen industry, 160; on mortality of white sailors in slave trade,
166; Canning to on Brazilian
trade, 170-71; imaginary interview with Coupland, 178; letter
of Ramsay to, 180; character of,
181-82; on emancipation, 182;
on Pownall amendent, 183; letter of Liverpool to on abolition,
189; son of, 192
Wilkinson, John, 106, 129
Williamson, J. A., 10
Winthrop, Governor, 110
Wood, William, on slave trade, 51;
on value of labor in W. I., 53; on
mainland trade with foreign W.
I., 118-19
Wool, triangular trade and, 65-
68; technological changes in, 68;
superseded by cotton, 68, 130;
expansion of, 130; Australian,
131; exports of to China, 134;
opposition to W. I. monopoly,
160-61
Wordsworth, William, 136, 195